Nathan Solomon Joseph

Religion, Natural and Revealed

A Series of Progressive Lessons for Jewish Youth

Nathan Solomon Joseph

Religion, Natural and Revealed
A Series of Progressive Lessons for Jewish Youth

ISBN/EAN: 9783337027438

Printed in Europe, USA, Canada, Australia, Japan

Cover: Foto ©ninafisch / pixelio.de

More available books at **www.hansebooks.com**

RELIGION,

NATURAL AND REVEALED.

A SERIES OF PROGRESSIVE LESSONS FOR
JEWISH YOUTH.

BY N. S. JOSEPH.

———◆———

LONDON:
TRÜBNER & CO., LUDGATE HILL.

1879.

LONDON :
PRINTED BY WERTHEIMER, LEA AND .CO.,
CIRCUS PLACE, FINSBURY CIRCUS.

NOTE.

———

THE late JACOB ABRAHAM FRANKLIN bequeathed by Will to five Trustees the sum of Five Thousand Pounds, for the promotion of certain stated objects in connection with the advancement of Judaism.

One of those objects was the publication of Religious Treatises and Text-books.

The Trustees having had the present Work submitted to them, and finding it in accord with the views of the benevolent Testator, have purchased the copyright, and now publish the work, at a price to cover the cost of printing only, in the hope and belief that it will prove a valuable Text-book for the instruction of Jewish youth.

JULY, 1879.

PREFACE.

THIS book has been written in scanty moments of leisure, snatched from the pursuit of an arduous profession. It therefore, doubtless, contains many imperfections, which would not have existed if the work had been the result of a steady and continuous effort.

It was commenced some years ago, at the suggestion of a dear departed friend, the Rev. BARNETT ABRAHAMS, and was discontinued when his death deprived me of his promised co-operation. It was resumed a few months since, the necessity of such a work having been, for many years, constantly pressed upon me, first, during my connection with many of our communal institutions, and lately in the education of my own children. This last exigency gave the most powerful impulse to the progress of a work for which a too scanty leisure hardly qualified me.

While there is no lack of excellent books professing to teach our Religion, they all partake of a more or less dogmatic character, little in harmony with the enquiring spirit of the age. The rationalistic tendencies of modern thought have administered a rude shock to all religions. They have caused many good, truth-loving parents to be less zealous than of old about the religious education of their children, the modern notion being that Religion and Reason are in some degree antagonistic. Children, hardly free from the restraints of the nursery, quickly imbibe, or perhaps inherit, the prevailing spirit of enquiry, and ask intelligent questions which would have surprised and horrified our grandfathers, but which must yet be answered.

The day for dogmatic religious teaching is at an end. For infants it may suffice. In the undeveloped intellect of the little child it may fill a temporary gap; but to the mind of an intelligent child, accustomed by the modern system of education to the exercise of the reasoning faculties, the teaching of Religion by a purely dogmatic method is useless, perhaps mischievous. The lesson, if swallowed, is not digested. If retained in the memory, it is, perhaps, retained only to crop up in years of maturity, not as a part of a living Faith, but as a pretty fiction, an exploded belief of credulous childhood.

With our Holy Religion this should not be. For, starting with few postulates, it makes but small demand on blind faith, and is essentially a reasonable Religion, that can bear the bright glare of enquiry. There is, therefore, no excuse with us, as with other creeds, for dogmatic teaching.

The object, then, of this work is to present a rational view of our Religion—to give the "reason why," wherever possible, for its prin-

ciples, its ordinances and practices, and so to
raise our Faith to the higher dignity of a firm,
intelligent Belief.

Although the principal ceremonial observances ordained in the Pentateuch will be
found to have a place in these pages, the
work must not be regarded as a compendium
of our Ritual. It would have been impossible
to render it such, without touching upon debatable ground, and alluding to points upon
which our co-religionists are not altogether
unanimous. The omission of these debatable
subjects (which probably few will notice) is
therefore not accidental but intentional, the
work having been written in a sense that may
render it acceptable to Jews of all shades of
opinion. The omission, however, to those who
notice it, will be useful, as showing that the
differences which divide the Jewish camp are
really insignificant, and that upon all truly important points of doctrine and observance,
Jews are unanimous.

A few words must be said about the scope of the work, the style, or rather styles, in which it is written, and the mode in which it should be studied. The book is intended to teach our Religion *progressively*, under the two heads—Natural and Revealed Religion. The first principles and most important observances and laws, enunciated in the simplest language, suitable to the capacity of the youngest children, will be found in the earlier Chapters of both parts of the work. As the work progresses, the subjects become less easy; and as those subjects are not intended for the perusal of very young pupils, the child-like language of the earlier Chapters is dropped, but a sufficiently simple style is preserved. The later Chapters (except Chapter XII.) and the Appendices, treating of subjects of inherent difficulty, are meant only for the perusal of advanced pupils, and consequently no attempt has been made to couch these in language of strained simplicity. Hence the variation in the mode of treatment, which, though it may affect the unity of the style, will probably enhance the utility of the work.

I have, in conclusion, to express my grateful acknowledgments to the Rev. Dr. HERMANN ADLER, for the important assistance he has rendered me in revising the manuscript of this work, and for many most valuable suggestions for its improvement. It is, however, only due to him to add, that he must not, by the fact of such revision, be held to identify himself with every opinion expressed in these pages. My sincere thanks are also due to the Rev. SIMEON SINGER, for his valuable services, most carefully and conscientiously rendered, in revising the work for the Press.

TABLE OF CONTENTS.

PART I.

NATURAL RELIGION.

PART II.

REVEALED RELIGION.

APPENDICES.

RELIGION, NATURAL AND REVEALED.

PART I.

NATURAL RELIGION.

CHAPTER I.

THE EXISTENCE OF A GOD.

EVERYTHING in the world must have had a maker. You cannot imagine it possible that anything, however simple, made itself.

If I showed you a piece of stone, and told you that the stone made itself, you would laugh, and tell me that you could not believe such nonsense. And you would be quite right. You would tell me that the stone had no power to move, or to think, or to do anything—much less to make itself.

And if I showed you a plant, with some pretty flowers growing on it, and I told you that the plant made itself, you would laugh still more, and would say that you knew better. You would tell me, perhaps, that the plant had grown from a little seed, and that the little seed had come from another plant, just like the plant I was showing you, and that the first seed that ever became a plant, could never have been clever enough to make itself in such a wonderful way that the seed should bring forth a plant, and the plant a flower, and the flower a seed, and the new seed a plant again, and so on, year after year, till now.

And if I showed you an animal—say a bird—and told you that the bird made itself, you would laugh at me again. You would tell me the same as you told me about the plant. You would say that the first bird could never have been clever enough to make itself in such a wonderful way ; and that if the bird had made itself, it would have been clever enough to keep itself alive for ever, which we know no animal can do. And of course you would be right.

But, suppose some one told you that all the world, as you see it, came by chance—that the mountains and valleys, the beautiful trees, and the sweet-smelling flowers, the beasts of the field, and men and women, and you too, all came by chance, you would think this idea still more laughable. You would say that chance never did anything half or quarter so orderly. You would call to mind that when you upset your box of toys by accident or by chance, the toys tumbled out in the most disorderly way, and you would have been very much astonished if it had been otherwise. You would call to mind that the things you see in the world are very regular and very orderly. You would remember that you never saw trees grow upside down, or the sun shine in the middle of the night, or anything heavy refuse to fall to the ground—all which might happen, if things were arranged by chance.

You would also remember, (and if you did not, some one ought to remind you,) that all the things we see around us on this beautiful Earth, seem to be arranged for one *design* or purpose, for the good of living creatures, and above all, of man. And we know very well that if there is a design or purpose in anything, that thing cannot be said to be the work of chance, but must have had some one to design it.

I dare say you have, at some time or other, seen a steam-engine : and if you have, I doubt not that you have thought it a very wonderful thing. Even if you look at it from a distance, as it almost flies along the iron rails, dragging after it waggons piled with goods, and carriages full of people, it seems a living wonder. But if you walk close up to it, while it is standing still, you will think it yet more wonderful. For you will see that it is made up of an enormous number of parts, some very strong, and some very delicate ; and if you ask how many pieces there are in it, you will be told that there are nearly four thousand, and that each one of those four thousand pieces is necessary to make the great giant move. And then you will think to yourself how clever the men must be who could make such a wonderful machine.

And if any one were to tell you that the steam-engine came together by chance, or that it was not made by an intelligent or clever maker, you would tell him he was a stupid fellow to talk such nonsense. You would say, "I see here four thousand pieces of metal of different shapes and kinds, some large and some small, and I see that they fit into one

another exactly ; so they could not possibly have
come together by chance ; and I see also that there is
a design or intention in their being so put together—
namely, *to move;* and as there is a design or intention,
there must have been somebody to design or intend,
and that person, whoever he was, may be termed the
maker of the engine, without whom that engine would
never have been made." And this would be a very
sensible answer for you to give.

I have been talking about a steam engine ; because
it is a thing that most people have seen and looked
at closely, and because also they know (or can learn
by asking) how or by whom it was made.

But now I am going to talk of engines much more
wonderful than the steam-engine. Perhaps you may
see them with less wonder, because they make less
noise ; but when you look at them attentively, you
will see in them even more to admire. And the more
you look, you will find there is the more to be seen ;
and though, unlike the steam-engine, you will not
find the maker's name written in letters of brass
upon them, you will not be slow to find out who was
the maker.

The engines I mean are the glorious sun and the
tranquil moon, the twinkling stars, and the beautiful
Earth on which we live. And I call them engines,
because they are known to move, to be always
moving ; not like the steam-engine, by fits and starts,
when water is poured in and heat applied ; but ever
moving, ever working, never stopping to take rest,
never even slackening speed for an instant.

Then, too, there are engines on the Earth itself,

which we may look at more closely than we can at the sun, moon, and stars ; such, for example, as the animals that live on this Earth. Yes ; these, too, are engines, and many of them have more parts than the steam-engine itself, and these parts are much less likely to get out of order, and they need fuel or food less frequently, and they are capable of repairing themselves over and over again, when they wear out or get damaged, till they get so old that there is hardly anything left worth repairing.

Now, as we cannot talk of more than one of these engines at a time, let us take one as an example, one with which I believe you are better acquainted than any other; I mean—*yourself*.

You will remember that the steam-engine is a running-machine. It moves, and drags a train after it ; but it can do nothing else. You, however, are something more. You are a reading and writing machine, a tasting and smelling machine, a seeing and feeling machine, a hearing and talking machine ; but the greatest wonder of all is that this machinery of yours is under the control or management of a something within you, which you cannot see, and which is called the *Will*, and that this Will is guided by another unseen something within you, which we call *Reason*.

But as we can see neither the Will nor the Reason, we will let them alone for the present, and talk about the machinery only.

Look at your hand. How beautifully it is fitted for its purpose ! It can carry your heavy load of books, and it can thread the finest needle with the finest thread. It can hurl a heavy cricket-ball a very long way, and it can make the thinnest up-stroke with the finest pen. It can throw; it can carry; it can pull; it can push; it can lift; it can crush; it can bind; it can loosen. Look at that great stout workman. He has just been lifting a hundred-weight of grain with his brawny hands! Look at him now. He is using the same hand to take out a little particle of dust that has been blown into his fellow-workman's eye!

I called you just now an engine. I think I must have been wrong. Why, your hand alone is a hundred engines all put together; for it can do a hundred *different* things, and many quite *opposite* things.

Just look at your hand, and ask yourself if you think it became a part of your body by chance, or without design or express intention. Of course you will reply, that it was designed for the express purpose of doing all the things which we see it doing, just as the steam-engine was designed for the express purpose of *moving* and *dragging*. Therefore, we cannot help saying at least the same of the hand as we felt obliged to say of the steam-engine, that the hand must have had a very clever maker; and I think you would feel inclined to add that, as the hand is so much more wonderful than the steam-engine, and as no man, however clever, can make a true imitation of a hand with all its powers and movements, the maker of the hand must be far more clever than he who invented or made the steam-engine.

Now the hand is only one part of you, my little engine. There are hundreds of other parts of the body quite as wonderful ; and the more you look into and investigate these matters, the more you will see to admire, and the more certain you will become that the maker of all these wonderful contrivances of your body must be a Being of mighty skill.

Perhaps you never thought before what a wonder you are. If not, I hope what I have told you will not make you conceited ; for let me tell you that there are other animals which, so far as their bodies are concerned, are quite as wonderful. There is the elephant, for example ; he has a trunk which can tear up a huge tree and can also pick up a pin. There is the camel, too, with an extra stomach, capable of holding enough spare water to enable him to travel a long distance in the desert without drinking.

There is not an animal that can be named, whose body is not truly wonderful in every point of its structure. And then, if we look more closely into the peculiarities and habits of each animal, we shall find how beautifully the body of each is suited to the climate in which it is to live : how some are clothed with fur, others with wool, others with bristles, according to the heat or cold to which each is likely to be subject.

Then also we see how wonderfully it is contrived that life should be preserved as long as possible. For example, we know, that all animals are liable to accidental injuries, and that they would soon die if those injuries were not repaired. But we see that the animal has in itself the materials for its own cure. If part of a steam-engine be broken or damaged, engineers must come with tools to mend it. The engine cannot mend itself. But animals are machines that can and do mend themselves. If the skin be broken in a living animal, or the flesh torn, there is a matter produced by the wound itself which heals it. Even if the bone of a living animal be broken, the broken edges give forth a liquid which soon hardens into solid bone, making the broken parts, if placed together, stick to one another, and form one sound bone again.

Is not that wonderful? And wherever we look we find something to admire, something to wonder at. I do not mean to say that we can always tell the design or object or use of everything, when we see it. But that is caused by our ignorance. At one time, people were much puzzled to know what could be the use of certain poisonous plants; but now they have found out, that these plants which destroy life may, if used in a particular way and in very small quantities, serve as medicines to cure disease and so preserve life. And thus it may be with many other poisons and many other things whose object we cannot at present understand. Perhaps, when the world becomes wiser, we shall know all about them too.

And, after all, those things which puzzle us are not the greatest or the most important points in the universe. The things we see every day are the greatest wonders. Sunrise and sunset, rain and snow, wind and hail, the change of the seasons, the growth of plants, and animals—lifeless seeds becoming living flowers; lifeless eggs becoming living birds; life everywhere, in the sea, in the fields, in the rivers, in the forests, in the air; living things made to last till their place is taken by other living things like themselves ; and every one of these living things full of machinery which seems perfection—these are wonders indeed !

You will remember we made up our mind that the steam-engine must have had a very clever maker. Now what shall we say of the World ?

Do you know that, when I ask myself that question, I begin to have quite a poor opinion of the steam-engine? For I never knew a steam-engine to lay eggs, and bring forth a brood of little steam-engines, like that fine old hen with her large family of chickens. Nor did I ever know a steam-engine that was capable of doing anything else than *move;* nor did I ever know a steam-engine, that was out of order, get itself in order again without being doctored by an engineer. And still the steam-engine is a very wonderful thing, and must have had a very clever maker. ·

Well, what shall we say of the World ?

I am sure you will agree with me in coming to this conclusion, that the World and its contents must have had a maker possessed of an intelligence, power, and cleverness, to which the intelligence, power, and cleverness of the engine-maker cannot bear the least comparison.

This great and wonderful Maker of the World and its contents we call GOD ; and what I have tried to prove to you is THE EXISTENCE OF A GOD, who designed and created the World.[1]

[1] See Appendix I. (intended for teachers and advanced pupils).

CHAPTER II.

THE UNITY OF GOD.

PERHAPS you may ask, How am I to know that the world had only *one* Maker? How am I to know that there is only *one* God?

You might perhaps point to the steam-engine I talked about, and tell me it was made by several makers, and you might ask how you are to know that each wonder of the World had not a separate maker.

You would not be the first person who asked such a question. Indeed in olden times, there were several nations who believed in almost any number of gods.

I am going to prove to you that these people were very foolish, and that it is right and reasonable to believe that there is only one God, the Creator of the whole World and of everything therein. This is what is meant by the Unity, or oneness of God.

Let me take you back to our old friend the steam-engine. Now, it is certainly true that the engine was made by several people; but one man only designed it. That is to say, there was one man only, who first made a drawing or picture of it before it was begun. And that same man it was, who settled how large it should be, and how strong it should be, how much weight it should be able to drag, how fast it should be able to run, and how large and how small every one of the four thousand pieces of metal should be. And all the men who were employed in making the engine were just like so many machines, obeying the orders of the master engineer, not daring to disobey, but following exactly the picture or design he had set before them.

It was only by this strict obedience that the engine could ever have been finished, and turn out to be a moving machine; for if one of the workmen took it into his head to make one of the parts larger or smaller than was intended by the master engineer, the engine would have turned out weak or unruly, or perhaps would never have been able to move at all.

So you see, after all, the whole engine might be said to be the work of one man; for, in making it, the common workmen, who put it together, had no more to do with the *design* or *intention* than the miners who dug out of the earth the metals of which it was made.

Indeed, if we look at the finished steam-engine, we shall at once see that one man only must have had the arrangement of it. If it were not so, the enormous number of parts would not fit into one another so exactly.

It is this exact fitting of the various parts, all pointing to one object or intention, which makes us feel sure that, however many hands put the engine together, one master-mind designed or arranged it.

Now, if I can show you that the Earth, nay, that the whole World is in this respect just like the steam-engine, that every little or great part exactly fits into some other part, and that each part, as well as the whole which is made up of the parts, points to one great object or designed intention, I think you will believe that, however many powers may have been used in making the great World, there was only *one God*, who was the Master-engineer of the World, who designed, ordained, arranged, and regulated it all.

Let us begin with the Earth itself. What do we find therein? We find coal in abundance, to warm our homes and cook our food ; then iron, the material of all those tools with which we till the ground, make our clothing, our furniture, indeed everything that has to be shaped ; the stone to build our houses, and lime and sand to join the stone together ; and then, not the least of the treasures of the earth, we find springs of pure water bursting out of the hard rocks, flowing in little streams, and swelling into large rivers always ready and at hand to quench our thirst. All for the good of the inhabitants of this Earth.

Then let us consider the Sea. It is the great cistern, from which the sun and air draw up moisture. The moisture collects into clouds, the clouds fall in refreshing showers of rain upon the fields and forests, making the earth bring forth corn, and fruit, and flowers in abundance. And then the surplus water runs into rills, and the rills run into ditches, and the ditches into brooks, and the brooks into rivers, and the rivers into the sea ; and so the water which came from the sea returns to the sea, so completing its circle of usefulness, and ready to begin anew a like circle of silent, useful work ; and all for the good of the inhabitants of this Earth.

Next, let us consider the living things that swarm in the sea. There are shoals of fishes which yield food, sea-monsters which yield oil, and sea-weeds which manure the fields near the sea-coasts; all for the good of the inhabitants of this Earth.

Then let us consider the Air. How wonderfully it is arranged! We are always breathing a part of it, So, too, are the plants. Now you might think that, in course of time, all the air would be spent, or would become impure, through so many plants and animals breathing it; and so it would, if it were not for a very beautiful arrangement.

The air, (which, you know, you cannot see, and which you only feel when it blows against your face and when you call it wind,) is made up of several parts, or different kinds of gas or air, mixed together. One of these parts (oxygen) animals inhale or breathe *in*, and when it has passed through their lungs, fanning and keeping alive the flame of life, they exhale it or breathe it out again, and it is then found to be entirely changed, and to be exactly like another part of the air (carbonic acid gas) which the plants breathe. And so, you see, the animals breathe out the very kind of air which the plants require.

But I have not told you all the wonders yet. This carbonic acid gas, which the plants and trees breathe, also becomes changed in passing through them, and when they have done with it, and exhale it or breathe it out, (for plants, and trees also, breathe, although with organs quite unlike our lungs) it has become changed back again into oxygen—the very kind of air that we and all animals require to breathe.

Now, is not this wonderful? You see it cannot matter how many animals there are upon the earth to be supplied with air. For, however impure they make it, the plants and trees are quite sure to set it right again.

Surely such a fact as this is quite enough to show that the animals, the plants, and the air they breathe must have had one and the same Maker. For how could we imagine it possible that the animals were made by one maker, the plants by another, and the air they breathe by a third, and yet that this clever and beautiful arrangement could exist.

The example which I have here given is not an exceptional instance, but is one of many instances showing that, throughout the world, things depend one upon the other; and,—still more wonderful,— that what is useless to one object is thrown off from it, but is immediately taken up by another object, to which it is not only useful, but positively necessary.

And this is the great fact that we find in nature— *there is no waste.*

Now, if you enquire into the cause of this, you will find how it is that there is no waste. You will see that the objects of the animal kingdom, the vegetable kingdom, and the mineral kingdom—in plain words, animals, plants, and the lifeless materials of the earth —have a way of changing places one with another. I will explain what I mean by an example.

Suppose we sow some beans; the rain moistens them; in course of time they will sprout. There is something in the seed which we call *life* (but which we do not at all understand) giving it the power of taking up a portion of the air, and of the water, and of

the lifeless earth, and so the seed grows into a plant.
It becomes larger and larger. At last it flowers;
then the flowers drop off, and gradually the beans
appear in their stead. A stem, a root, a number of
leaves, a flower, and a quantity of beans (themselves
seeds for a new crop of beans) seem all to have come
from a simple seed. But they have really come from
many things besides the seed. Something has come
out of the earth, and something out of the air, and
these somethings, which were before lifeless, have
mixed with the little seed, and become part of the
living plant. How, we do not know, and perhaps
never shall.

Now, what becomes of the plant. Let us watch
and find out. Suppose a horse eats the beans. The
beans will become part of his flesh and blood, and
muscles and bones, and so such part of the plant as
is useful for food becomes part of an animal. As
for the remainder, it is not wasted. The leaves will
fade and the stalks will wither; but the leaves will
crumble into dust at last, and become part of the
earth again—a very fertile part, known as leaf-mould.
The stalks and roots will do the same, if left to
themselves; but the farmer will, perhaps, burn them,
and use the ashes for manure, which brings them to
the same useful end; for they become part of the
earth again, ready next year to serve the same useful
purpose; perhaps not as part of a crop of beans, but
for wheat, or barley, or mangold-wurzel, or something
of that sort.

And, pray, bear this in mind. It is the *same*
earth, the *same* lifeless soil, which becomes part

of the beans, or part of the wheat, or part of the barley.

We have seen how the lifeless earth changes into, and forms part of, the living plant, and how a portion of the living plant changes into, and forms parts of, the living and moving animal. Let us watch the further changes.

The horse which eat the beans, of course, breathes; and it has been found that part of his food goes to form the air which he exhales or breathes out.[1] So certain portions of the beans go back to the air, which, you will remember, was part of the nourishment of the growing bean. And more than that, as I told you before, it goes back just in the very state, fit and ready for the plants to breathe.

Then the ordure from the horse will contain those portions of the beans which were not able to be changed into flesh or blood or muscle or bone; and we know that this is turned to a very useful account as manure, forming part, and a very fertile part, of the ground, although so nasty and offensive to the smell. And perhaps, after all, the nasty smell is an advantage; for it is a hint to us to bury the offensive matter in the ground, where it may be useful. Otherwise we should probably let it lie about, and it would not only be of no use, but would render the air of the neighbourhood unhealthy.

But what becomes of the horse? In course of time it will die of old age. Its skin will be used for one purpose, and its hair for another, and, perhaps, its

[1] Namely, the carbon of the carbonic acid gas which he exhales.

flesh will feed other animals; but its bones will be burnt and ground for bone-earth, a most valuable manure; and such parts of the poor old horse as cannot be turned to some profitable purpose will be buried in the earth, where it will become dust, very fertile dust, ready, like the bone-earth, to grow a crop of beans, or wheat, or barley of extra-fine quality.

So you see the changes take place, but never come to an end; for nothing is wasted. One thing depends upon the other, like the links of a chain. The chain is complete between the animal, the vegetable, and the mineral creations. They change places over and over again. It is the same matter, the same substance—call it what we may—mineral, vegetable, or animal. Only, in one case life is wanting; in the other two life is present.

Now let us sum up the few facts we have noticed. We have found that the same matter runs through the earth, the plants, and the animals; that these make all sorts of exchanges one with another; that all the exchange-process is transacted by that wonderful agent which we call life; that during all this never-ending business nothing is lost, but that what one throws away as useless is immediately snatched up and used by another.

Does this look as if these things had more than one Maker? If there were two or more makers, would it be likely that the work of one would exactly fit into the work of the other in every respect? that the object or intention of one would exactly agree with the object or intention of another? that the material used by the one would be the same as, or capable of changing with, the material used by the other?

If there were more than one Maker, would it be likely that the earth and every particle in it would be acted upon by one fixed and never-changing law or rule; that the great planets, which twinkle only like little sparks in the sky, would (as we know they do) all follow the same law or rule;[1] that all the animals would be made in such a way as to breathe *one* air, and all the plants in such a way as to breathe one *other* air; and, above all, that there would be plain and evident in all the works of creation on our earth *one* main object, namely, the good of all living creatures?

The thing is impossible. Two or more makers cannot be. If such a work as the steam-engine required one master-mind to design it, what shall we say of the world, where we find thousands of objects—each more wonderful, more lasting, more perfect than the steam-engine—and all fitting exactly into one another, and pointing to one object—*Life?*

There can be but one conclusion—that the world must have been designed by *one* Master-mind; that there is but *one God*, the Creator and Ruler of all things created.

After reading all this long argument, and coming to this conclusion, I dare say you wonder how it was that,

---

[1] The law of gravitation. And recent discoveries by means of spectrum analysis have shown that the same chemical elements that form the material of the earth, form also the material of stars whose distance is beyond computation.

in olden times, there were so many people—and some very clever people, too—who believed in several gods.

I will try to explain to you how it was. And when I have finished, I think you will find that the explanation affords another proof of the Unity of God.

The nations who worshipped several gods saw the works of the Creation with eyes like our eyes, but not with thoughts like our thoughts. They would view the sun as the source of light, which made their fields fertile and their gardens gay. Then they would view the rain as a source of gloom, and as an enemy of the sun, because it often, when in excess, spoilt their crops, undoing all the good which the sun had accomplished. Then they would consider the wind as an enemy of the rain, because it dried it up, and thus undid the rain's work.

So when they saw the different powers of nature fighting with each other, and one undoing the work of the other, they thought each power had a separate god which ruled it.

And this idea they carried still further. They saw that men were ruled by different virtues, vices, and passions. They saw one, all of whose deeds were caused by the ruling passion of Revenge, another actuated by Love, another by Hatred, another by Ambition, another by Avarice, another by Patriotism, another by Philanthropy, and so on ; and they found such very different results produced by these different men, that they imagined the various virtues, vices, and passions which led them or drove them on to these different results, must each have a different god.

Besides, they often saw in one and the same man,

perhaps in themselves (as we find in ourselves) good passions and bad passions, fighting with one another, sometimes the one and sometimes the other gaining the victory.

And thus it happened that they had a multitude of gods ;—a god of the sun, a god of the rain, gods of the winds, and a god of the waves ; for they saw so many different and opposed effects produced, that they were led to think each effect must have had a cause which was itself a distinct creator.

Of course you and I know this idea to have been very absurd. And I really think that many of the clever people of those days must have thought so themselves ; for some of them, in their books, made their gods cut a very funny figure, representing them as doing all sorts of ungodly things. But certainly there were millions who really believed in all these gods. And we must not laugh at them ; for, in truth, they knew no better.

You see how their idea of a number of gods arose. They noticed the sun, and noticed the rain, and noticed the wind ; they saw the effects of each, but did not think of the effect of all put together. They saw that one power moistened the earth, and the other dried it ; that one parched the earth, and the other cooled it ; but they did not see that it was the moistening and drying, the parching and cooling, which, all put together, made the crops grow.

So, too, in the affairs of men ; they saw the love and the hatred, the charity and the revenge, the avarice and the ambition, the good and the evil, pulling different ways ; but they did not see that all these opposites put together kept the world of men always in movement, always in that state of activity of mind and body which is a necessity of man's nature. In a word, they did not look at the world as we have been looking at it—as a *whole;* and did not notice—indeed, did not know—how all these parts fitted into each other, and formed the whole.

But, happily, we know better. We know that these powers of Nature, which by themselves would produce such opposite effects, together balance one another; and it is this *balance of power* which affords another proof that there is but one Creator and Ruler of the world.

I will try to explain what I mean by an example taken from the affairs of men. I dare say some of you read a newspaper; and those who do not, hear now and then what is going on in the world. Now, you will almost always find a great fuss being made about some ambitious nation or another becoming too strong, or trying to become too strong, or endeavouring to master its weaker neighbour. When such things take place, you will generally find that the rulers of the other nations put their heads together and say that the thing ought not to be, lest it should disturb the " balance of power "; in other words, lest the ambitious nation should become too powerful, and swallow up all the little nations. So, you see, the " balance of power " is maintained by one nation watching the other very closely, and keeping it in check.

Well, sometimes the ambitious nation says, " I *won't* be kept in check; I *will* swallow up my weak

neighbour." And perhaps he will try to make out
that his weak neighbour is wicked and barbarous, and
deserves to be swallowed up ; or perhaps he will try
to show that his weak neighbour doesn't mind being
swallowed up, and, indeed, rather likes it.   Then
there begins a terrible dispute, and perhaps the nations
come to blows, and there is a long and frightful war.
Generally it ends in changes which are scarcely im-
provements, and usually the "balance of power" is
maintained ; but sometimes it has ended in the ambitious nation becoming more powerful, till it goes on,
year after year, greedily adding fresh provinces to its
empire.   Such a state of things never lasts, but while
it lasts it is very inconvenient and very burdensome.

Perhaps you now see how important this "balance
of power" is, and how difficult it is to preserve it in
the affairs of men.

But in Nature—that is in the works of God—it is
very different.   There, the balance of power is quite
as indispensable ; for, without it, we should now and
then have all our houses blown down by a hurricane,
all our fields burnt by the sun's heat, or all the inhabitants of the earth swept away by a deluge ; for,
without speaking of the other forces of nature, the
winds, the sun, and the rain would be quite strong
enough to produce such results, if they were not held
in check.

Yet all the forces of Nature are so nicely balanced
that, while each performs its work, it works without
destroying.   Now and then, indeed, there are slight,
very slight departures from the balance of power,
but very soon it restores itself by some convulsion,

affecting but a small portion of the earth, such as an earthquake, a whirlwind, or a thunderstorm. These are destructive sometimes, but they are no doubt for the general good, evil though they may at the time appear to be. We know and see the good of a thunderstorm; perhaps we may some day, when we shall have grown more clever, see the good of an earthquake.

Be that as it may, the balance of power is the rule of Nature, and the exceptions above named, if carefully examined, will be seen to have for their object the enforcement of the rule.

Well, what do you think this proves? I know what your answer will be. I am sure you will say that the forces of Nature cannot have separate and independent rulers, as the kingdoms of the earth have; that, as all the forces of Nature pulling in different and sometimes opposite ways, and each performing different useful work, still balance one another, and balance one another *exactly*, there must be but One Creator who created these forces, but One who governs them.

And so you will believe in the Unity or oneness of God.

CHAPTER III.

WHAT WE KNOW ABOUT GOD.

IF you had a friend living a long way off, whom you had never seen, but who had always been very kind to you, frequently sending you presents, and paying you great attention in various ways, you would, I think, be very desirous of knowing all about this unseen friend.

You would try to find out what his likings and dislikings were, so that you might do something to please him. And if you had some idea that, one day or another, this unseen friend intended to send for you, and that if he then were pleased with you he would make you very happy, you would, I am sure, be most anxious to get all the information you could about this good friend.

You would enquire whether he received any news of your sayings and doings, and would endeavour to discover every peculiarity of his character. You would, moreover, try to find some one who had seen this friend, so that you might learn all about him ; but if you could not discover any person who had seen him, you would endeavour to find out his character in another way. You would think over all the presents he had sent you, and the manner in which they were sent, and the quantity in which they were supplied, and the purpose of each, and you would thereby be able to arrive at a pretty good guess of what your friend's character was like.

All this is supposing that you had never received from him any messages or letters, which would save you the trouble of guessing in the way I have described.

Now you and I have such a friend, and his name is GOD, and I have already shown you that we have only *one* such Friend. Neither you nor I have ever seen Him, but we receive presents from Him every day.

I dare say that you feel grateful to this good Friend, and would like to please Him. I dare say, too, that you have some sort of notion (which I hope will soon ripen into a belief) that He will one of these days send for you; and you, therefore, would like to act in such a way, that you will stand well in the opinion of this great Friend—the one and only God.

But before you can do this, you feel that you ought to know something about His power, His nature, His character, His likings, and dislikings. This is what we mean when we talk of the *attributes of God.*

Well, let us see if we can find some of the information we want from the splendid gifts this great Friend has sent us. We shall afterwards see that He sent us several messages, a long time ago, and that from them we can learn still more. But we will talk of the messages another time, and just now think only of the gifts.

God has given us the earth to live upon. What a magnificent present! Of how many thousands of presents does it consist! If we lived hundreds of

years, we should never be able to count the treasures it
contains, never grow tired of the beauties it exhibits.
Well, I believe we shall conclude, after thinking a
little about this splendid present, that He who gave
it to us is good, kind, wise, and merciful. Let us try.

What a beautiful world it is! There is everything
to charm the sight. The face of Nature is so fair
that we never tire of it. The fields and the forests,
the heavens and their hosts, the glorious sea—the
grandest thing on earth—all delight our senses,
whether we look broadly over the whole, or minutely
into each little part.

Think of the flowers, so sweet to the smell, so
charming to the sight, filling our houses with fragrance
and cheerfulness! Think of the food so bountifully
supplied—necessaries of life, but yet so agreeable to
the sense of taste as to render the satisfying of hunger
one of the great pleasures of life! Think of the fresh
air of Heaven, how balmy, how grateful to the senses,
as we breathe it without an effort, or as its gentle
breezes play upon our faces, enliven our limbs, and
fan the flame of life! Think of the joys of the heart
and of the soul, the emotions of love, of gratitude, of
realised hope, and the proud sense of right in a conscience satisfied. It is a splendid place, this world of
ours!

But I fancy you saying:—" Pray stop; do not go
on so fast." I fancy you reminding me that you have
heard of such things as disease, want, suffering in
many frightful forms, hatred, crime—many, many
shocking things that will hardly bear thinking about.
I fancy you reminding me, too, that though the

mountains look so beautiful, there are such things as volcanoes, pouring out devouring torrents of liquid fire; that though the sea is so grand, so splendid a sight, there are such things as shipwrecks; that though the birds sing so sweetly, and though their plumage is so lovely, there are such things as vultures and eagles who live only by the death of other animals.

Well, well! You are quite right to remind me of all these things. We shall never get on if we shut our eyes to the truth.

Let me tell you, then, that there are many matters which we can never know during our life on earth, and among these there is none so impossible to know *for certain* as the reason for so much evil in the world. But a little thought will bring us to a conclusion probably not far from the truth.

Something within us tells us that there is a world beyond this; that when we die, we shall live elsewhere in a happier and a better state. We are taught this at home and at school; and to you and me, who have learnt this from other sources than our own thoughts and feelings, it may be difficult to think that this idea of a future state would come into our heads naturally, without any teaching. Nevertheless this would be the case. The most savage nations, and those neglected members of the civilized races, who are perhaps more degraded than savages, have the notion of a future life implanted in their breasts, not merely as a hope, but as a conviction.

It would seem, moreover, that this world is a place of preparation for the future world; that here we have to make ourselves fit for the enjoyment of ever-

lasting life, and that our enjoyment of the next
world will depend on our conduct in this. This
notion is perhaps as deeply implanted in the mind as
is the main idea of a future state. The most savage
nations think that their heroes who die in battle—
according to their ideas, the most noble end—will
have the rewards dearest to them in the world to
come; and in civilized communities, even the most
uneducated and neglected of human beings, who perhaps never think of a God ruling the world, yet have
some vague idea that their crimes will be punished
in a world beyond this.

You and I believe in a future state, in which we
shall be rewarded or punished in accordance with our
conduct in this world; and if we are asked why we
believe it, we shall perhaps find no better nor more
valid reason than the wonderful fact that *we are
prepared to believe it without a reason.*

If this world be regarded as a mere place of preparation for the next world, there is not much difficulty in accounting for the presence of so much evil.
Let us try to account for it by a familiar illustration.

Suppose that, at school, you were not compelled to
learn, but were allowed to do whatever you liked, so
that if you felt inclined to talk, or to have a game,
or to go out for a walk during school hours, you could
do so, without your master finding fault with you;
would the master who so indulged you be really
kind? Silly and thoughtless children might perhaps think he was; but you know better. You know
that you go to school for the purpose of learning
those things which will be useful to you when you

grow older. If you attend to your studies at school, you will get on in the world; you will become clever and good, and people will respect and love you.

It is, therefore, the duty of your master to see that you do attend to your studies. The good master will always do this. Sometimes he will encourage you by fair words, by smiles, and by presenting you with prizes; at other times, he may find it necessary to speak angrily to you, to frown at you, or perhaps even to punish you. Now, the sensible master, who occasionally frowns and punishes you, is your best friend; while the foolish instructor, who always indulges your fancies and your frolics, is in fact your enemy.

I know it is difficult for you to see this at the time. While you are being punished, you feel angry with your teacher, and think him too harsh; but the time will come, when you will see things in their true light. When you have left school, you will feel thankful to him who checked your indolence by wholesome punishment, and will despise him who encouraged it by his indulgence.

Now, if you consider this life as a place of preparation for a happier and better life, you must regard the world as a school in which your soul is to be educated and trained, so as to fit it for a happy destiny in the next world. Thus it is that God acts towards us as a wise instructor. He calls into activity the noble impulses of our soul, and checks its evil tendencies. Sometimes He causes the light of His countenance to shine upon us, showering down blessings upon us, and prospering our undertakings; at other times He finds it necessary to frown upon us, to disappoint our hopes, to afflict us with disease, loss of property, or other misfortunes. But all is done for our own eventual good. You may depend upon it, that God knows how to teach us the all-important lesson, how to prepare for the future life—that He knows when to encourage, and when to chasten. You may rest assured that it would not be for our advantage, if we always had things as we would wish them to be.

As if to convince us of this, God has, from time to time, allowed a few individuals in high positions to enjoy almost unlimited power and wealth. History shows us that nearly in every such instance, the individuals so gifted were spoiled by their good fortune. Nero, for example, was not an inhuman man before he became Emperor of Rome. It is stated that at the beginning of his reign he could with difficulty be induced to sign the death-warrants of murderers and other criminals. Yet, after he had enjoyed a few years of great power and prosperity, he caused his mother, his wife, and his tutor to be murdered in cold blood.

And Nero is not a solitary example of the evils resulting from unchequered good fortune. Even as children sometimes require to be checked and corrected, lest they become selfish and wilful, even so do men require trials and disappointments to recall them to a sense of duty and to improve their soul; and God is far too wise and too good a teacher to withhold the needful correction. So you see how the seeming imperfection of our earthly existence conduces to our eventual happiness; for by our very nature we require occasional sorrow and suffering.

But perhaps you may ask—Could not God, who created us, have so formed us as to have different natures? Could He not have made us so naturally inclined to do good that we should not have needed correction? I would answer, that we really know too little of God's plan to be competent to solve fully and with certainty such difficulties. We see but a very small portion of God's works; we can have but a very faint idea of the working of the providential scheme. Man is but an atom on this earth, and the earth itself is but an atom of the whole of God's great universe. When we shall see the *whole*, when the future spiritual world, with all its hidden wonders, shall be revealed to us, then we shall doubtless see that God has ordained and arranged all things for the best, and that no other arrangement could ensure so much happiness to so many creatures.

Although the full solution of this great mystery—the mystery of the existence of evil—cannot be expected in this our little life, yet some faint glimpse of the truth may be further obtained by the help of an extension of our illustration.

Suppose that the schoolmaster offered prizes to those of his pupils who would answer a number of examination-questions. Suppose that, contrary to the usual custom, he were to set very simple questions, and (to make it a very easy matter to answer them) allowed his scholars to refer to as many books as they pleased, and even to copy the answers from them. I know what you would say to this. You would object altogether to be examined on such terms. You would say :—" I should not care for a prize so easily gained.

The examination would not prove my merit at all. Any dunce could answer as well as I could in such circumstances. So I would rather be excused from being examined. If I gained the prize, I should not deserve it, and so would not value it."

Now suppose a contrary state of things. Suppose the schoolmaster were to give such questions as he thought his pupils ought to be able to answer, if they had worked hard and used their time well; and suppose he left them entirely to their own resources, thinking that, with the knowledge he had conveyed to them, they ought to be well able to answer even the most difficult questions. What would you say then? You would say, "This is a very different affair. I shall be glad to be examined upon these terms. I know I shall have to work hard to deserve the prize; but, if I work hard, I shall gain it. And when I shall have gained it, how glad I shall be! Such a prize will be worth having."

Let us apply this illustration. Life is our school; God our great Schoolmaster; everlasting happiness the prize He offers to us, His pupils. If it required no exertion on our part to obtain this prize; if life offered no difficulties and no temptations, so that we could hardly help doing good, where would be our merit? Our happiness would be spoilt by the thought that it had not been earned by our exertions. Therefore God, in His goodness, has ordained it otherwise. Like the wise schoolmaster, He has made the examination hard, and consequently the prize worth having. He has placed difficulties and temptations in our way, that we might battle with them and obtain the victory.

To some He has made life a struggle for existence; but doubtless He has made them proportionately strong to enable them to carry on the struggle. Everyone has his sorrows, his pains, his heart-burnings, his temptations, and his difficulties. Even the most favoured are not free from them. Let us not cry over them. Let us rather remember that they are as the difficult examination-questions.

And if we think how proud is our feeling of triumph, when we have resisted a temptation, overcome a difficulty, struggled and conquered, perhaps we may therein catch a faint glimpse of our future prize— eternal happiness casting its beauteous shadow before.

Then if it be true—and who shall doubt it?—that there is an eternal life, where eternal happiness is the prize of the good, there is no difficulty in accounting for the existence of evil in this world, and we see therein another, and a signal mark of the goodness of our Creator. *The evil is there for man to conquer.*

And God has given him the power to conquer it. The passions are strong within us; but the will is stronger, and can vanquish them. The voice of temptation is loud; but the voice of conscience is louder, and can drown it. And so, too, in the world of matter. If the enemy be famine, man finds some mode of giving new fertility to the barren ground. If it be tempest, he has at hand the means of warding it off and protecting himself from its ravages. If it be the loss of worldly possessions, he has within himself the energy of character to take heart and to try to replace them with new. If it be disease, he finds remedies wherewith to baffle it, and even to prolong the span of life. If it be death, he has it in his power so to live as to make death itself the gate of eternal life—a passing evil for a lasting good.

Yes, there are evils in the world; but they are the main-springs to our exertions, the incentives to our toil. They are the giants with whom we have to contend boldly, manfully, and honourably. To conquer them by honest strength of purpose, is the aim and end of the great battle of life.

Thus, then, we see how evil tends to our eternal welfare. It is mixed in small proportions with the good things of this earth, gently, wisely, and kindly; not dealt out in quantities to crush mankind, but tempered with the good, so as to strengthen the immortal soul, and make it worthy of everlasting happiness.

If, then, we have to guess the disposition of our Great Friend—the One and Only God—from thinking about the gifts which He has presented to us—the earth and its contents, what shall be our guess?

Shall we guess that the Being who has given us such a beautiful place to live in, endowed us with such powers of enjoying its beauties, mingled good and that which seems to us evil so wisely, so mercifully and so kindly, ordained apparent evil as universal good, made us so marvellously, fashioned our body and mind so wonderfully, and adapted all things to our eternal welfare, is a Being immeasurably good, merciful, and wise?

Shall we guess this of our great Friend? If we do, we are not likely to guess wrong.[1]

---

[1] A portion of this chapter was written for the author by the late Rev. Barnett Abrahams, B.A.

CHAPTER IV.

MORE ABOUT GOD.

YOU are satisfied that the One and Only God, who created you, is good and merciful and wise. But I wish you to know still more about Him.

1. GOD IS ETERNAL ; that is, He always *did* exist and always *will* exist. How do we know this? We have already come to the conclusion that this beautiful world and all therein must have had one great Creator, who brought everything into being. Now, if this Great Creator did not always exist, there must have been some time when He was Himself created by some one else; but that would be nonsense, for when we speak of a Creator, we mean a being who was the first cause of everything. There could not have been a Creator prior to the first cause or Creator of All, and, as we cannot imagine a beginning to time, we cannot imagine a beginning to God. Hence we say, we believe that God has existed for ever.

But how can we tell that God always *will* exist? We can only judge of the future by the past, and we cannot conceive the possibility of a Creator who has always existed ever coming to an end. We cannot conceive it possible for Time and Creation to come to

an end, and, while these exist, there must always be
a Creator to rule and govern the world.

2. GOD IS IMMUTABLE ; that is, He never changes.
How do we know this? You might perhaps think,
that because the works of the Creator exhibit constant change, the Creator Himself must be change-
able. But I can show you that this would be a very
false conclusion to arrive at.

It is quite true that we see change everywhere in
nature. Without it there would be no life. But that
change is always produced *in precisely the same
manner*, following always in the same order. The
mode or manner of change is unchangeable.

Let us give one or two examples. If you take a
pound of ice and pour boiling water upon it, the ice
will change, it will melt ; but, however often you try
the experiment, you will find that it will always
require exactly the same quantity of boiling water to
melt the pound of ice. Again, if you mix sand and
potash in certain fixed proportions and put them in a
furnace, they will produce the substance we call glass;
but, unless you keep to those fixed proportions, the
glass will not be produced.

And as it is with small matters, so is it also with
greater ones. The earth itself, and all the planets,
revolve around the sun, each in a period peculiar to
itself, a period which is always the same. We know
exactly, by calculation, to a second, when an eclipse
will take place, long before it occurs. We know
exactly to a second, when there will be new moon
or full moon. Indeed, everything in nature has
always been found to be so regular that people in

olden times called any fixed order of things, observed
everywhere, "a law of Nature." They ought to have
called it a law of the Creator.[1]

If the laws of the Creator are thus unchangeable,
what must the Creator be? What must He be, who
made these laws, who rules His Creation by the same
fixed, everlasting rules, and who supplies daily and
hourly the power or force, which keeps creation in
action ever in the same way. Surely He too must be
free from all change—Immutable.

3. GOD IS INCORPOREAL; that is, He does not
possess bodily form. If God is unchangeable, He
cannot be composed of matter, or have any bodily
form. For all things formed of matter, or having
bodily form, are liable to change. The hardest rocks
crumble to dust in course of time. Metals rust away
to powder. Everything natural or formed of matter
is changed by time. If then God is unchangeable,
He must also be incorporeal; He must be without
bodily form.

You will perhaps ask, if God has no bodily form,
what is He like? Now this is a question, which no
mortal can possibly answer. For we cannot form a
perfect idea or give a correct description of anything
except by connecting with it some material qualities,
such as size, shape, hardness, weight, and so on. And
since God is incorporeal, and has no such material
qualities, no one can say what He is like.

---

[1] It is not necessary here to take into account the few recorded
departures from the ordinary course of nature known as miracles;
for a law of nature is not the less a law in consequence of its
exceptional suspension. See Appendix III., "Miracles and
Revelation."

And if we picture to ourselves God, the Creator and Ruler of the world as some great giant with enormous power, we shall be doing very much the same as ignorant idolaters did, thousands of years ago, and we shall be committing a great sin. We must not think of God in that way at all. When we think of our parents, and love them, we do not think so much of their looks or of their form, but of their goodness and kindness to us. Probably no one ever loved his mother any the less for her being ugly, or any the more for her being beautiful. And so we should think of God, not with regard to any bodily likeness, but with regard to His qualities. We should think of His goodness and kindness to us, shown in His providing for our daily wants; of His wisdom and power, shown in the government of the world; of His mercy and forbearance, shown in His permitting sinners to live that they may repent of their wickedness; and if we think of all these qualities, we need no other picture of God.

4. GOD IS OMNISCIENT AND OMNIPRESENT; that is, He knows and sees everything that happens in the world that He has created. He, who creates and regulates all things, must surely have a perfect view and knowledge of all that goes on through His vast creation, and not only a knowledge, but, as there is design in all He has created, also a fore-knowledge, a knowledge of things before they take place, a fore-knowledge of the result of His work.

For how could it be otherwise? To regulate the works of the Creation and the course of events, requires a knowledge of all things existing, and of every power, thought or instinct, moving or influencing them. Surely the great Creator must know everything which He has formed, and His power must be present everywhere among His works, though we see Him not ; for we discern His watchful care in all things. He who is the Creator of every cause, and who has ordained the law by which that cause should produce a certain fixed effect, must surely be aware of the effect ; for both effect and cause are of His creation. So God must know everything. He or His mighty power must pervade all space. How careful then should we be of our actions ! How careful even of our thoughts ! For they are ever open to the gaze of the God who made us.

5. GOD IS OMNIPOTENT ; that is, He is all-powerful. Let us first try to understand what this means. We mean that nothing that can be imagined possible to be done, is too great or too wonderful for the power of God to accomplish.

I use the words " possible to be done" not to put a limit or boundary to God's power, but to put a limit or boundary to our own belief; for no one should ask you to believe a thing that is impossible. For example, we cannot believe it possible for anything to be wet and dry at the same time, hard and soft at the same moment, white and black at the same instant. We cannot believe it possible for two bodies to occupy the same space at the same time, or for the part of a thing to be greater than the whole. Such things you would call *impossible;* and if anyone told you " You only require Faith to enable you to believe those things to be possible, which seem to you physically impossible," you would reply, " Faith cannot make a man believe that to be possible which cannot be even *understood* to be possible. I cannot believe a thing which is inconsistent with all belief, and which even contradicts itself. I set no bounds nor limit to the power of God, but I cannot profess to believe a thing which appears to me impossible, because self-contradictory."

This would be a very proper answer for you to make.

When, then, we say that we believe that God is Omnipotent, or All-powerful, or Almighty, we mean that nothing possible is too wonderful or too great for Him to do. We see His mighty power wherever we turn,—in the giant mountains and in the vast deep, in the peaceful valleys and in the flowing streams, in the swift whirlwind and in the rolling thunder, in the rustling breeze and in the gentle dews. We see His power in the life which lives and reproduces life, in the birds and beasts and fishes, in the trees and shrubs and flowers, and in *ourselves*, favoured above all beings. We see His power in the earthquake and volcano; in the splendid sun, the gentle moon, and all the hosts of heaven—countless beyond number, great beyond measure, stretching through space beyond limit.

Looking at these His glorious works, and remembering, too, that He rules and regulates all of them by His own Power and Will, who shall say that there can be a limit to the power of God? He moves worlds, and keeps them ever moving. Can we imagine anything requiring greater power? He gives life, and makes that life bring forth fresh life, without end. . Can we imagine anything greater than the power of the Great Being who works such wonders? Surely not! And therefore it is that we say that God's power is immeasurably great ; and that is what we mean by saying that God is Omnipotent, All-powerful.

* * * * *

Thus we have learnt the attributes of the Creator from His works. We have examined the presents He—our Great Friend—has sent us, and learnt therefrom His character. They show us, that He is One, that He is good, merciful, and wise, that He lives for ever, that He never changes, that He possesses no bodily form, that He knows and sees everything, and that He is Almighty.

When we think of these attributes—all centred in One Mighty Being, the Creator of the World—and then think of ourselves, short-lived, weak, ignorant, and imperfect, we wonder gratefully at the goodness of the Eternal God, and feel that it should be a pleasure and a duty to love, honour, and reverence Him, and to strive to obey His Holy Will, if we do but know it.

CHAPTER V.

MAN AND HIS POSITION.

IF I ask you what you are, you will reply, "A human being;" and as the words escape your lips, you will feel a certain sensation of pride in making this reply. You may, perhaps, remember that you are a very helpless creature; very weak, very small; oh, so small compared with the great earth—so ridiculously small compared with the mighty universe; but the idea will still be uppermost in your mind, "I am superior to the handsomest bird that soars through the skies; I am nobler than the noblest beast that roams proudly through the forests."

If this idea rises in your mind, as I hope it will, you will be right to give play to it—right to encourage it. But your pride must not be the pride of the rich man who looks down with disdain on persons of lowly station, exclaiming, "See how rich I am! what a wonderful fellow I must be!" It should be the pride of the rich man who wonders to himself, "How is it God has made me so rich? Proud as I am of my riches, I should be prouder still, if I knew how to use those riches well. What shall I do to deserve such blessings?"

Oh, how rich you are! Let us count your riches. The beasts of the field and the fowls of the air have no speech. The wild beast roars ever the same note;

the birds sing ever the same tune. Their enjoyments
are few, because their wants are so few. They live,
they eat, they drink, they sleep, they bring forth
young, they die—that is the life-history of every bird,
beast, reptile, and fish, since the Creation till the present day. No improvement, no progress. The bird
builds its nest to-day precisely as did its forefathers
five thousand years ago.

But with you, how different! Let us count your
riches. You have speech—the power of conveying
your thoughts, your feelings, and your wishes to
those around you. Your voice is unlike any other
voice in creation. What varieties of feeling it can
express! With it you may laugh, or you may cry;
with it you may express your admiration or your
disgust, your love, your pity, or your scorn. The
same words spoken in different tones will have
different meanings.

Then think of the music of the voice. The cuckoo
never tires of her two notes, and knows no others; the
nightingale, with a voice of wider range, yet only
knows one song. But man can do much more. He
can combine his notes without limit, and make sweet
music to echo every thought; as many songs as
thoughts—without number.

Then reflect upon your face. You may be plain or
handsome, it matters not; there is that in your face
which is a treasure beyond price—the power of expression. The voice utters words, but it is the face
which speaks. The voice of pity is sweet; but how
much more eloquent the pitying look, the moist eye,
the face suffused with sympathy! The voice of anger

is terrible; but what its effect without the lowering brow, the flaming eye, the pouting lips, the distended nostrils, the fallen countenance?

Then think of the noble form of man. He is the only animal that stands naturally upright. Some animals there are, indeed, which, from their habit of climbing, assume something like the erect attitude; but it is always forced and unnatural; and the creature seems to be glad to walk on all its legs again. Those long fore-legs which, as they swing gracelessly by the monkey's side, seem to try to make us believe that they are arms, soon drop listlessly to the ground. The legs will be legs. The animal must walk bent to the earth. Even the gorilla, that nearest approach to man, though its strength is enormous, soon becomes fatigued when it walks in an erect position. The beast looks downwards, man upwards. There is something noble in the attitude of even the meanest man.

But if man has cause to be proud of his superiority over the brute creation, on account of his form, his attitude, and other qualities of his body, he has still greater cause for pride in the qualities of his mind; for they are qualities which he alone of all animals possesses, and which are wholly absent in the brute creation.

On man alone is bestowed the gift of Reason—that power by which you can put facts together, and draw therefrom conclusions, or new facts arising from those with which you were previously acquainted. Some have maintained that the brute shares this gift with man, but only in a less degree, and that what we call instinct is but a low kind of reason. But it matters little by what name you call it. You know full well, that the most sagacious brute never does anything which could indicate what you call reasoning. Its senses are keen, and it readily distinguishes friend from foe; its appetites are keen, and its senses guide the creature to the means of satisfying its cravings. It has its attachments and aversions, memory, hatred of a foe, and gratitude to a benefactor; but in spite of its experience and memory, it shows no increase of intelligence, after it has once reached maturity.

Man alone is an improving animal. You improve, because you have the desire to improve, and Reason and Free-will afford you the means of improving. Man does not accept the position in which he is born as a fate. His Free-will gives him the power of rising superior to adverse circumstances. No man is ever truly contented. The striving for something higher is the blessed distinction of our race. Without it, you would settle down in life like the beasts of the forest, careless of the future, callous to improvement. The desire of improvement spurs you to healthy action, gives you a relish for the duties of life, and bids you try to leave the world better than you found it.

But that same desire of improvement does not end its mission when it has tended to the increase of knowledge, and the advancement of those arts which mark the distinction between civilized and barbaric life. The desire of improvement gives birth to that noblest of all desires—the hope of a future and better state.

And here again you feel the proud position of man. You feel that you have a Soul within you, a Spirit which can never perish, which must live, when your body will have decayed and crumbled into dust. You feel that it is this soul, that sets in motion all your thoughts, your feelings, your reasoning, your judgment, and all the powers of your mind. You feel that it is this soul that bids you improve, that makes you dissatisfied even with the greatest worldly happiness, that tells you that the fulness of happiness is in a world beyond this.

If there were need to prove that this soul is immortal, you could not have a better proof than your own hopes—the hopes of all men. You would feel horrified if you were told that when your life here comes to an end, your soul would perish, and be annihilated. Your soul recoils from such an idea. Your fond hope, and the hope of every human being is a happy immortality. And this universal hope is one of the best proofs of the immortality of the soul; for surely that God, whose greatest attribute is kindness, would not have breathed into you and every man so noble a hope, and so holy an aspiration, without giving you the means and power of realising them. Your soul must be immortal, because an all-merciful Creator has bid you hope for immortality.

If a further proof were wanted of the soul's existence in a life hereafter, we might find one in the history of every human being, however lofty or however lowly his position. Everything in creation has an object and purpose. If there be no hereafter for man, what is the object, what is the purpose of his life?

Surely not the objects and purposes he attains in this world.

Take, for example, the life of a poor labouring man. He works hard all the days of his life, and all his wages are a morsel of bread. He has few enjoyments, few comforts; and the older he gets, the more difficult he finds it to earn a livelihood, the more burdensome his existence becomes.

Perhaps he is more fortunate than such men usually are. Perhaps, as he grows old, his children love, honour, and cherish him, and he thus has few troubles to weigh down his hoary head. But, however fortunate the lot of such a man, as he grows older, he will find in the world fewer and fewer attractions. Everything becomes irksome. He used to like the music of children's voices; he cannot bear it now. He used to like a nice gossip with his neighbours; he does not care for it now, for his tongue is sluggish and his memory fails him. He used to like to read what was going on in the world; but now he can read no more: his sight is too weak; and if anyone reads to him, he is nervous. Ask him, "What would you like, my good old man?" and he will reply, "Nothing, thank you. Let me sit quietly in my old arm-chair, next a roaring fire. Let me sit there quietly, doing nothing; only thinking."

Can this be the end for which this good old man has been labouring hard, and working well all his life?

Take another case. Take, for example, the life of a great statesman. He has worked very hard for the public good. Early and late he has laboured to improve the condition of his fellow creatures. Suppose the most favourable state of things. His services have been successful, and have been fully valued. The nation honours him; the great men of the earth court him; and people say he is one of the greatest men of the age. And he has a loving family who almost adore him. As for riches, he has more than he can ever care to increase. What more can he have of the good things of this world? And yet—and yet, though this great man has attained the summit of his worldly ambition, he is not happy. He is growing very old. He cannot help himself. He can scarcely walk. He goes to the Senate, the scene of his former triumphs, and people listen to a tremulous voice from lips which used to thunder forth fervid eloquence; and as they listen, fondly catching every syllable, mutter to themselves, "What a wonderful old man! but how different from what he was!" And then he knows himself how he has changed. He sees that the words of younger men have greater weight than his. So he enjoys the world no more. Day by day he becomes weaker. Even his high position weighs heavily upon him, bringing him responsibilities which he is too weak to bear. What can he do but follow the example of the poor old labourer, and sit quietly by the fireside, musing on the past?

And can this be the end, for which this great and noble old man has been labouring hard and working well all his life? Impossible. There must be a higher end in a world beyond this. There must be an existence in a future state, where the worker of good meets an eternal reward.

The two examples we have cited have been the most favourable examples that could be named— examples of men who, as far as their worldly hopes could reach, have, each in his own sphere, had those hopes amply fulfilled. But you must know well that the majority of the human race are not so fortunate. We are not all born to a happy life, not all destined to be heroes. The great bulk of the human race is made up of hard workers, whose life is almost a struggle for existence, whose happiness is chequered with many misfortunes, and whose worldly hopes are seldom half fulfilled. Surely, then, the aims and objects of their lives are not to be found in this world.

And worldly happiness is, at best, but a very partial kind of happiness. One man longs to attain riches, and thinks he will have arrived at the summit of happiness, if he becomes a rich man. He works hard, and becomes rich. And when he is rich, do you think he has attained happiness? Another man longs for knowledge—a more worthy longing. He studies hard; he travels; he searches for truth everywhere, and becomes a very learned man; and when he has acquired all this knowledge, what is his happiness? He has the small gratification of feeling that he knows a little more than his fellow-creatures; but he has learnt, among other things, the humiliating fact, that the more knowledge he has acquired, the more extensive has the field of knowledge become to him. The more he explores, the greater the extent of unexplored territory that rises before him.

And so with the object of every earthly hope, every

earthly ambition that we foster in our heart. It looks beautiful, it seems perfect happiness at a distance. But when attained, there seems always something wanting to make the happiness complete. We always crave for something more.

What does all this show? Does it not distinctly indicate that if happiness be the wages for toil, our wages are not paid in this world? Does not the very fact that our powers of enjoying worldly pleasures diminish as we grow older, plainly indicate that the great storehouse of happiness is in a future world?

Yes. Wherever we look, we see facts which point clearly to the conclusion that this life is a preparation for another life ; that happiness may certainly be found on earth, but that perfect happiness cannot be attained in this life ; that we are constituted to improve, that we are placed here to improve; that our improvement leads to our happiness ; that this world is a world of work, but that the real wages will be paid in a world beyond this.

CHAPTER VI.

REWARD AND PUNISHMENT.

THE real wages will be paid in the world beyond this. In the world to come, every man will receive the reward or the punishment to which his actions in this world entitle him.

But you will say, "We know nothing of the next world. How can we talk about such matters?" To a certain extent you are right. No one has ever come back from that great unknown territory to tell us what is the reward of the pious, and what the punishment of the wicked.

And it is well that our knowledge upon this subject is wrapped in uncertainty. For if we knew exactly the nature and extent of the reward or punishment payable for each of our actions, there would be no such thing as pure motive, and consequently there would be no merit in doing right and avoiding wrong.

Men would balance and weigh their sacrifices and their restraints here against the happiness resulting therefrom in a future state, would probably find it worth their while to be good and moral, and would be so not because it was right, but because it was profitable. But would the happiness resulting from such a commercial kind of virtue be pure happiness? I think not.

Suppose you go to school with your work well prepared, and that you have accomplished the task set you by dint of great industry and perseverance; and suppose that your teacher is so pleased with your work, that he gives you a prize, which you never had the least idea he would bestow, you will feel delighted at receiving such a reward. Your delight will be of the purest kind; for you will feel not only pleased at receiving the prize, but you will feel proud at having received it as a *token* of your industry, and not as a *payment* for your industry. The knowledge, which you will thus have acquired, will also give you an unusual degree of satisfaction; for you will feel that you have acquired that knowledge for the love of knowledge, and not for the sake of any benefit that you might derive from it.

Next, suppose that your teacher set to his class this very same difficult task, telling you and all his pupils that whoever performed the task to his satisfaction should receive a prize, I dare say you would try to gain it, and I hope you would succeed. But if you did, I am sure your pleasure would be very different from what it was, when you gained the other prize, without it having been promised to you. You would work for the prize, not for the knowledge; and when you took the prize, you would feel as if you had taken a sort of bribe to do something which was, after all, only right and proper that you should have done without any bribe. And, besides the happiness being less pure, the knowledge acquired would be less pure, and, probably, more easily lost.

And so it would be, if our great Master, our Creator, had announced to us the reward in store for us in a future life for every good action, and the punishment for every sin. The happiness derived from the reward would not be pure happiness. But, with the uncertainty of our knowledge as to the reward and punishment, virtue is truly its own reward on earth, and the happiness, be it great or small, which will be our prize in heaven will be a pure, a holy, an unsullied happiness. It will be unsullied by the sordid feeling that we had been bribed to do the right thing.

So you see that the uncertainty as to the nature and extent of reward and punishment in a future state is a positive advantage to us. But notwithstanding this uncertainty as to nature and extent, that such reward and punishment must exist is sufficiently clear. Let us reflect upon the subject, and see how it is that we must believe it.

In every-day life, we frequently see bad men prospering, and good men suffering the greatest misfortune. We often see men, who defy every principle of morality, leading a very pleasant life, growing rich and powerful, and apparently untouched by the least pang of remorse, and exhibiting no symptom of unhappiness. Everything with them seems to prosper, and good fortune seems to grow even out of their wickedness. On the other hand, we often see men, who lead a good and virtuous life—honest, industrious, and religious men—whose labours end all in disappointment, who are stricken by poverty or disease, and who are ever bowed down under the weight of their misfortunes. I dare say these cases are exceptional, but they are sufficient for our argument.

God is just; and even though these cases may be

exceptional, He cannot be unjust even in these exceptional cases.   Now, if there were no punishment in a
future life for the wicked man who prospers in this
world, and no reward in a future life for the good man
who is unfortunate in this world, would such a state
of things be consistent with the perfect justice of God?
We know not fully the ways of God; but we know
for certain that He is just; and justice requires that
the wicked man who prospers here shall be punished
hereafter, and that the good man who is unfortunate
here should receive the reward of his good deeds in a
future state.

And even apart from these considerations, when
we reflect upon the evident aim and object of our life
we shall come to the same conclusion.   If we believe
in the immortality of the soul—and who can doubt
it?—we must believe that we are here in this world
for some purpose connected with the everlasting state,
which is to follow our present life.   For what other
purpose can this be than to test the qualities of our
soul, to prove our worthiness to receive heavenly happiness, and, above all, to enable us to *earn* that happiness by deserving it?   Just as the bread is sweetest,
for which we have to toil the hardest; just as the
child is dearest, for whom we have to suffer most
anxiety, so is the happiness greatest for which we
have to work the most.

So we are here to earn the everlasting happiness,
which will only be true happiness if we shall have
fairly earned it by working for it and deserving it.
We all have trials and temptations placed in our way;
and he deserves eternal reward the most who over-

comes them. We all have passions and vices, and he earns best his title to everlasting reward who conquers them. We all have opportunities of doing good to our fellow-creatures, of improving our own minds, of contributing also, each in his own small way, to the improvement of the world. He who does this work well, deserves and earns the highest reward of immortal life.

But if, on the contrary, we submit to the dictates of our passions, if we encourage our vices, if we lead a selfish life, setting a bad example to those who are sure to copy us, if we abuse our opportunities, if we are dishonest to our neighbours, if we stifle the voice of conscience, if we transgress the laws of morality, if we forget all else in our love of wealth and worldly position, can we expect a reward in a future life from a just God? Must we not rather expect a punishment for spending a life ill, uselessly, mischievously, and wickedly, for neglecting golden opportunities, for abusing the wonderful powers with which we are endowed?

We know not what may be the nature or degree of the reward or of the punishment. These are

> Things which the invisible King,
> Only omniscient, has suppressed in night.
> *Milton.*

But reward certainly awaits the good, and punishment certainly awaits the wicked. Every man is responsible for his deeds. According to his work, so will be his wages in the world to come.[1]

[1] The arguments on this and the preceding chapter will be found further developed in Part II., Chap. xii.

PART II.

REVEALED RELIGION.

———◆———

CHAPTER I.

WHY RELIGION WAS REVEALED.

ALL that we have proved so far about God and His ways, we have learnt from looking into God's works, within and without us—in other words, from looking into Nature; and so the religion we have at present learnt is known as Natural Religion.

And I dare say you think, that the conclusions we have come to are also natural in another sense; for they have nothing unnatural or unreasonable about them; and you will be right in so considering them. Indeed, I should not be surprised if you imagined, too, that what I have taught you is so plain and so clear that it would be impossible for any men to come to any other conclusion about God and His ways than those which we have arrived at.

I wish you were right in thinking so. I wish I could tell you that all the world believes as you believe, and that the "Natural Religion," which you consider so very natural, was the religion of the whole world. I am sorry to say it is not.

Perhaps there might have been a time, when the

world was young, when all men's ideas about religion were as pure and natural as your own. Of this we cannot be sure; for there is a great uncertainty about all history, especially about the early history of the world. But this we know—that before the world was very old there were all sorts of religions, and that people were not satisfied with the simple and beautiful Natural Religion—the religion taught by Nature—which declared One only God, to be the Creator of Heaven and Earth.

How it all occurred no one can say with certainty. But in course of time almost all men worshipped idols, images of wood or metal or stone, of their own making, or worshipped the sun, or fire, or animals, instead of the great and unseen God.

Perhaps it was because the Great God was unseen that they at first made idols only to remind them of Him. Perhaps, when they at first worshipped and bowed down to the sun, they thought they were doing honour to God, its Creator.[1] But, however that may be, in course of time some worshipped the sun as if it were their Creator, and others bowed down to idols, the work of their own hands, as if the idols had made them. All this is very curious—so curious that you will probably find it difficult to believe that people could have been so silly; but it is nevertheless true; and you may see hundreds of those idols preserved in the British Museum, some of wood, some of metal, and some of stone; and there are learned people who

---

[1] The Parsees now worship God in this same manner, and with the same idea. The common notion that they are Sun-worshippers is not true.

could tell you much about each of those idols, and about
the people who worshipped them ; and not the least
wonderful fact about the matter is, that many of the
people who worshipped those idols were very clever,
and were only silly in their religious belief and
practices.

Now, if people simply believed in a foolish unreasonable religion, and in other respects were good
people, always doing right and acting justly, their
silly belief would, perhaps, do no great harm to any
but themselves. But unfortunately it happened, that
idolatry, or the worship of idols, led to all sorts of
wickedness.

I could not tell you a hundredth part of the dreadful sins that idolaters were guilty of; but they often
committed frightful sins in the name of their religion,
and did all sorts of wicked things, saying that their idols
or gods bade them act thus. And, worst of all, they
committed murder, in the name of religion. The fire-
worshippers, for example, used to sacrifice men and
women and even children to their fire-god, burning
them in fiery furnaces as offerings.[1] Captives of war,
instead of being kindly treated or kept as slaves, were
slain in like manner as offerings to the idols, and, such
was sometimes the madness of idolaters, that many of
them sacrificed their own lives or the lives of their
own dearest children to those idols they declared to
be their gods. What silly folks to think that this
could please the Great Creator of Heaven and Earth !

All this went on for very many years, for hundreds
of years. Religion ran wild in idolatry, and as the

---

[1] Deut. xii. 31.

religions of idolatry grew, all kinds of wickedness grew, till at last the world became so wicked that it could never have lasted in such a state.

But God ordained it otherwise. He could not leave men to make their own religion, for the results had been too dreadful; so God Himself had to teach the religion that was true and good and fit for mankind, not only to make known His own existence, His own ways and works, but to make known His Will, His Law, His code of right and wrong. The making known or revealing to man this knowledge is called the *Revelation*.

CHAPTER II.

How Religion was Revealed.

You will read in the Bible how this was done.

It was not done in a moment. It was the slow work of many, many years.

God revealed Himself to Noah immediately after the flood, giving the world, through him, a few leading laws, intended to prevent a repetition of those acts of violence[1] which, before the deluge, had disgraced humanity.

God again revealed Himself to Abraham, the son of Terah, an idolater. He bade him leave his native land, his kindred, and his father's house, and travel in distant countries; and assured him that through him all the nations of the earth should be blessed. And wherever he went, Abraham proclaimed the Name of the True God, and by his noble example of goodness, kindness, virtue, and unselfishness, showed the world that his religion must be the true one; and that his God must be the One and only True God.

I will not recount to you all the events of the life of Abraham; for you can read the history for yourselves in your Bible; you can also read some beautiful stories about him which are translated from the Talmud; and you will not then be surprised to hear, that Abraham made many converts to his belief.

[1] Gen. vi. 11.

Abraham had several sons, one of whom—Isaac—
was alone worthy to succeed him in his mission. He,
too, travelled about, working, like his father, to make
known to the world the fact that had been so long
forgotten, and which has since his time been so often
lost sight of, that Religion and Morality are one, and
cannot be divided; that as God is all Goodness, so
there cannot be godliness without goodness; and that
the love of God is best shown by the love of God's
creatures. The Bible tells you all about the history of
Isaac in such beautiful words, that I will not attempt
to imitate them; so I will leave you to read his history
for yourselves in the Bible, and you will also find some
charming stories about him among those Talmudical
tales to which I have already referred.

Time went on; and Isaac had two sons, of whom,
one—Jacob—was considered, notwithstanding many
faults, worthy to follow his father in his task of
improving the world. He, too, became a wanderer,
and there is no doubt that he, too, made known the
one true Religion wherever he went.

The Bible tells the eventful history of Jacob in
terms so beautiful and so wonderful, that you will
read it with the greatest interest. The Bible, ever
truthful, tells you of all his faults, and failings. But
in spite of all his faults and failings, the sacred
history shows Jacob to be a grand example of
confidence and belief in the goodness and power of
God.

How he served faithfully for many long years as a
humble shepherd; how in time he was blessed with
large possessions and a numerous family; how he

returned to his native land a wealthy prince; how he lost his favourite son Joseph, and after the long lapse of years, again found him, having become, by the wonderful course of events, the greatest man in all Egypt, who had, under God's wise Providence, saved the whole country from the effects of a terrible famine, and how he and all his children and grandchildren—seventy souls—went down to Egypt and settled there—all this you will read for yourselves in the Bible, and you will find the history more stirring and marvellous than any tale you ever read.

Jacob died, and so, too, after many years of prosperity, did his son Joseph, and all his other sons. While they lived, they and their descendants were loved and respected by the Egyptians; but when they died, the great good which Joseph had worked for Egypt, was soon forgotten: a new king arose, who knew not Joseph; and all the Israelites, or descendants of Jacob, were cruelly treated.

For they were too prosperous. They increased in numbers; and as they increased, so the knowledge of the True God probably spread throughout the land, and threatened to put an end to the idolatry of Egypt. The Egyptians grew alarmed at this. Their idolatry was very peculiar. They worshipped living animals, birds, beasts and reptiles. One would scarcely believe it; for the same history which tells these facts gives full particulars of the wonderful learning of the Egyptians, and shows how they were wiser in science and in the arts than any people of that age.

For a long, long time, the Israelites were oppressed by the Egyptians, used as slaves, over-worked and tormented ; but in spite of all this ill-treatment, they did not join the idolaters of Egypt ; they remained steadfast to their Religion ; and when they suffered, they cried to the Lord God of their fathers, the One True God, whom they had been taught to regard as the sole Creator and Ruler of the world.

Their cry was heard. For God sent them Moses to deliver them from the oppression of the Egyptians ; and it was this same Moses, who was to be the instrument of God's revelation to Israel, the man who was to make known God's Law to His people and through them to the whole of mankind.

The Bible will tell you all about the early history of Moses ; how he was preserved from drowning, when an infant ; how he was brought up at the court of Pharaoh, the king of Egypt, by the king's own daughter ; how he went out and saw the sufferings of his people and pitied them ; how he protected the weak against the strong ; how God appeared to him, and told him of his mission, declaring that he was to be the herald of His sacred Name, and the deliverer of His people ; and how He gave him the power of working miracles, so as to show that he was indeed a messenger of God.

You know what a miracle is. You know that it is an exceptional departure from the ordinary course of things, a temporary suspension of some law of nature. We do not see such miracles occurring in our times, and therefore it is to some people difficult to believe that miracles ever took place. But it surely ought not to be difficult to believe that the same God who made the world, and who has boundless power, can, if He so wills it, for some special purpose, alter or suspend for a time the established order of nature.[1]

You will read in the Bible how Moses followed the commands of God ; how he communicated his message of deliverance to His people ; how he begged Pharaoh, often and in vain, to allow the Israelites to leave Egypt ; how the wicked king afflicted the Israelites more and more ; how Moses threatened him with the anger of God ; how Pharaoh persisted in his wickedness ; how Moses worked miracles in the sight of the king, to show that God indeed had sent him ; how ten terrible plagues were sent, one after the other, to punish Pharaoh and his people for their ill-treatment of the poor Israelites ; and how on the night of the tenth plague, when the first-born of every Egyptian family was struck dead, the children of Israel, who, living in the midst of these awful plagues, had remained uninjured and untouched by them, were allowed, amid the scene of death and suffering, to pass out of the cities of the Egyptians, unhurt and without hindrance.

But the crowning miracle was to come—the miracle which more than any other was to show the Israelites the power of the Great God who had brought them out of Egypt. For the Egyptians, recovering from the blow inflicted upon them by the death of their first-born children, and finding the Israelites gone, pursued them ; and Pharaoh, with all his hosts of horsemen and foot-soldiers, overtook them on the brink of the Red

---

[1] See Appendix III., " Miracles and Revelation," for a further development of this argument.

F

Sea. Imagine the position of the poor Israelites! Behind them the teeming hosts of a cruel enemy, ready to destroy them or capture them ; before them the cruel sea ready to engulf them. But suddenly, by the Divine command, the waters of the deep arose from their bed—stood erect like walls on their right hand and their left, permitting the Israelites to pass between, on the dry bed of the sea, and to reach the opposite shore. The Egyptians followed in pursuit. They too trod the dry bed of the sea ; but before they could reach the opposite shores, the waters returned to their place, and Pharaoh's mighty hosts were drowned in the rolling waves.

One can well understand that the nation of some two million Israelites, unexpectedly rescued by this miracle, would love and reverence and honour the Mighty God, who had saved them in so wonderful a manner, when all hope of deliverance had vanished, and by this miracle they would be induced, nay, compelled, to believe in the God who had saved them. Indeed, the Bible tells us, that when " Israel saw the Egyptians dead upon the sea-shore . . . the people feared the Lord, and believed in the Lord and His servant Moses."

Moses led the Israelites from the banks of the Red Sea into the wilderness of Arabia; and here they were fed daily with food which fell from Heaven. A pillar of cloud led them by day, and a pillar of fire showed them the way by night. They lived a life of miracle, for all their daily wants were supplied by an unseen Hand, and by no work of their own.

After a few weeks of this miraculous life in the

desert, they came to the wilderness of Sinai; and their minds were thus well prepared to receive the great Revelation—the proclamation of the Will of God, and to believe it.

For they had learned to regard themselves as a special and peculiar people, protected by God, fed by His Hand without effort of their own; they were prepared to listen and to believe.

And when they came near the mountain of Sinai, where God was about to reveal Himself to them, He called to Moses and bade him prepare them for their mission. He was to tell them, " If ye will obey My voice, indeed, and keep My covenant, then ye shall be a peculiar treasure unto Me above all people, for all the earth is Mine. And you shall be unto Me a kingdom of priests, and an holy nation." And when the people heard these words, they answered together, " All that the Lord has spoken we will do."

Three days after, the Voice of God was heard on Sinai amidst thunders, clouds, and lightning, and the sound of trumpets, declaring the Law which was to be for ever the guide of mankind. You must read for yourselves in your Bible the narrative of this wonderful event—the greatest event that ever took place in the world's history—fully to understand the awful solemnity of the scene. Fancy six hundred thousand men, with their wives and children, crowding round the foot of the mountain, the mountain blazing and smoking like a furnace, the earth quaking, the lightning flashing, the thunder rumbling, the trumpets sounding long and loud—waxing louder and louder —and God revealing Himself and His holy Will to

His people, through His servant Moses, not secretly to a few, not in a dream by night to a small and selected number, but in the open day, to a whole nation, to six hundred thousand men, their wives and children!

CHAPTER III.

THE TEN COMMANDMENTS.

1. I am the Lord thy God, who have brought thee out of the land of Egypt, out of the house of bondage.

2. Thou shalt have no other gods before me. Thou shalt not make unto thee any graven image, or any likeness of any thing that is in the heavens above, or that is in the earth beneath, or that is in the waters under the earth. Thou shalt not bow down thyself to them, nor serve them ; for I the Lord thy God am a jealous God, visiting the iniquity of the fathers upon the children unto the third and fourth generation of them that hate me: and shewing mercy unto thousands of them that love me and keep my commandments.

3. Thou shalt not take the name of the Lord thy God in vain: for the Lord will not hold him guiltless that taketh his name in vain.

4. Remember the sabbath day to keep it holy. Six days shalt thou labour and do all thy work: but the seventh day is the sabbath of the Lord thy God : thereon thou shalt not do any work, thou, nor thy son, nor thy daughter, thy man-servant, nor thy maid-servant, nor thy cattle, nor thy stranger that is within thy gates: for in six days the Lord made heaven and earth, the sea, and all that in them is, and rested on the seventh day : wherefore the Lord blessed the sabbath day, and hallowed it.

5. Honour thy father and thy mother ; that thy days may be long upon the land which the Lord thy God giveth thee.

6. Thou shalt not kill.

7. Thou shalt not commit adultery.

8. Thou shalt not steal.

9. Thou shalt not bear false witness against thy neighbour.

10. Thou shalt not covet thy neighbour's house, thou shalt

not covet thy neighbour's wife, nor his man-servant, nor his
maid-servant, nor his ox, nor his ass, nor anything that is thy
neighbour's.

WHEN children are young, their wise parents do not
teach them too many things at first, lest they might
forget them; but they tell them first the few things
which are the most important; and as they get older,
they go on teaching them more and more, little by
little.

And God treated the children of Israel in the same
wise way. He did not tell them all the Law at once,
but began with the Ten Commandments, because,
although the most important, they were quite easy
and simple, and able to be understood and obeyed by
everyone. And that is the reason why I have quoted
them in full.

The First Commandment.

You will notice that God began the Commandments
by telling the Israelites that He—the God who was
speaking to them—was the same God who saved them
from the Egyptians. God might have told the
children of Israel that He was the God who had
created them and all the world. But they could not
have understood that half so well as the great fact,
which they themselves had so lately experienced—
that He was the God who had saved them from
slavery, and that He alone was to be the Lord their
God.

The Second Commandment.

In the Second Commandment you will find that

God tells the Israelites that they shall have no other
God but Him; that they shall make no idols,
nor bow down to images. And then God tells them
something about Himself. He tells them that He is
a just God who punishes the wicked people and such
of their children as hate Him, and that He is also a
merciful God, who is good and kind to all who love
Him and obey His laws.

Now, if you are asked what is the chief difference
between Jews and other people, you might safely say,
that the Jews believe and obey all that is in the Second
Commandment, but that members of most other faiths
do not, although perhaps they fancy they do. For
the followers of most other religions believe that there
is somebody besides God who saves sinners from
punishment. But God tells us in this Second Commandment that He alone is God, that there is none
beside Him, that it is He alone who visits or punishes
iniquity and sin, that we have to answer to Him for
our actions, good or bad, and that it is to Him alone
we must look for mercy.[1]

And so we have in these first two Commandments
the main principles or chief points of our belief—that
the God who gave us the Law on Sinai is the One
and only God, who will reward us or punish us according as we are good or wicked.[2]

---

[1] We find the same declaration in Deut. xxxii. 39. "See now
that I, even I, am He, and there is no god with me: I kill, and
I make alive; I wound, and I heal: neither is there any that
can deliver out of my hand."

[2] The Jewish Creed may be reduced to these three principles:
(1.) That God is ONE; (2.) That He gave us the Law; (3.)
That He will reward the good and punish the wicked.

The Third Commandment.

The Third Commandment forbids us to swear falsely; forbids us indeed to swear at all, unless it be necessary to do so in the interest of truth.

In courts of law people who give evidence, or tell all that they know of the matters enquired about, have to promise to speak the truth, and they call God to witness that every word they are about to speak is true. This is called swearing, or taking an oath. If, after taking the oath, they say anything untrue, they are guilty of perjury or false swearing.

People must never swear except when ordered to do so by law. If they swear without it being necessary, they take the name of God in vain; and God will consider them guilty.

An oath is a very sacred thing, and if you ever go into a court of law, you will see how important it is, where all sorts of weighty matters—often matters of life and death—are in question, that witnesses, or persons who give evidence, should speak the exact truth. And so, in this country, they have to promise to speak "the truth, the whole truth, and nothing but the truth," and then they have to kiss the Bible to show that they believe in the God of the Bible, and that they know and feel that He hears all that they say, and that they believe that He will not hold them guiltless if they say anything untrue, and so take His name in vain. I shall tell you more about this, when we come to the Ninth Commandment.

But taking the name of the Lord God in vain has yet another meaning. If we pray to God without think-

ing about what we are saying; or if we pray in a
hurried, careless manner, only anxious to get through
our prayers, or if we laugh or gossip in synagogue,
we take God's name in vain.

Children, and indeed grown-up people too, often get
into a bad and silly habit of "saying their prayers"
instead of praying. If you beg your parents to do
you some favour, you will speak to them in an earnest,
careful manner, and will not stare about you while
you are addressing them. And if you caress them,
and tell them how much you love them and how duti-
ful and obedient you will be to them, you will speak
to them as if you meant it, and will not be thinking
of something else while you are talking to them. But
people who ask favours of God, and who address Him
in words of praise and thanksgiving, often let their
words fall from their lips without thinking of what
they are saying, or of the meaning of the words they
utter, but think meantime of all sorts of other things.
This is *saying prayers*, not *praying*. This is taking
God's name in vain. And God tells us that He will
not hold us guiltless, if we thus pray without turning
our thoughts to Him.

The Fourth Commandment.

The Fourth Commandment is a very long one; but
you will know almost all about it without my telling
you.

You who have lessons all the week will no doubt
think this a very pleasant commandment, and one
very easy to obey; and perhaps you will think that

God need only have ordered the Israelites to rest on the seventh day without giving such a long commandment, and going into so many particulars.

You know how pleased you always are when Friday evening comes, and what a treat it is to have no lessons to learn till Sunday morning, and how glad you are to see your parents with you all Saturday, doing all they can to make you happy; taking you with them to synagogue to hear the prayers and the singing; taking you with them afterwards for a nice walk and a pleasant talk, and not troubling you at all about lessons or books, except just a little piece of the Bible or a short Bible story, which you like too much to call a lesson, and which you would not miss for the world.

And I dare say you will wonder very much when I tell you that plenty of people break this law, and keep no Sabbath, but go on, by their own free will, week after week, working, and working, and working, without having any day of rest. And perhaps, when I tell you this, you will exclaim, " Poor people, how I do pity them !" Well, so do I; but they are not all poor people in the sense you mean the word. They are generally people who are very fond of money, and who think that if they stop working on Sabbath, they will lose the chance of gaining a little more, and they either forget or will not remember that they are disobeying God.

Now in the Fourth Commandment, God tells us very plainly that we must and ought to be industrious, and do all our work on six days of the week ; but that the seventh is the Sabbath or day of rest, and that neither we nor our servants, nor even our cattle, should do therein any sort of work; and He tells us that, after having made all things in six days, He Himself rested on the seventh day, and thus hallowed the Sabbath by His own Divine example.

If you will just think a little about the wonderful world and the creatures in it, I fancy it will strike you, as it has often struck me too, that the most wonderful thing in all God's creation is that which He created at the close of the sixth day—Rest.

The world is so full of life and work and movement, that we are apt to forget how great a blessing and how great a wonder is rest. You, young people, who revel in your sports, whose joyous spirits find their vent in merry laughter, while you run or leap or vault as if your legs were made of springs (as indeed they are to some extent), what would you be, I wonder, without rest? How do you think you would get on, if, when tired out, you were to lie down and be unable to sleep, or if, when dreadfully fatigued, some cruel person were to come and tell you you must go on playing or running or jumping, whether you liked it or not? Do you think you would enjoy it, when tired out and ready for a nice refreshing sleep? I think not.

And is it not wonderful how, without any trying, you go to sleep? and how you wake up, feeling so fresh and vigorous and ready for fun, just as if you had never been fatigued in your life? or how, after a long tiring walk, you sit down and rest, and then feel quite strong again and ready for another long walk? Ah, rest is a wonderful thing, perhaps the greatest blessing in the world; so you need not wonder that God should have blessed the Day of Rest and made it holy.

But if you, who only have to learn lessons or do needlework, and do no very hard work with your head or your hands, find rest so pleasant and so good for you, how must it be with grown-up people, who have to work hard for their living all the week? How delighted they ought to be when Friday evening comes, and they feel that they need not, cannot, and dare not do any more work for a whole day! Not only do they enjoy the rest for which they have worked so hard, but when the time comes for them to set to work again, they enjoy their work all the more, just as you feel all the more inclined for a nice romp, after you have awoke from a sound sleep. It is a splendid thing—this Sabbath—which God has given us as a holy day of rest, and you may feel quite sure that those who do not keep the Sabbath do not half enjoy their lives.

Now, most religions besides ours, have a Sabbath; although, as you know, some keep it on a different day; but they don't keep the Sabbath as we do: and I dare say you will ask how we ought to keep it.

You might be inclined to say that, as it is a day of rest, people should lie in bed all Sabbath, and so have a nice long day of idleness. But if you look at the Fourth Commandment you will find that the seventh day is called the "Sabbath of the Lord thy God," also that God blessed the Sabbath day and hallowed it, or made it a holy day. Now, this shows that we

ought to spend at least some part of the Sabbath in
the service of God, in reflecting about Him and His
wonderful works, in praising and thanking Him for
His goodness, and in thinking about our position as
His creatures. And this being a day on which we
have no lessons or business to do, we have plenty of
time to examine ourselves, and ask ourselves whether
we have done right during the past week, and, if not,
how we can do better next week.

But you must not for one moment imagine that
God's Sabbath is to be, as some of our neighbours
make it, a sad day, on which you may not laugh, or be
merry, or read pleasant books. Judaism is a happy
religion and a natural one, and you are meant to
be happy and natural on the Sabbath day. When
you have done your religious duties, you may play as
much as you like. Only there are things which you
may not do, even though they be for enjoyment. For
example, you may not cook or do anything with fire ;
nor may you buy anything, nor carry any burden ;
nor write, nor do needlework, because all these things
are done on the working days as matters of labour.
Nor may you drive or ride on the Sabbath, because God,
mindful alike of all His creatures, and wishing that
man should be merciful to the poor dumb beast, commanded that the cattle should also rest. But putting
aside all these things, there are plenty of pleasures
left to you for the Sabbath, and it must be not only a
day of rest and quiet thought, but a day of joy and
gladness.

The Fifth Commandment.

I once heard a little girl say that God need not have troubled Himself to give the Fifth Commandment at all ; and when I asked her why, she said she could not imagine any people who did not honour and love and obey their father and mother.

I wish this little girl was right. But unfortunately there are many children, and many grown-up people too, who are apt to disobey this simple commandment.

To honour one's parents means much more than merely paying them respect. It means that we must do whatever they tell us willingly, and even without asking why. It means that we must follow their good advice. It means that we must tend them lovingly when they grow old or ill or infirm, as lovingly as they tended us when we were young and helpless. It means that we must bear in mind their wishes when we are away from them, and even long after they are dead. It means that we must never do anything to dishonour their good name.

And if we obey this command, God promises us that our days shall be long in the land that He giveth us.

The Sixth Commandment.

"Thou shalt not commit murder," is one of the most important laws in the Bible. It was not a new law when God gave it on Sinai. He gave the same law to Noah when he and his family came out of the ark.

Obedience to this law makes the great difference between barbarous and civilized men. Among bar-

barians, life is never safe. One man hates another or envies his property, and he thinks nothing of killing him, if he be the stronger man. But God put an end to the reign of "might against right," when He declared, " Thou shalt not commit murder; " and even earlier still, when He told Noah, " Whoso sheddeth man's blood, by man shall his blood be shed." Human life was to be sacred, it being the great gift of God. We are to do all in our power to protect and save life. We may not stand by quietly and see a fellow-being perish if we can assist him. Our wise men remind us that as we are all descended from one man, Adam, he who saves a single life is as if he had created a world. So when you read this commandment, you must not think that it does not apply to such as you, to whom the horrid thought of murdering a fellow-creature would never occur; but you must remember too, that it bids you assist your poor and suffering fellow-creatures, and do all that is in your power to help them to live.

You will find in the Bible very many other laws, having for their chief object the protection of human life ; such, for example, as the laws relating to dangerous animals,[1] the commandment to build battlements or parapets on the house-tops, lest persons might fall therefrom and be killed,[2] and the laws of the cities of refuge,[3] which were intended to shelter those who had by accident killed a fellow-creature.

The Seventh Commandment.

This commandment forbids husbands and wives to

[1] Exod. xxi. 28.　　[2] Deut. xxii. 8.　　[3] Deut. xix. 1—10.

be unfaithful, or untrue, or unkind to one another; and the importance of this you will understand better as you advance in age.

The Eighth Commandment.

This law is a very short one; but it tells us a great deal in a few words. There are unfortunately a great number of people who steal rather than work for a living. If they are found out, they are sent to prison, or otherwise punished; and you will probably be surprised to hear, that there are people who have actually spent the greater part of their lives in prison, having been so often found guilty of theft. Perhaps they have been the children of bad, dishonest parents, and have seen all sorts of wickedness in their young days. Not that this excuses them; but it accounts for their wickedness, which to you would otherwise appear hardly comprehensible.

Now you, and children like you, who have been well and carefully brought up, would feel horrified at the idea of stealing even the most trifling article; and I am sure, when you grow up, you will feel just as horrified at the notion of taking anything that belongs to anyone else. But I ought to tell you that there is a good deal of stealing done in an indirect or roundabout way, but which is none the less a crime because the law cannot touch it so easily. I mean dishonest dealing and deceitful trading.

If a shop-keeper tells a customer a lie about some article he is selling, intending him to think it more valuable than it is, or if a servant wastes his master's time or property; or if a man borrows money which he knows he cannot repay; or if he sells a faulty article, charging the price of a perfect one; or if a tradesman sells short weight or adulterated goods; or if he buys property which he knows, or suspects, has been stolen—all these are dishonest dealings, and are offences against the law, "Thou shalt not steal," quite as much as stealing a piece of money directly from a neighbour's pocket.

I told you that the *protection of human life* was one of the greatest marks of distinction between savages and civilized men. The *protection of property* is another such mark of distinction. If property were not safe, no one would care to work hard to make money or amass wealth; and people would only care to work enough for their use from day to day, lest some one stronger than they should come directly they had saved a little, and rob them of all they had saved. Saving, or "thrift," as it is called, is of great importance to the welfare of the world; for without thrift in good times, we might starve when the bad times come. And indeed this really happens in barbarous countries even in our own days. Property not being safe against thieves, the people do not care to save, but eat and use all that they produce. When a bad harvest comes, they have saved nothing, and they starve to death. So you see the importance of thrift; and as thrift cannot exist unless property is safe, you see also the importance of the law, "Thou shalt not steal."

Other parts of the Bible contain laws on the same subject, and give us particulars of the punishment of

G

theft. In Leviticus,[1] and Deuteronomy,[2] we are commanded, to be just in business matters, and to give full weight and true measure. A thief, if the article stolen were found with him, had to pay twice the value of what he had taken ; and if he stole a living animal, and slew it, he had to "restore five oxen for the ox, and four sheep for the sheep."[3]   If he had not the means of paying, he was sold as a slave,[4] and this was the origin of what we now call "penal servitude," *i.e.*, imprisonment for a certain term of years, with hard labour.

The Ninth Commandment.

You know already something about the Ninth Commandment—"Thou shalt not bear false witness against thy neighbour,"—because, in telling you about the Third Commandment, I told you what a witness is, and what perjury, or false swearing, means.

The worst of all perjury is that in which a man bears false witness, or gives untrue evidence against his fellow-man. It is a crime terrible enough when his false evidence is likely to deprive another of his rights, or of his property; but it is a thousand times worse when his false evidence is intended to deprive another of his character, or his liberty, or perhaps his life.

I have told you of the form of oath used in this country. When the Jews lived in their own country, in Palestine, and a witness gave evidence affecting the

---

[1] Levit. xix. 35, 36.   [2] Deut. xxv. 13, 14, 15.
[3] Exod. xxii. 1, 9.   [4] Exod. xxii. 3.

life of a prisoner, the Judges reminded the witness of
the duty of speaking the exact truth, and told him
that he who destroyed one single human life was as
guilty as if he had destroyed a whole world.

It is almost impossible to imagine anyone guilty of
so terrible a sin as bearing false witness against
another; and yet there have been many such cases,
and not a few, too, in which people have even been
condemned to death upon evidence falsely given.

In another part of the Law,[1] God ordains what
shall be the punishment of the perjurer. He is to
suffer the same punishment as the intended victim
would have suffered, if the perjurer's evidence had
held good : "If the witness be a false witness, and
has testified falsely against his brother, then you shall
do unto him as he had thought to have done unto his
brother."

But, although you may find it difficult to imagine
anyone wicked enough to bear false witness against
his neighbour in a court of justice, you will have less
difficulty in imagining people wicked enough to transgress this law in other places. Indeed, when you
reflect a little, you will call to mind that bearing false
witness against a neighbour is rather a common,
every-day sin.

When you hear children speaking against one
another, making much of their playmates' little
faults, or taking away their schoolfellows' characters,
although they are not perjurers, yet they bear false
witness against their neighbours. As you grow older,
you will find that nothing is more valuable to anyone

---

[1] Deut. xix. 18, 19.

than *character*. And yet nothing is so easily injured by a chance word, perhaps carelessly or thoughtlessly dropped. Gossips, who are too idle to work, are never too idle to talk, and they dearly love a little scandal about their neighbours. They mean it to be harmless enough, and have, perhaps, no notion of hurting anyone; but the harmless scandal, every time it is repeated, becomes greater and greater, exaggerated each time it is spoken, till at last it is by no means harmless; for it destroys a good character.

It is always a safe rule never to speak ill of anyone. People will often call you dull and stupid, if you refuse to join them in talking scandal and laughing away the characters of their neighbours. But you must not mind that. The people, who are really dull and stupid, are those who have nothing sensible and amiable to talk about, and who talk scandal because there is nothing else in their silly heads.

The Tenth Commandment.

A great deal might be written about the Tenth Commandment; for covetousness is the root of almost every sin.

We are ordered not to covet anything that is our neighbour's; and many people have thought this rather an unreasonable law, because they have not understood it properly. They say: Why should not a man be ambitious, and like to have things as good as his neighbour has? If his neighbour has a nice house or a nice ox, why should it be a sin for him to

say, " I wish that house were mine !" or, " I wish that
ox were mine ! "?

Now, if he were to say, " I wish I had a house like
his !" or, " I wish I had an ox like his !" he would be
doing no great harm; because, although it is always
well to be happy with what one has, there is nothing
to prevent a man working hard and earning money;
and, when he has earned enough, he may buy or build
a house exactly like his neighbour's house; and there
are oxen enough in the world; so that he can buy
quite as fine an ox as his neighbour has. The sin
of coveting, then, consists not in your wishing for a
similar article, but for the same article that your neighbour has. His house, for example, could not be yours
unless you somehow dispossessed him of it, and in
order to do this, you might be induced to do him
some wrong.

If you read the history of King Ahab, you will find
that this was the sort of covetousness that led him
and his wife to commit a terrible sin. He coveted the
vineyard of Naboth; and because Naboth would not
sell it to him, the King's wife, Jezebel, procured some
wicked men to give false evidence to the effect that
Naboth had committed a fearful crime against God,
and the poor man was stoned to death; and then
Ahab took possession of the vineyard he had so
longed for.

Ahab and Jezebel were both very wicked people :
so you are, perhaps, not much surprised at their being
covetous. But, when you read the Bible, you will
find that even the great and good King David, in a
moment of blind passion, committed a terrible sin,

almost if not quite equal to murder, through coveting his neighbour's wife, and that he was fearfully
punished in consequence.

So you see what covetousness may lead us to.
Understand, there is no harm in being ambitious—
that is, in wanting to improve our position, to grow
greater, or richer, or more comfortable, and to have
nice things about us. The harm is in letting the
ambition become a passion, and letting the passion
so get the better of us, that we don't mind what we
do so long as we get what we want.

It is always best to be contented; but if you are
ambitious, there is one way of checking ambition so
as to prevent it becoming a passion. While you are
trying your best to grow rich, you should try at the
same time—and still harder—to grow wiser, and
more learned, and more pious; and if your wisdom
and knowledge and goodness grow as your riches
grow, your riches will do you no harm. Then your
ambition for wealth, position, or comfort will never
lead you to covet anything that is your neighbour's.
You will earn your money honorably, and perhaps
become as well off as your neighbour, without wishing
him or doing him any harm. You will spend your
money well and wisely; for your great ambition will
be to do all the good that is possible with the means
with which God has blessed you.

But in all your efforts, you will never covet what is
your neighbour's. War and murder and theft and
misery, and, indeed, almost every evil in the world
would vanish, if people would only obey the Tenth
Commandment.

CHAPTER IV.

ABOUT THE LAW OF MOSES.

YOU will read in the Bible, that when the children of Israel heard the Voice of God proclaiming the Ten Commandments, when they perceived "the thunderings and the lightnings and the noise of the trumpets and the mountains smoking," overcome by fear, they removed and stood afar off. And they begged Moses to go near and listen to all that God had to order them, and promised Moses, that if he would tell them the commands of God, they would obey in all things.

And so "the people stood afar off; and Moses drew near unto the thick darkness where God was." And then God said to him, "I will speak unto thee all the commandments and the statutes, and the judgments which thou shalt teach them." And thus it happens that the Law which God gave to our forefathers is called the "Law of Moses," or the "Mosaic Code," because, after God had proclaimed the Ten Commandments on Mount Sinai, He gave the other laws by the mouth of Moses, who taught them to the people, through the chiefs of the tribes and the wise men, during the forty years' wanderings in the wilderness.

These laws were not given to Moses all at once; but they were given at different times, and as occasion required; and when the forty years' wanderings were over, and Moses was about to die, he repeated the most important of them, and also added some, which, for various reasons, had not been mentioned before.

It thus happens, that the various laws are spread about the books of Exodus, Leviticus, Numbers, and Deuteronomy, mixed up with the history of the wanderings, and with the events which gave rise to many of those laws; and, surely, no better way could have been found of teaching a people so many laws, than by giving them a few at a time, and putting them in practice as they were given.

For you must remember that in those times—thousands of years before printing was invented—the Israelites could not each have, as we have, a nice, neat little book, containing all the laws of God; so the laws had to be so taught as to be well kept in memory, and there is no better way of remembering things than by practising them.

You will find also some of the laws in the first Book—the Book of Genesis—laws which God gave to the patriarchs Noah and Abraham, and these too are embodied with the laws given to the Israelites by Moses, and so the whole five books, Genesis, Exodus, Leviticus, Numbers, and Deuteronomy, are together called the *Torah* (תּוֹרָה), or Law; not that these books are all law-books, for indeed they are history and law combined—the word *Torah* (תּוֹרָה) meaning much more than " law," for it means instruction,[1] or what we now call education.

---

[1] The word *Torah* תּוֹרָה is derived from the verb יָרָה " to teach."

So when you read the Pentateuch,[1] or Five Books of Moses, you must not be surprised to find that the laws are not arranged, like Acts of Parliament, in a Statute Book, one after the other, in what you would call regular order; and still, if you read carefully, you will find that there is, after all, a certain amount of system or regularity in their arrangement, and that though the history and the laws appear mixed up together, there is good reason for it, there being usually some connection between any one piece of the history and the series of laws which are next to it.

I do not propose to tell you all the laws of the Mosaic Code. If I did, I should perhaps tire you; for there are 613 laws, and you could not be expected to remember so many.

What I wish to do is, to tell you something about the principal laws, just as I have already done as regards the Ten Commandments, so that when you read the Bible for yourselves, you will be able better to understand their meaning.

But, before commencing, I ought to point out one thing, which I have already hinted at, and which you must always bear in mind, when you read about the Law of Moses. It is this—that the Israelites to whom the Law was given were meant to be distinguished from all the rest of the world; they were meant, as I have already told you, to be "a kingdom of priests, a holy nation." They were to be a pattern of goodness and virtue for all the nations of the earth, and it was with that intention that God gave the Law.

[1] Pentateuch—a Greek word which means Five Books.

When you come to the end of Deuteronomy, you will probably say, " Surely it was not intended that all the world should obey all these laws !" and you would be right. But it was intended that the Israelites should obey them ; for God had told them that He had set them apart to be a peculiar people, to be His own chosen nation, so that all the world should look up to them as examples. For this reason He told them that they should be holy, since He the Lord their God was Holy. For this reason He told them to set aside the evil customs they had learnt in Egypt, and to follow only the customs which He taught them ; not to adopt the laws of the nations among whom they were about to dwell, but to follow only the Law which He revealed to Moses, different from any law which up to that time had existed.

When you read ancient history, you will find how different this Law was. You will find that the laws and the customs which existed among the ancient pagan nations were terribly cruel, and in many respects terribly wicked. Those laws were the laws of " might against right." The slave, for example, had no rights—not even the right to live, if his master wished him to die. The creditor had full power over the life of his unfortunate debtor. The helpless had no protection for their lives ; for old people who were past work were put to death ; and little babies who were delicate at birth were exposed to cold and hunger, and thus neglected till they died. You will be shocked indeed, when you learn how cruel were the nations of ancient times, and what wickedness was sanctioned by their laws.

So you see how necessary it was that, besides a model religion, there should be a model code—a complete set of laws—which should be followed by a model nation, and form a pattern for all other nations to copy, so far as it might apply to their special position and wants. True, the whole world was not meant to be a "kingdom of priests" like the Israelites ; so it was not expected that the whole world should follow all those special customs and observances, which were intended to make the Israelites, outwardly and inwardly, different from all other nations ; but the whole world could look up to the "kingdom of priests," and copy their charity, their brotherly love, their justice, their morality, and their steadfast faith ; and this was what God meant when He four times declared to Abraham, "Through thy seed shall all the families of the earth be blessed." All religion and all morality were to be taught through us, the descendants of Abraham.

When you grow older, and read all about those two great religions,[1] which, in spite of their many differences and faults and fallacies, have originated in our own Holy Faith, you will understand better how God's promise to Abraham has been fulfilled. And when you read history, you will understand, too, how it is that the Jews have, notwithstanding all their failings, yet deserved the name of the "kingdom of priests." For, dispersed among nations which have changed their religions and their morals according to the whim or fancy, or fashion of the times, the Jews alone have remained the guardians of God's Holy Law, never

[1] Christianity and Islam.

allowing a word or a letter to be changed, and not simply guarding and preserving the Book as a volume of venerable antiquity, but keeping it as the ever-living Word of the Ever-living God, *keeping it by keeping its laws*,[1] observing the self-same Law as did our forefathers three thousand years ago—the Law of Moses.

[1] Excepting only such laws as were connected with the Temple service, or with the ancient Israelitish polity, and which the destruction of the Temple, and consequent dispersion of Israel, rendered impossible of fulfilment.

CHAPTER V.

OBSERVANCES.—SACRIFICE AND PRAYER.

YOU, children, who have good and affectionate parents, must often feel a great longing to *do* something to show how you love your parents. You are not satisfied to keep the emotion of love in your heart and mind—to keep it as a pleasant thing, only to be thought about. You feel that you must *tell* them how dearly you love them. You must embrace them, and make them feel that you return their love. And perhaps, at times, you will bring them from your own small possessions some trifling gift, a gift great in proportion to your little all, but yet an absurdly small trifle if they estimated it by its money-value.

We are all children of God,[1] and I hope we all love Him, and feel that we cannot do enough to show how we honour Him. But He, living for ever in the High Heavens, is so far above us, who dwell only a few short years upon this little earth of ours, that we know not how to approach Him to show our love. And yet we must do something to show it. We cannot rest satisfied with feeling that we love Him, or with thinking of His goodness. For as we are composed of soul and body, when the soul feels the emotion of love, the body must express that love; and so we must *do* something to show God our love.

[1] Deut. xiv. 1.

Even when the world was very young, men experienced this great want, and they did very much the
same as little children do, who bring sweet-meats to
their parents, thinking that what they themselves
like best must be acceptable to their parents. And so
we find that Cain and Abel brought to God offerings
from their own substance—Cain from the fruit which
he had tended, Abel from the firstlings of his flocks.[1]
Soon afterwards, in the time of Seth, we find that
"men began to call on the name of the Lord."[2]   They
found a vent for their gratitude in the language of
prayer and praise.   And thus both sacrifice and
prayer existed very early in the history of the world.

These were the first " religious observances."

I have already told you[3] what these observances—
sacrifice and prayer—led to.   I have told you how,
in course of time, the people became idolaters, and
how they at last came to sacrifice men and women,
and even their own little children, in the absurd belief
that if they sacrificed that which was dearest to themselves, such sacrifices would be pleasing to their gods.

So one of the first things that God had to teach the
children of Israel was to give up the terrible practices
of idolatry.   To stop sacrifices altogether and all at
once would not have been advisable—perhaps hardly
possible; for the desire to give something to God
could not be checked; so that desire had to be made
harmless and even useful; and thus it seems God
instituted the system of sacrifices that we find in the
Mosaic code.   Thus it was that in the first laws
which God gave the Israelites after the Ten Com-

[1] Gen. iv. 3, 4.   [2] Gen. iv. 26.   [3] Part II., Chap. I.

mandments, He forbade their making gods of silver and gold, but explained to them how they might bring sacrifices.[1] "You shall not make with Me gods of silver, neither shall you make unto you gods of gold. An altar of earth thou shalt make unto Me, and shalt sacrifice thereon thy burnt-offerings, and thy peace-offerings, thy sheep, and thine oxen."

The Israelites were not upon any account to sacrifice human beings. They might bring as offerings beasts or birds; but these were to be of particular kinds—clean animals without blemish. Even then the offerings had to be made in certain fixed and particular ways, and those who brought the sacrifice might not offer it themselves. It had to be offered by a priest, one of the descendants of Aaron, who were all considered holy servants of God.

Later on,[2] you will find that any animal required for food by the Israelites during their abode in the wilderness, had to be taken to the priest, slaughtered by him, and the blood and fat offered as a sacrifice. All this was to show how sacred a thing is life. It was to show that even the life of a brute was not to be taken lightly, inconsiderately, or wantonly; and thus the people would be led to think that if the life of a beast be thus regarded, how sacred must be the life of a human being !

You will read for yourselves in the Bible all about the sacrifices, and you will doubtless be surprised that the laws of God contain such minute details as to the manner in which the offerings were to be made. You will find that the latter part of the Book of

[1] Exod. xx. 23, 24.   [2] Lev. xvii. 3, 4, 5.

Exodus is filled with particulars of the manner in which the Tabernacle, the Ark, the altars, and all the vessels of the Tabernacle were to be made; how Aaron and his sons were to be set apart and consecrated as priests to minister to God and offer up sacrifices, and you will find a large portion of the Book of Leviticus filled with particulars of the various sacrifices, and the manner in which they were to be offered.

You will read about the burnt-offerings, the meat-offerings, the peace-offerings, the sin-offerings, the trespass-offerings, and the offerings of consecration.[1] You will read also[2] about the daily offerings, the offerings of the Sabbath, the Festivals, and the Day of Atonement,[3] and you will be surprised, perhaps, at so many small particulars being given as to each.

And, indeed, it is surprising till you see the object. The object was to compel a fixed form of sacrifice, to admit of no wild departure from a certain routine, so that the Israelites might never wander away to the wicked idolatries and human sacrifices which they had been accustomed to see in Egypt; and yet the forms of sacrifice prescribed were sufficient to satisfy their religious feelings and cravings and wants, however fervid and zealous they might be.

See how this was accomplished. God bids them make a beautiful Tabernacle, that He may dwell with them. He invites them to bring free-will offerings of "gold, and silver, and brass; and blue, and purple, and scarlet, and fine linen, and goats' hair, and rams' skins dyed red, and badgers' skins, and shittim-wood ;

---

[1] Lev. i. to vi.   [2] Numb. xxviii. and xxix.
[3] Lev. xvi.

oil for the light, spices for the anointing oil and for sweet incense ; onyx stones, and stones to be set in the ephod and the breast-plate." [1]

The gifts of the grateful people poured in ; for they were delighted to offer tribute to the God who had saved them from slavery, and now intended to dwell in their midst. The gifts poured in to such an extent that Moses had to restrain them. " For the stuff they had was sufficient for all the work to make it, and too much." [2]

Then the work of constructing the Tabernacle is commenced. God gives every particular and detail of how it is to be made, and how furnished ; and so it is prepared and fitted under the very eyes of the people, without mystery or concealment ; unlike the religious systems of other nations, in which the priests made a mystery of everything, lest the people should see the deceptions they practised.

Read carefully the account of the Tabernacle, and you will be struck with the idea that it must have been very beautiful, but very simple, and you will also be struck with the idea that everything was so made that the worship therein was to be open and public to the whole assembly of Israelites. The priest was to be seen when he went into the sanctuary, and when he came out. There was no hidden mystery. The priest was one of themselves, one of the kingdom of priests. The priest was to minister to God, not as a mediator between God and His people, but solely as a servant of God, performing the service of God, according to fixed rules and ordinances.

[1] Exod. xxv. 3—7.   [2] Exod. xxxvi. 7.

When you read the laws relating to the sacrifices,
and especially the laws of the sin-offering, the trespass-
offering, and the offerings of the Day of Atonement, it
will probably appear to you very strange, that God
should accept merely the blood of an animal as an
atonement for men's sins; and it certainly would be
very curious, if it were true; but it is not true. The
common notion is that the sacrifice of the animal
constituted the atonement, and that God accepted the
life of the animal instead of the life of the man who
had committed the sin.   But this notion is altogether
wrong.   How such a silly idea came into people's
heads you will one day understand, when you read
about a religion[1] which is entirely based upon this
mistaken idea of atonement by sacrifice.   If you
reflect a little, you will at once say that nothing could
be more ridiculous than the idea that a man, who had
committed some terrible sin, should receive the forgiveness of God by simply bringing to a priest an
animal to be slaughtered ; and when you read for
yourselves in your Bible the law of sacrifices, you will
at once see that there is nothing to warrant so absurd
an idea.

When you carefully read the 5th and 6th chapters
of Leviticus, you will discover the spirit and meaning
of sacrifices.   You will find that if a man committed
a sin against God, he had first to make a confession
of his sin, and afterwards to bring as an offering a
lamb or a kid ; and if he could not afford a lamb or
a kid, he might bring two turtle-doves or two young
pigeons ; and in case he could not afford these little

---

[1] Christianity.

birds, he might bring as his offering a tenth part of an ephah of fine flour, and the priest burnt on the altar a handful of the flour. In the last case—the sacrifice of the flour—there was no life taken, so there was evidently no sacrifice of blood. And thus you see the taking of life and the sacrifice of blood were not essential to the atonement. The really important part of the proceeding was the confession of the sin—the open demonstration of the sinner's penitence.

Reading a little further, you will find that if a man sinned against his neighbour by dealing falsely with him, or by robbing him, or by deceiving him, or by detaining lost property that he had found, or by swearing to a neighbour's injury—then he had to bring as a trespass-offering a ram without blemish; but, before bringing it, he had to make good to the neighbour he had injured all that he had wronged him of, and to give him in addition one-fifth part of the value. In this case it is clear, that the really important part of the transaction was not the offering, but the making good the injury.

If we wish further to see how small a value God placed upon sacrifices, compared with the spirit in which the sacrifice was brought, we have only to refer to the prophets and sacred writings.

Samuel tells Saul, who, contrary to God's orders, had saved alive the sheep and oxen of the Amalekites to sacrifice to the Lord at Gilgal, " Behold to obey is better than sacrifice, to hearken than the fat of rams."[1]

[1] I Sam. xv. 22.

Isaiah exclaims thus—"To what purpose is the multitude of your sacrifices unto Me? saith the Lord. I am full of the burnt offerings of rams, and the fat of fed beasts, and I delight not in the blood of bullocks, or of lambs, or of he-goats. . . . . Wash you, make you clean; put away the evil of your doings from before mine eyes; cease to do evil; learn to do well; seek judgment, relieve the oppressed, judge the fatherless, plead for the widow." [1]

In like words God proclaims, through his prophet Jeremiah, that the aim of the Law was obedience and not sacrifice. " I spake not unto your fathers nor commanded them in the day that I brought them out of the land of Egypt, concerning burnt-offerings and sacrifices. But this thing commanded I them, saying, Obey my voice." [2]

The prophet Micah speaks in the same strain. He asks,[3] "Wherewith shall I come before the Lord, and bow myself before the High God? Shall I come before Him with burnt-offerings, with calves of a year old? Will the Lord be pleased with thousands of rams, or with ten thousands of rivers of oil? Shall I give my first-born for my transgressions, the fruit of my body for the sin of my soul? He hath shewed thee, O man, what is good; and what does the Lord require of thee, but to do justly, and to love mercy and to walk humbly with thy God?"

Again, in the 50th Psalm, God declares, "I will take no bullock out of thy house, nor he-goats out of thy folds. For every beast of the forest is mine, and

[1] Isaiah i. 11, 16, 17.   [2] Jer. vii. 22, 23.
[3] Micah vi. 6, 7, 8.

the cattle upon a thousand hills. I know all the
fowls of the mountains; and the wild beasts of the
fields are mine. If I were hungry, I would not tell
thee; for the world is mine, and the fulness thereof.
Shall I eat the flesh of bulls? or drink the blood of
goats? Offer unto God thanksgiving, and pay thy
vows unto the Most High."

King Solomon, too, in the 21st chapter of Proverbs declares, "To do justice and judgment is more
acceptable to the Lord than sacrifice."

I have quoted these passages from the Bible to
show that the performance of other duties, such as
obedience to God, was considered of greater importance than the bringing of sacrifice.

And I think you will now understand that, though
these sacrifices occupy so large a portion of the Law
of Moses, their main intention was to fill up what
would otherwise have been a great gap in the daily
action of our ancestors' lives.[1] They had been accustomed in Egypt to see sacrifices—wicked, sinful
sacrifices—sacrifices to idols, even human sacrifices.
They had to be weaned from such customs; accordingly sacrifices, which should be not only harmless
but beneficial, had to be ordained; sacrifices, which

[1] The view here given is that stated by Maimonides, *Moreh
Nebuchim*, Book III., chap. 32. It is, however, right to add
that this view is combated strongly by some of the highest
Jewish authorities; amongst them, Nachmanides, who maintains, upon Biblical grounds, that the institution of sacrifices
was intended to possess a permanent character. Following
this opinion, the compilers of our liturgy have embodied in
the prayer-book many prayers for the restoration of the
sacrifices.

would serve as an outlet for their gratitude, or as a proof of their penitence, or as a reminder of the everlasting presence of a watchful God, willing to receive the love and adoration of His creatures.

And so all the little details of the sacrifice were fully prescribed, so that nothing like idolatry should be practised. Nor were they to deceive themselves with the idea that they could sin, and atone by a sin-offering, and sin again, as often as they pleased; getting absolution from the priest as often as they pleased, simply by bringing an offering, and so making wrong-doing a profitable business. No; the offering had to be accompanied by a public confession, and by restitution, with one-fifth added as a penalty; so that wrong-doing could not be made profitable or pleasant in its results, if a man ever wished to be at peace with his Maker.

But the words which I have quoted from the Prophets will show you further that, though we have at present no sacrifices and no priests, there are other means accessible to all men at all times of making themselves acceptable to God. By penitence, prayer, and praise; by acting justly, mercifully, and charitably.

Of this last-named duty, acting justly, mercifully, and charitably—a duty which includes many hundred duties—I cannot speak here at length, but will treat of it in its proper place.[1] But the act of prayer and praise is an observance—was one of the first observances; and as we are led to the subject by the words of King David, who bids us offer to God thanksgiving instead of sacrifices, it is right to tell you now something about prayer.

---

[1] Chapters ix and x.

"What is the good of prayer?" some of you may ask. Can we expect that the praises we offer to God are pleasant for Him to hear? Can we hope or expect that He, who made all the world, listens to our puny voices and feeble words? It seems at first hardly possible; but we know that it is not only possible but certain; for God Himself commands us to pray to Him and to praise Him. He tells us: "When thou hast eaten and art satisfied, then thou shalt bless the Lord thy God for the good land which He hath given thee."[1] He tells us also: "to love the Lord your God, and to serve Him with all your heart and with all your soul."[2] Also He commands His servants the priests to pray for the welfare of the people in the well-known form of blessing:[3] "The Lord bless thee and keep thee. The Lord make His face to shine upon thee, and be gracious to thee. The Lord lift up His countenance upon thee, and give thee peace." And so in our prayer and our praise we are to look to God as the source of all blessing, to acknowledge Him as the Great Power who supports, rules, and sustains us. This acknowledgment is the great principle of every religion.

When, therefore, Ezra and the men of the Great Assembly ordained that we should worship God three times a day,[4] and that we should offer thanks to Him

---

[1] Deut. xii. 10.

[2] Deut. xi. 13. Upon this text our ancient teachers comment thus, : הֲרֵי אוֹמֵר זוּ תְּפִלָּה ? שֶׁהִיא בְּלֵב עֲבוֹדָה הִיא אֵיזוֹ—"How can we serve God with our heart? By devout prayer." *Taanith*, 2, a.

[3] Numb. vi. 24, 25, 26.

[4] Following the words of King David, "Evening and morning and at noon will I pray" (Psalm lv. 17).

before and after every meal, and utter a blessing
on every suitable occasion, their object was a wise
one. They intended that we should always have
before us the thought of an ever-present God, who
sees our every act. They intended that in every act
of our lives we should acknowledge the greatness
and goodness and providence of God, so that the
thought that He is always and everywhere at hand
should keep us from sinning, and so cause us to lead
a good and godly life.

But even if the Law of God and the ordinances of
our wise men had been silent on the subject of prayer,
and had given us no hint of that great duty, the dictates
of our hearts would prompt us to utter words of praise ;
for gratitude must find vent in open expression. If
you have a favourite dog, whom you feed and carefully tend, he will lick your hand and dance around
you in delight, and show you his gratitude in many
ways. If you have a little bird to whom you daily
give his dole of grain and drink, he will warble out
his notes of gratitude every time he sees you. How,
then, can man, who alone has the gift of words,
forbear to bring the homage of his heart and the
offering of his lips to the Creator, who made him
and supports him? That we should pray to God is a
law of God, but also a law of Nature, which every
man, woman and child gladly obeys. Perhaps God
is pleased with our songs of praise, just as you are
pleased to hear the warblings of the little bird you
tend.

Foremost amongst the blessings derived from
prayer is the feeling that we are holding communion

with our Supreme Creator, and that, by the contemplation of His perfections, our hearts become elevated, our moral tone improved, and our impulses braced and strengthened for the performance of good and noble deeds.

King David, who taught all the world the language of prayer and praise, tells us, "It is good to sing praises unto our God; for it is pleasant, and praise is comely."[1]   And, lest we should think that the Great Creator of the universe would not concern Himself with the petty wants of us puny mortals, and would not hearken to our prayers, he tells us, "The Lord is nigh unto all them that call upon Him, to all that call upon Him in truth.   He will fulfil the desire of them that fear Him; He also will hear their cry, and will save them."[2]

The Prophets teem with similar declarations as to the power of prayer. "Before they call I will answer; whilst they are yet speaking, I shall already have heard."[3] "Call unto Me and I will answer thee, and show thee great and mighty things."[4] "I called upon Thy name, O Lord, out of the low dungeon; Thou hast heard my voice."[5]

Sceptics have often raised the objection, that we cannot hope to alter the pre-ordained design and intention of God by our puny prayers. But in truth the same objection might be raised against all other human exertion; and a blind fatalism would result. And, after all, it may so happen that prayer is one of

[1] Psalm cxlvii. 1.
[2] Psalm cxlv. 18, 19.
[3] Isaiah lxv. 24.
[4] Jerem. xxxiii. 3.
[5] Lam. iii. 55.

the means ordained by God to produce the legitimate ends we long for, and that God delights in granting such of our prayers as are worthy prayers, as a kind father delights in granting the reasonable wishes of his children. Certainly this is the case with all prayers which we sincerely offer for our own moral improvement. "There is an apparent connection, at least, between prayers for the greatest moral good and its attainment. Prayer for virtuous dispositions and conduct, for resignation, trust and tranquillity of mind, does certainly tend to procure them. The very posture of the mind in prayer tends to produce them."[1]

[1] Sir J. B. Byles's "Foundations of Religion," p. 77. We may also quote the following paraphrase from the Tenth Satire of Juvenal :—

" Still raise for good the supplicating voice,
    But leave to Heaven the measure and the choice ;
    Safe in His hands, whose eye discerns afar
    The secret ambush of a specious prayer.
    Implore His aid, in His decisions rest,
    Secure whate'er He gives, He gives the best.
    But when a sense of Sacred Presence fires,
    And strong devotion to the skies aspires,
    Pour forth thy fervours for a healthful mind,
    Obedient passions and a will resigned ;
    For love, which scarce collective man can fill,
    For patience, sovereign o'er transmuted ill,
    For Faith, that, panting for a purer seat,
    Counts Death kind Nature's signal for retreat—
    These gifts for all the laws of heaven ordain,
    These gifts He grants who grants the power to gain ;
    With these celestial wisdom calms the mind
    And makes the happiness she cannot find."
                                    JOHNSON'S *Vanity of Human Wishes.*

Now, perhaps you will think it rather strange that the Law of Moses, which tells us so many things, does not tell us what prayers we should say. It gives us full particulars and details of the sacrifices, but ordains very few forms of prayer. In the twenty-first chapter of Deuteronomy, you will find a special prayer to be said if a man be found slain, and his murderer cannot be discovered; and, in the twenty-sixth chapter of the same book, you will find prescribed the prayers which were to be said on bringing the first-fruits, and on offering the tithes; but these are rather confessions than prayers; and in the sixth chapter of Numbers you will find the priest's prayer, of which I have already spoken. But besides these, there are really no forms of prayer specially ordained in the Law of Moses.

Why was this? Because prayers were to be the natural outpouring of the heart. In later times, forms of prayer were composed for common use, and certain Psalms were sung in the Temple by the Levites. Later still, when the Jews returned from the captivity, Ezra, aided by the prophets and scribes of his time, prescribed the Order of Service, consisting principally of the prayers and psalms then in common use; and these you will find in your prayer-book, together with very many others of much later date, all in Hebrew, except a few which, having been composed in Babylon, during the dispersion, were written in the Aramaic or Chaldee dialect, then the mother-tongue of the exiled Jews.

You will readily understand why our prayer-book should be in Hebrew. It is not only our own language, but the language in which God spake to our forefathers; and it is the language which we hope to resume as our own when we return to the Holy Land. You would not be able to compose Hebrew prayers for yourselves; so it is fortunate that you have some ready prepared for you; and, though these prayers are only *forms* of prayer, there is much in the reflection that they are the same that have been used by our people in their synagogues, and their homes, during many generations, and that they have served during so many ages to bring pious and holy thoughts into the minds and hearts of millions of our forefathers, and to comfort them in their sorrows.

But all these prayers are of no avail to you, unless, in praying, you think of their meaning, and unless you add to these set forms, composed by other people, prayers of your own, which need not be in Hebrew, and need not even be in words—I mean, loving thoughts of God, grateful thoughts for all His kindness towards you; hopes that He will guide you and give you strength to do your duty and resist temptation; earnest longings that He will make you worthy of His goodness, and help you to improve day by day, and so enable you, small and humble though you be, to work His will on earth, and earn a place in Heaven.

CHAPTER VI.

OBSERVANCES.—SABBATHS AND FESTIVALS.

FROM what I have told you, I think you must already understand that Religion consists of two parts—belief and observance; belief being the act of the mind, observance the act of the body with the help of the mind; and I think you understand, too, how the first religious observances—sacrifice and prayer—arose quite as a natural necessity, from men's anxiety to *do* something to show their gratitude to God and their dependence on Him.

Now, when a system of religion was ordained, it was necessary to fix particular periods and seasons when men should completely rest from their daily labours, and so withdraw themselves from the business of their lives as to enable them to turn their thoughts to God and to His service; and it was for this reason that the Sabbath and Festivals were ordained.

And perhaps there was also another reason, namely, that men should not, in their great love of God and their strong wish to serve Him, neglect their worldly duties. And so God, in fixing those particular days for His service, wisely set *bounds* and *limits* to the religious fervour of men. We are not, like the priests and monks of other religions, to spend our lives in penance and in prayer; we are meant to work, and religion is meant to sanctify our work. And thus it is that we find the Commandment of the Sabbath in almost every case preceded by the words " six days shalt thou labour." Work was to be the first of duties, and a holy life was to be no excuse for a lazy life.

THE SABBATH.—Of the Sabbath itself, I have already spoken at some length when telling you about the Fourth Commandment; so I need not say much here upon this subject. But I ought to tell you, that it is the most important of all those observances, which distinguish our people from the other nations of the earth. How important God regards it, you will understand from the remarkable fact that the Law of the Sabbath is so many times repeated in the Books of Moses.[1] You must read for yourselves all the references given at the foot of this page, and you will find that, though the wording of the Commandment differs slightly in different places, the principle of the Sabbath is the same in all—rest on the Sabbath-day for everyone, for yourselves, your household, your servants and your cattle.

When you read the Bible for yourselves, you will find how terrible a sin Sabbath-breaking was considered. You will read how the man who gathered sticks on the Sabbath-day was stoned to death.[2] You will read how the prophets Jeremiah and

[1] Exod. xvi. 23 ; Exod. xx. 8, 9, 10, 11 ; Exod. xxiii. 12 ; Exod. xxxi. 13—17 ; Exod. xxxiv. 21 ; Exod. xxxv. 2, 3 ; Lev. xix. 3 ; Lev. xxiii. 3 ; Deut. v. 13.

[2] Numb. xv. 32-35.

Ezekiel[1] denounced the Sabbath-breakers; and you will find how the chief prophets, especially Isaiah,[2] promised the highest reward to those who keep the Sabbath holy.

God tells us, "it is a *sign* between Me and you throughout your generations," and this continues to be true even to this day. The observance of the Sabbath is truly a "sign"—it is truly a test whether a man is one of God's chosen people. The man who, though he may incur great loss or inconvenience thereby, always keeps holy the Sabbath-day, shows himself to be a truly sincere Jew. It is a "sign" between the Jew and his God. It is a sign that God looks upon Israel as His chosen people, and it is a sign that the Israelite looks upon God as the Guardian of himself and of his race, the Source of all earthly blessings, the Sustainer of every living creature.

And so the Jew brings a sacrifice of one-seventh portion of his time to the observance of the Holy Sabbath, in the sure hope and confidence that the time so given to God will not be lost; in the perfect trust that He who ordained the Sabbath will not bring to poverty or want those who keep His Sabbath holy.

THE FEAST OF PASSOVER.—Many of you may suppose that one day in seven ought to be quite enough to be set apart as holy, and you may perhaps wonder why, besides the Sabbath, so many other holy days were ordained. I will try to tell you why.

[1] Jer. xvii. 27; Ezek. xx.   [2] Isaiah lvi. 2.

All nations have certain days in the year which they celebrate as anniversaries. Just as you celebrate every year the anniversary of your birth, many nations celebrate, as each year comes round, the events which they call to mind with pride or pleasure. But these events are not always such as are worthy of being remembered, and these anniversaries are not usually celebrated in the most sensible manner.

When you read ancient history, you will learn what shocking sports, what cruelties and what wickedness were practised on some of the anniversaries in Greece and Rome. Even in civilized Europe, people now celebrate the anniversaries of victories and other historical events by the absurd practice of firing guns; and here in enlightened England, the great winter anniversary, which is half national and half religious, is celebrated amongst many classes as a period of gluttony and excessive indulgence in strong drinks, certainly not in a mode worthy of human beings.

It was to be different with the Israelites. Their early history was full of events worthy to be remembered ; and the commemorations were to be worthy of the events. The glorious departure from Egypt, the giving of the Law, the wonderful travels in the wilderness—these were events which were worth remembering, and they were to be commemorated, not by cruel sports, not by races, not by gluttonous feasts, but by joyful thanksgiving, by intelligent enjoyments, and by charitable deeds.

We shall see, in detail, how this was ordained in the Holy Law, and shall commence with the Feast of Passover.

I can almost fancy some of my readers making up their minds to skip the next few pages, feeling sure that I can tell them nothing about this festival that they don't know already. And it is quite likely that they are right, and that the only good I can hope to do will be to set them thinking a little, not only about the observances themselves, but about the reason why. For, in these days, the " reason why " is all-important. And so it ought to be ; for what is Religion without reason ?

Now, if I ask you why you keep the Passover, you will tell me at once that you keep it to remind you of the great deliverance of our fathers from the bondage of Egypt. You will be quite right in so answering ; but you will not have told me nearly all in those few words.

We, who live in this happy land, free to worship God according to our conscience, free to do as we please, to go where we please, to work as we please, can hardly imagine what it was to live as did our forefathers in Egypt, under the rule of the wicked Pharaohs. To be slaves ; to be obliged to work not for ourselves but for others ; to have nothing of our own ; to be beaten by cruel taskmasters, who give impossible tasks, so that the worker cannot escape punishment ; to work in fear and dread, without hope and without the comforts and joys of home—this was the state of the poor Israelites. And, worse than all, the lives of their offspring were not safe ; for the cruel King, at one time, doomed all the male children to destruction. Such was the state of bondage from which God delivered our ancestors.

I

But why should we, year after year, and after so many centuries, call to mind, by the observance of Passover, these terrible trials of our forefathers? To show our gratitude to God, is doubtless one reason. But there is yet another reason—to declare to the world the right of man to be free. Passover is the Festival of Freedom. We read the history of our ancestors in Egypt, and relate their wonderful deliverance and the fall of the mighty tyranny which had oppressed them; and we thereby declare that God ordained Man to be free—free in body, and free in mind, and we offer a warning to slave-owners, to tyrants, and to oppressors, that God will break their power.

For you, living in this free and happy land, must not suppose that, all the world over, people are now free and happy as you are. You must know that slavery still exists in many parts of the world, and that, in Egypt itself, there is even now, a servitude of the *fellaheen*[1] or native peasantry—not much better than the slavery which afflicted our forefathers. You must know, too, that there are many countries where Jews are still oppressed, their lives and their property in constant danger; and other countries where our people cannot meet for public worship, nor even permit it to be known that they are Jews.

Pharaoh's hosts were drowned in the Red Sea; but in every age there have been other Pharaohs who have

[1] "The wretch is caught, bound and sent off to work, without wage, at the canals; his wife is taken and chained; his children are stripped and plundered."—*The Khedive's Egypt*, by Edwin de Leon. 1877.

sprung up in his place, tyrants who have enslaved at times the bodies, at times the souls of their subjects.

When you read History, you will find that the power of the tyrant has always been, in the end, broken. Tyranny after tyranny has collapsed, power after power has perished, nation after nation has disappeared; but one nation alone has remained alive through all these thousands of years—scattered about the world, but yet alive and full of life—the Jews; and these, year after year, celebrate with joy and gladness and gratitude the great Festival of Freedom.

You know well, all of you, how the festival is celebrated; how, before the festival begins, the home is cleansed from leaven, so that no particle of it remains; how the first-born sons fast on the day before Passover, to commemorate the miraculous escape of the Israelitish first-born from the tenth Egyptian plague; how the כֶּדֶר (Seder) night is observed, every household joining in solemn prayer and praise, reading the narrative of the Exodus,[1] seated around the table whereon are spread the memorial of the Paschal Lamb,[2] the unleavened bread and the bitter herbs;[3] how at that table all sit as equals, parents and children, master and servant, host and guest; how, for

[1] As commanded in Exod. xiii. 8.

[2] See Exod. xii. 11. It is worthy of remark that, even now, the Samaritans, who live in Nablous (in Palestine) celebrate the Passover by actually slaying and roasting the paschal lamb, and eating it with all the ceremonial details ordained in the twelfth chapter of Exodus. A highly interesting account of this observance may be found in Dean Stanley's "History of the Jewish Church," Appendix to Vol. I.

[3] Exod. xii. 8.

more than a week, unleavened bread is eaten,[1] and
no leaven is allowed in our homes ; how we meet in the
Synagogue to praise God for His mercies ; and how,
on the seventh day of the Festival, we there read the
narrative of the wonderful passage of the Red Sea,
and sing the Song of Moses in the same words
used by our forefathers, when they had just trodden
a path through the bed of the mighty waters, and so
escaped from the ruthless sword of Pharaoh.

When you thus keep Passover, how happy, how
joyous, how grateful must you be ! When you look
on the memorial of the Paschal Lamb, and think of
the salvation worked for the Israelites, at the hour
when the sprinkling of the blood of the first Paschal
Lamb caused the destroying angel to pass over[2]
their houses, and to leave unhurt their first-born from
the plague which killed the sons of the Egyptians;
when you eat the unleavened bread, "the bread of
affliction," and think of the first unleavened bread
which our forefathers made in their hurried departure
from Egypt; when you eat the bitter herbs, and think
of the bitter hardships our ancestors suffered in the
"land of bondage"—how thankful you must feel that
your lot has fallen on better days, and that you are
free and happy !

How proud you must be that you are Jews and
Jewesses, declaring before the world the greatness,
and goodness, and glory of God, in that you are the
living witnesses of His greatness, and goodness, and
glory ! For every Passover, year after year, for thousands of years, have those same words of prayer and

---

[1] Lev. xxiii. 6.   [2] Hence the name "Passover."

praise been sung, which you sing; those same customs
been observed which you observe; thus joining the
past with the present, and making you feel, in
the words of the *Hagadah*, as if you yourselves
had just come out of Egypt, the objects of God's
special mercy and special providence!

THE FEAST OF WEEKS.—Why is that pleasant
festival of early summer called the Feast of Weeks?

You know the beautiful custom, *the counting of the
Omer*, which we observe on forty-nine evenings, commencing on the second evening of Passover. This
custom is ordained in the Law of Moses,[1] and you can
read for yourselves all the particulars in the words of
the Bible. Its object is to impress upon us all a due
estimate of the value of time, that precious possession
of which not one of us, old or young, can tell whether
we have much or little; and to remind us, at a season
when time is of the highest value to the worker, that
we are answerable to God for the use or abuse of our
time.

You will find that on the second day of Passover,
when the sickle was first put to the corn, and the
wheat harvest began, the Israelites were to bring as
an offering " a sheaf of the first-fruits of the harvest;"
that, for seven weeks afterwards the days were to be
counted, and that on the fiftieth day, when the seven
weeks were over, the Feast of Weeks was to be kept;
there was to be a " holy convocation," and it was to be
observed " with a tribute of a free-will offering."[2]
The " first of the first-fruits " was to be brought to

[1] Lev. xxiii. 15, 16 ; Deut. xvi. 9.   [2] Deut. xvi. 10.

the House of the Lord ;[1] and so this festival is not
only called חַג הַשָּׁבוּעוֹת "the Feast of Weeks," but
יוֹם הַבִּכּוּרִים "the Day of First-fruits."

In Palestine the summer is much earlier than here.
The barley was ripe at the Passover season, and the
corn was all reaped when the Feast of Weeks had
arrived. On this festival the first-fruit offering was
brought into the Temple, consisting of "two wave
loaves of two tenth deals baken with leaven."[2]

After this festival the first-fruits were brought by
each Israelite to the Temple.

How the first-fruits were brought, and what prayer
was said when they were brought, you will find in the
26th chapter of Deuteronomy.[3]   It is a remarkable
prayer, one of the few set forms of prayer ordained by
the command of God, and it is, perhaps, rather a
declaration than a prayer ;—a declaration of the early
history of our race, a narrative of the miraculous redemption from Egypt, and a confession that all our
possessions come from God ; for it concludes with the
words, "And now, behold, I have brought the first-
fruits of the land which Thou, O Lord, hast given me."

These last words, again, involve that great principle of our religion—the recognition of God in every
act of our life, in every good thing that we receive, in every happiness that we enjoy.

The prosperous farmer, fresh from his harvest-
field, might feel puffed up with a sense of his importance, might grow too proud of his possessions,
and might think that it is to his own industry
and talent that all his wealth is due. But the

[1] Ex. xxxiv. 26.   [2] Lev. xxiii. 17.   [3] Deut. xxvi. 2—10.

Day of the First-fruits draws near. He obeys the Divine command and brings his offering to the Holy place. He joins the procession which, as the Mishna tells us, came from every city and village of Palestine, bringing to the Temple of Jerusalem the choicest first-fruits, decked with the finest flowers, amid the sound of music and the voice of song, echoing the words, "O come, let us go up to Zion, to the Lord our God." [1]   No matter how rich he may be, he himself must carry on his shoulder his own first-fruit, and, standing before the priest, he recites the ordained prayer, and finishes with the words, "And now, behold, I have brought the first-fruits of the land which Thou, O Lord, hast given me!" The pride half rising in the heart, the boast half rising to the lips of the successful farmer, would be suppressed at the humble confession of his lowly origin, and at the prayer which acknowledges God as the Source of all good.

To us, who have lost our Sanctuary, and who live in a climate where the wheat-harvest is gathered several months later than in Palestine, the Feast of Weeks, held in May or June, can present only a shadow of its former beauty; and instead of bringing, like our ancestors, our first-fruits, we are forced to content ourselves with adorning our Synagogues with choice flowers as a memorial of Nature's productiveness and God's loving bounty.

But, from another point of view, the Feast of Weeks is as much to us as ever it was to our forefathers. It is the anniversary of the giving of the Law on Sinai, the anniversary of the greatest event that the world

[1] *Bikkurim*, III.

has ever witnessed—the Revelation of God to His people.

Of this Revelation I have already treated at some length, so I need not here do more than impress upon you the importance of the Festival which calls to our remembrance so great an event. And I feel sure that, when you have recited in the Synagogue the narrative of that marvellous Revelation, your hearts will be full of gratitude to the Great God, who chose us from all nations to receive His Holy Law, and who has kept us alive amid dangers and persecutions to be the witnesses of His Word and Will to the whole world.

THE FEAST OF TABERNACLES.—We are commanded in the Holy Law to dwell in booths for seven days, commencing on the fifteenth day of the seventh month, to remind us that God caused the children of Israel to dwell in booths when He led them out of the land of Egypt.[1] These seven days are the Feast of Tabernacles,[2] and the eighth day was ordained to be kept as a "solemn assembly."

We are commanded, too, to take on the first day of the festival "the fruit of a goodly tree,[3] the branches of palm-trees, the boughs of thick-leaved trees,[4] and

---

[1] Lev. xxiii. 34, 43.

[2] The word "tabernacles" in the name of this festival must not be confounded with the term "tabernacle" as applied to the "tabernacle of the wilderness," which was quite a different structure. To avoid confusion the Feast of Tabernacles should, perhaps, be called the "Feast of Booths."

[3] According to tradition, the Citron.

[4] According to tradition, the Myrtle.

willows of the brook, and to rejoice before the Lord seven days."

You will find it interesting to read in the Book of Nehemiah[1] how, after a long interval of neglect, the Feast was observed by our ancestors under Ezra the scribe; how they published and proclaimed in all their cities and in Jerusalem saying: "Go forth unto the mount and fetch olive-branches, and pine-branches, and myrtle-branches, and palm-branches, and branches of thick trees to make booths, as it is written," and how the people went forth and brought them, and made themselves booths everyone upon the roof of his house, and in the courts, and in the Court of the House of God.

In this climate it happens, unfortunately, that the season when the Festival falls is usually a rainy and inclement time of the year; and thus the command to dwell in booths or temporary huts is not so generally observed by our people as it should be. But there are yet many zealous Jews in this country who, in spite of the great inconvenience, yet make an effort to observe the command as ordained; and who erect tabernacles wherein they eat their meals and spend a portion of their time during the Festival.

Perhaps there are few of you, my young readers, who have never seen such a Tabernacle, with its shifting roof and its ceiling of evergreens; and some of you may probably have lively recollections of many happy hours spent in such a frail and slight abode. Those who can afford it decorate their Tabernacles with lamps and pictures and flowers and fruits,

[1] Nehem. viii. 15.

making their little temporary home truly a thing of
beauty. The Law of Moses does not tell us how to
make a סֻכָּה (*Succah*) or booth; but, according to
tradition, the main characteristic of the *Succah* is
the roof, which must be formed of green leaves
arranged in such a manner that the sky may be seen
between the leaves, so as to indicate the temporary
character of the structure as distinguished from the
permanent ceiling of an ordinary habitation.

This slight and temporary home is not only to
remind us of the wanderings of our ancestors in the
wilderness, but also to bring to our minds thoughts
of gratitude towards the God who loads us with His
bounty. At the feast of ingathering, when we might
perhaps be filled with pride at our worldly success,
we are told to leave our warm, substantial homes, and
to take up our abode in the frail booth, roofed like
the hut of a wanderer.

Looking at this leafy roof, we see the sky, and call
to mind the Heavenly Hand that made and fashioned
us, and gave us all we have: we see the starry hosts
of heaven, and understand our own nothingness; and
the frail covering, which scarcely keeps out rain and
wind, makes us think of those poor distressed creatures
who would have no roof to shelter them, but for our
timely aid.

The beautiful trophies of nature, too, which we are
commanded to take during the Festival, are meant to
lead us to like thoughts of duty, and humble gratitude. The palm, emblem of uprightness;[1] the citron
and myrtle, emblem of that charity that spreads its

[1] Psalm xcii. 12.

fragrance far and wide, giving much and yet losing nothing; and the willow, emblem of true humility —these choice gifts of nature we are to gather, and, looking at them, learn from them a holy lesson.

And in all our rejoicings we are to be mindful of others besides ourselves. Not only "shalt thou rejoice," says the Bible; but "thy man-servant, and thy maid-servant, and the Levite, the stranger, and the fatherless, and the widow, that are within thy gates,"[1] are to share the bounties of nature, and to take part in the joys of the happy harvest-home.

The eighth day of solemn assembly, which follows the Feast of Tabernacles, has no defined object stated in the Bible, but it would seem to have been intended to inspire us with gratitude at our having been permitted to celebrate the solemn series of holy days of the month of Tishri.

It is the custom of the Synagogue to signalize the close of these holydays by a festivity, thoroughly characteristic of our religion, known as *Simchath Torah,* שִׂמְחַת הּתֹּורָה, "the rejoicing in the Law." You are aware that on every Sabbath during the year a section of the Holy Law is publicly read in our places of worship,[2] in such manner that the entire Pentateuch

---

[1] Deut. xvi. 14.

[2] During times of persecution, the public reading of the Law was prohibited under pain of death. Our people, thus debarred from reading the weekly portions from the Pentateuch, read, as a substitute, lessons from the prophets which contained some reference or resemblance to the respective portions from the Law they were compelled to suppress. This is generally considered to have been the origin of the *Haphtoroth,* or lessons from the prophets, which are now read weekly in the Synagogue after the *Sedrah,* or portion from the Pentateuch.

may be completed in one year, and that the last
section (comprising the last two chapters of Deuteronomy) may be read on this Festival.

Directly the Pentateuch is thus completed, it is
again commenced, the first chapter of Genesis and
part of the second being read with great solemnity.
On this occasion the synagogue is made to wear its
most festive aspect; the sacred scrolls of the Law,
decked in gorgeous vestments, are carried in procession round the holy edifice, while hymns of praise
and thanksgiving, attuned to joyous music, testify
our gratitude to God for His goodness in having
permitted us again to complete the perusal of that
Law which is our greatest treasure.

CHAPTER VII.

OBSERVANCES.—THE NEW YEAR'S DAY AND DAY OF ATONEMENT.

AT the commencement of the last chapter I told you that it was an essential part of the system of our Holy Religion to set aside certain days upon which we should turn our thoughts to God, and that this was one reason why the Sabbath and Festivals were ordained. But besides these, God ordained for a like purpose two other Holy days—the Day of Memorial (or New Year's Day) and the Day of Atonement—to remind us of our position, to recall us to our duties, if we have forgotten them, and to enable us to remove from our souls the burden of sin.

"Now what does all this mean?" some of you young folks will ask; for probably most of you will be ignorant of what I mean by the " burden of sin."

You young people, who, in your several pursuits and studies, have little worlds of your own, though I trust you may know little or nothing about great sins, will no doubt remember that there have been times when you have done wrong. I hope not often, but I doubt not it has sometimes happened so with all of you. And, perhaps, some of you may have known children who very often do wrong, and who seem to get worse and worse, the older they grow, till something shocking occurs to them, some illness, perhaps,

or some misfortune, which sets them thinking about
their wrong-doing, and makes them resolve to do
better in future.

Now, just as there are sometimes wayward, disobe-
dient children, there are sometimes wicked men and
women, who seem to forget God and His laws, and
who keep on sinning daily more and more. The souls
of such people are burdened with sin.

But though, happily, there are not many of these
awfully wicked people, there are yet a very great
number of people in the world who now and then
do wrong, who forget or neglect to do some duty,
or who do something that is forbidden, and who,
without being very wicked, are yet far from perfect.
Indeed, no mortal is perfect. Every one has his
faults—most of us very many faults—and these faults
would become, as we grow in years, sins—perhaps
even great crimes—if we did not from time to time
check them, and make up our mind to put a stop to
them.

Now, God ordained [1] the New Year's Festival to be a
Day of Memorial, or Day of Remembrance; that is
to say, a day on which He calls to mind everything
we have done during the past year, and passes judgment on us according to our work. And, as He has
placed within every one of us a conscience, He ordained that on that day the שׁוֹפָר (ram's horn) should
be sounded to awaken that conscience, so that all

---

[1] " In the seventh month, in the first day of the month, shall
ye have a sabbath, a memorial of blowing of trumpets, an holy
convocation. Ye shall do no servile work therein."—Lev. xxiii.
24, 25.

of us may on that day consider our acts, examine our own conduct, and judge ourselves truthfully, even as God judges us.

This duty—the duty of self-examination and self-judgment—is one of the greatest of the duties we owe to ourselves; and it is right that we should perform this duty not merely once a year, on the Day of Memorial, but every night when we retire to rest. King David tells us, "Stand in awe, and sin not; commune with your heart upon your bed,[1]" in the silence of night. And I have already told you that self-examination is one of the duties of the Sabbath-day.

Some of you will no doubt fancy such frequent self-examination quite unnecessary, and may think it likely to make you too serious, and rather miserable. But this is a mistake. Every morning, and perhaps twice or thrice in the day, you look at yourselves in the glass, to see if you are clean and tidy, and when you are satisfied with your appearance, the sight does not make you miserable or serious—perhaps, quite the reverse. And so, if the examination of your acts and thoughts, and the judgment of your conscience be satisfactory, and you feel you are good and clean and spotless in the sight of God and your conscience, the result is increased happiness.

But God, knowing how apt we are to forget this great duty of self-examination, ordained the Day of Memorial, so that, at least once a year, we should be judged by Himself and our conscience, and so be prepared for the great Day of Atonement, which is to

[1] Psalm iv. 4.

follow nine days after. Therefore, when in the synagogue you hear the *Shophar* שׁוֹפָר—the ram's-horn
sounding in plaintive and tremulous notes, remember
that it sounds an alarm.   It is meant to arouse you
from your fancied security, to awake your slumbering
conscience, to remind you of your position.   Year by
year, you are expected to improve, not alone in education and worldly knowledge, but in heart and mind
and soul.   Every year as you grow older, and draw
nearer to that day which will be the close of your life
here and the opening of your new life in the world to
come, you are expected to become purer and nobler
in spirit; every year to have fewer faults and greater
virtues ; every year to grow more godly ; and as each
Day of Memorial comes round, you have to satisfy
yourself that this improvement is taking place in your
soul, in that part of you which is immortal.

But if not, what then?   If, when the trumpet
sounds, and you review your ways and works, and examine your heart and soul, you find all vain and unprofitable—duties neglected, bad passions encouraged,
vices increased, days wasted—what then ?   Shall you,
in despair, go deeper and deeper into wickedness?
Shall you waste your time in useless tears ? No. God
has opened to you the door of escape from evil, has
given you the power of repentance and the chance of
forgiveness and reconciliation, by ordaining for that
purpose His great Day of Atonement. "For on that day
shall atonement be made for you to cleanse you, that
you may be clean from all your sins before the Lord."[1]

The Day of Atonement! What thoughts crowd

[1] Lev. xvi. 30.

into the mind at the mention of that day! It is the holiest day of the year, the day which we give entirely to God and to the purifying of our soul by repentance. During that day, no thought of the world or of its profits and pleasures may enter our minds. We are to spend the whole day in meditation and prayer. We are to afflict ourselves; and tradition has ordained that part of that affliction shall consist in abstaining from food and drink from sunset to sunset. For one whole day we are to forget our body, and to think only of our soul—that "living soul" which God planted within us, when He breathed into our nostrils the breath of life.[1]

You, young people, who would not on any account be seen with soiled hands or dirty faces, and who take just pride in your neat and cleanly dress, may well ask yourselves what is the use of being clean in the sight of man, if your soul is unclean in the sight of God? And just as you feel how refreshing it is to take a bath, to cleanse your body from impurity, so must you feel how refreshing it is to take means for purifying your soul, and causing your transgressions to pass away year by year, so that, at least once a year, "you may be clean from all your sins before the Lord."

And truly it is a great privilege, that God should have given us the great Day of Atonement, to remove from the soul the burden of sin, so that every year we may, as it were, begin a new life with a clean and spotless soul and a light and joyful heart.

Now, how is this accomplished? I have told you about the sacrifices, and especially about the sin-offer-

---

[1] Gen. ii. 7.

K

ings; so you know what was their meaning and what their intention. But now we have no temple and no priests, no altar and no sacrifices. How, then, can we celebrate the Day of Atonement so as to receive pardon for our sins?

The Bible tells us how this may be done. By confession, by penitence, by prayer, and by good deeds. If you read the ordinance of the sacrifices of the Day of Atonement, as found in the sixteenth chapter of Leviticus, you will see [1] that confession was a very material part of the Atonement-service. The high priest was to confess over the scape-goat "all the iniquities of the children of Israel and all their transgressions in all their sins." In your prayer-book you will find the form of public confession of sins, (וידוי), which probably includes every possible kind of transgression, and indeed many of which you probably do not even understand the meaning. But although it is right that every Jew, worshipping in public, should join with his fellow-worshippers in one general form of confession, yet this is not the confession which can satisfy us as individuals. Each one of us must make a confession of his own special sins, not to a priest, as is the custom with members of other faiths, but to God and to ourselves.

Confession is the first step towards amendment. We must feel and own that we are wrong, before we are likely to cease our wrong-doing. And the confession must be accompanied by a firm resolution never to repeat the wrong, and, so far as may be possible, to repair its effects.

[1] Lev. xvi. 21.

Penitence, then, does not consist (as many think it does), of mere sorrowful prayers for forgiveness, nor of mere empty confession. There must be *active penitence*, reparation for the past, and resolution for the future.[1] If we have injured or offended our neighbour, the injury or offence must be made good, before we can hope for forgiveness;[2] and if the wrong has been the neglect of a duty, we must do our best, by our future efforts, to remedy the effects of our neglect. This is the true penitence of the Day of Atonement. It is little better than a superstition—indeed it is a superstition—to suppose that our iniquities are removed by a miracle, as the result of our prayers and our fasting. The prayers and the fasting are but empty forms, without the active practical penitence, of which I have spoken. The prayers and the fasting are aids to true penitence, for they bring the penitent to a proper frame of mind. But they are useless, taken by themselves.

Indeed, one cannot imagine a great and kind and merciful God taking delight in our torturing ourselves by hunger, or in our crying aloud to Him for forgiveness, unless these be a means to an end, the end being *our improvement.* If you would learn the thoughts of God upon this subject, as expressed by the

---

[1] Among the ancient Egyptians, regret, without amendment, was accounted one of the forty-two deadly sins.

[2] The Talmud tells us עֲבֵירוֹת שֶׁבֵּין אָדָם לַמָּקוֹם יוֹם הַכִּפּוּרִים מְכַפֵּר עֲבֵירוֹת שֶׁבֵּין אָדָם לַחֲבֵירוֹ אֵין יוֹם הַכִּפּוּרִים מְכַפֵּר עַד שֶׁיְרַצֶּה אֶת חֲבֵירוֹ: "The Day of Atonement expiates sins between man and his Maker, but not sins between man and man; for these, the only atonement is the redress of the injury." *Yoma*, 85, *b.*

mouth of His prophets, you should read the 58th chapter of Isaiah,[1] and the 7th chapter of Zechariah. From the first of these I will quote a few verses, for nothing could be more forcible, and nothing can indicate better how futile are all religious observances —even the great fast of Atonement—unless accompanied by practical contrition, practical well-doing, and the practical virtues of Justice and Mercy.

" Ye shall not fast as ye do this day, to make your voice to be heard on high."

"Is it such a fast that I have chosen? a day for a man to afflict his soul? is it to bow down his head as a bulrush, and to spread sackcloth and ashes under him? Wilt thou call this a fast and an acceptable day unto the Lord?"

" Is not this the fast that I have chosen? to loose the bonds of wickedness, to undo the heavy burdens, and to let the oppressed go free, and that ye break every yoke?"

" Is it not to deal thy bread to the hungry, and that thou bring the poor that are cast out into thy house? when thou seest the naked that thou cover him, and that thou hide not thyself from thine own flesh?

" Then shall thy light break forth as the morning, and thine health shall spring forth speedily ; and thy righteousness shall go before thee ; the glory of the Lord shall be thy rereward."

" Then shalt thou call and the Lord shall answer ; thou shalt cry, and He shall say, Here I am."[2]

So if you observe the fast as Isaiah bids you

---

[1] The *Haphtorah* for the morning of the Day of Atonement.
[2] Isaiah lviii. 4—9.

observe it, the Day of Atonement will be to you a true blessing. Year by year each Day of Atonement will find you purer in heart and soul. Year by year, your penitence, prayer, and good deeds will have wrought for you the true atonement, will have brought you the approbation of your conscience—the Divine Spirit within you—and with it the grace and forgiveness of your loving and merciful Creator.

CHAPTER VIII.

OBSERVANCES.—OUTWARD DISTINCTIONS.

WHEN God made a covenant with Abraham, promising him that he should be the "father of many nations," that his descendants should be a great people who should possess all Canaan, and that He would be their God, He established the rite of circumcision, which was to be "a token of the covenant,"[1] an outward sign and bodily distinction between Abraham's descendants and the rest of the world.

This rite was again enjoined by Moses,[2] and has been observed by all Israelites down to the present time. But you can hardly understand its true meaning and significance till you grow older.

There are other laws of the Pentateuch, which may also be called laws of outward distinctions—the law of מְזוּזוֹת, *Mezuzoth*, the law of תְּפִלִּין, *Tephillin*, and the law of צִיצִת, *Fringes*. All these were to be signs of our allegiance to God, signs that we differ from all nations of the earth, and that we regard ourselves as God's chosen people.

I will talk of the *Mezuzoth* first.

Among the ancients, it was usual to set up images of their gods at the doors of their houses, so as to

---

[1] Gen. xvii. 11.   [2] Lev. xii. 3.

remind them of their duties every time they entered or left their homes. Some of the colossal idols, taken from the entrances of Egyptian palaces, you may see in the British Museum. Of idolatry and its frightful effects, I have already spoken; so you need not be surprised when I tell you that, in the Law of Moses, everything was ordained so as to root out idolatry.

You will find in the 6th chapter of Deuteronomy, from the 4th to the 9th verse, the שמע (*Shemang*), those well-known words, which form the declaration of the Israelite's faith :—"Hear, O Israel, The Lord our God, the Lord is One God. And thou shalt love the Lord thy God with all thine heart, and with all thy soul, and with all thy might. And these words, which I command thee this day, shall be in thine heart. And thou shalt teach them diligently unto thy children, and shalt talk of them when thou sittest in thine house, and when thou walkest by the way, and when thou liest down, and when thou risest up. And thou shalt bind them for a sign upon thine hand, and they shall be as frontlets between thine eyes. And thou shalt write them upon the posts of thy house, and on thy gates."

These simple words, declaring our allegiance to the One and only God, were to be written on the door-posts of our habitations. And now, after the lapse of more than three thousand years, the Israelite still follows this Commandment. Upon a strip of parchment are written the Declaration of Faith, the *Shemang* above quoted (Deut. vi. 4-9), together with a portion of the 11th chapter of Deuteronomy (verses 13-21), in which the same Commandment is repeated and the doctrine

of reward and punishment declared. The parchment is folded and enclosed in a case of glass or of
metal, the word שַׁדַּי *Shaddai* (Almighty) being alone
visible on the outside; and this enclosed parchment
forms the *Mezuzah*.

On the post of every door of every Jewish house
the *Mezuzah* is found, and, in many towns where our
people dwell, it is found *outside* the street-doors, as if
to declare to the world, " This is the house of one of
God's chosen people." Judaism has rightly been
called the religion of every-day life. It is intended to
permeate our life, to become part and parcel of our
existence, so that at every act of our lives we may
keep in mind the idea of an ever-present, ever-watchful
God, who sees us everywhere, and from whom we can
conceal neither our acts nor our thoughts.[1] The sages
tell us, " The consciousness of God's presence is the
great teaching of our Religion."[2] And so the *Mezuzah*,
which we cannot help seeing daily and many times in
the day, cannot fail to remind us of the God whose
Name, " Almighty," is inscribed thereon, and of our
allegiance to that God, as expressed in the words
written within the *Mezuzah*.

Next, the *Tephillin*, or phylacteries.

All of you must have seen, and many of you must
have used the little square cases of leather, enclosing
folds of parchment, on which are written certain passages from the Law, one case being attached to the

---

[1] God asks through the prophet Jeremiah אִם יִסָּתֵר אִישׁ
בַּמִּסְתָּרִים וַאֲנִי לֹא אֶרְאֶנּוּ " Can any hide himself in secret places,
that I shall not see him?"—Jer. xxiii. 24.

[2] שִׁוִּיתִי ה' לְנֶגְדִּי תָמִיד זוּ כְּלָל גָּדוֹל בַּתּוֹרָה :

left arm by long thongs of leather, the other to the forehead, just between the eyes, with a leather fillet or circlet, and long thongs of leather hanging therefrom. These constitute the *Tephillin*, and they are both worn during the time of Morning Prayer, except on Sabbaths and festivals.

The passages written on both the parchments are the two sections already referred to, as written in the *Mezuzah*, viz., the Declaration of Faith (Deut. vi. 4-9), and the promise of reward and punishment (Deut. xi. 13-21); and, further, the narrative of the miraculous redemption from Egypt and the sanctification of the first-born (Exod. xiii. 1-16). In these passages the command is four times repeated, that these words shall be bound as a sign upon our hands, and as frontlets, or as a memorial, between our eyes.

Now what is the meaning, and what the teaching of the *Tephillin?* I will try to explain.

In olden times, and indeed in days not far distant, it was a custom among most nations to wear amulets or charms. These were of different sorts and kinds, but they were usually little idols or images in human form, or sometimes (as among the Egyptians) representations of animals that were held sacred. These amulets or charms were worn upon the body, and were supposed to protect the wearer from evil.

You will be astonished at the absurdity of such a practice. But you will be still more surprised to know that even now the same custom prevails among many barbarous nations of Asia, Africa, and America, among the half-civilised tribes of Russia, and even in Spain, Italy, and other countries, among people

who claim to be educated and enlightened.[1]   In
Russia and Italy the priests are probably to blame
for this; for they traffic in such charms, bestowing upon
them their blessing, without which they are supposed
to be of no effect.   What a horrid idea!   What a
wretched superstition!   To suppose that men and
women can be protected from evil, not by the Almighty Hand that made them, but by a puny little
object fashioned by one man and blessed by another
man!

That the wearing of such charms is a form of
idolatry, I need not tell you; for everything which
derogates from our exclusive allegiance to our great
and all-powerful God is idolatry.   I have already
related by what stringent laws the Israelites were
guarded, and for what reason they were so guarded,
against any and every form of idolatry, or against any
custom that would lead thereto.

Now when the *Tephillin* were ordained, God told
the children of Israel, that if they would wear a charm
upon their hands or upon their heads to protect them
from evil, the words which He commanded them
should be that charm.   The constant remembrance
of His law was the only charm which could protect
them from evil.   This would be a charm different
from that worn by idolatrous nations.   Not a lifeless
image of man or beast, but God's living word was to
be their protection.   That word declared the Unity
of God, the doctrine of reward and punishment, and
the fact of the Divine redemption and revelation, which

[1] The Italians wear a charm to guard themselves against the
imagined mischievous effects of the *jettatura* or evil eye.

together constitute the chief articles of our faith. These were the words which were to be our protection through life; they were to encircle our brain, the seat of understanding, and be ever present in our mind; they were to be bound upon the left arm, near the heart, to remind us that we must curb every unholy desire, repress every impure thought, and that we must be filled with the love of God; they were to encircle our hands, and bind those hands to be righteous and godly in their work.

Of the *Fringes* or *Tsitsith* I need not say much; for their teaching is very similar to that of the *Mezuzoth* and *Tephillin*. In Numbers xv. 37—41, you will find that the Israelites were ordered to wear fringes on the borders of their garments. In Deuteronomy xxii. 12, we find that these fringes were to be on the outer garment, so as to be a distinctive mark before the world. These fringes are still used on the *Arba Kanfoth*, which every male Israelite should wear, and on the *Talith*, which is worn in synagogue. They are made of wool or silk, and are twisted in a peculiar fashion with a large number of threads. These threads are meant to be typical of the many commandments which form the Holy Law. And the text above quoted tells us, that the reason why we wear the fringe is, that we may "look upon it, and remember all the commandments of the Lord and do them."

It was a custom among many ancient nations, before the invention of the art of writing, to use coloured threads for the purpose of reminding them of the chief events of their history. Thus, the ancient Mexicans and Peruvians used the so-called *quipus*—cords composed of threads of different colours, tightly twisted together, from which were suspended a number of smaller threads, which formed a fringe; and these were used to record certain important events and facts in their history. It is difficult for us, with our widely different systems, to understand how this was done; but probably the mental faculty, which we style the association of ideas, enabled them to associate certain numbers, colours, and patterns of threads with certain dates and events.

The *Tsitsith* or fringes fulfil a function somewhat similar to that of the *quipus*. If we bear in mind, that these symbols have been instituted by God as memorials of His commands, they will, every time we look upon them, arouse in our minds pious reflections, and stimulate us to godly actions.

In olden times, a peculiar blue thread formed part of the fringes; but the special dye, produced from a worm—the *techeleth*—which was used for this purpose, is no longer procurable. This blue tint was intended to remind the Israelites of the blue vault of heaven, and of Him who is there enthroned, ever watchful of their every act and word and thought— for His eye is upon us continually; there is not a word on our tongue, but the Lord knoweth it entirely; not a thought in our heart, but it is laid open before Him.[1]

[1] See also " Sabbath Readings," No. 51, " The Fringes;" No. 29, " Tephillin ;" No. 75, " Mezuzoth."

CHAPTER IX.

Social Duties.

After God had given the Ten Commandments, He gave to Moses a series of "judgments,"[1] which were to form the basis or foundation of the moral and social laws of the Israelites; that is to say, the laws which were to regulate their manners and their dealings with one another. God might have said in a few words, "Be just and kind to each other;" and this would have included everything. But it would not have been sufficiently practical; so it was necessary to go into detail.

Laws relating to Servitude.

The first series of these judgments referred to slavery, or more properly to servitude. Now you might suppose, that one of the first laws that would have been given to a nation just released from slavery would have been a law for putting an end to all sorts of bondage; and many writers who have looked only on the surface of the Bible, have regarded the Mosaic Law as cruel, because they allege that it countenanced slavery. But it will be seen that, far from countenancing it, distinctly prohibits slavery—that is, slavery in the sense in which we

[1] Exod. xxi., xxii., xxiii.

understand it. God ordains that "he that stealeth a man and selleth him, or if he be found in his hand, he shall surely be put to death."[1] So slavery, such as we understand it, such as existed until lately in some parts of America, and such as still exists in certain Spanish possessions and in parts of Asia and Africa, never could have existed; for it was an act punishable by death to steal a human being.

Still there was a mild kind of slavery permitted; but it was so hemmed in by laws for the protection of the slave, that the words "servitude" and "servant" should be used to designate this condition of semi-bondage rather than the words "slavery" and "slave."[2] If you carefully read Exod. xxi. and Deut. xv. 12-17 you will understand the nature of these protective laws. Only under three conditions could such servitude exist. First, strangers who were taken prisoners of war could be bought and sold as bondsmen. Secondly, Hebrews who had been found guilty of certain crimes were sentenced to penal servitude,[3] and were liable to be sold as slaves, but for no longer than six years, unless they, of their own accord, renewed their servitude.[4] "In the seventh year he shall go out free for nothing."[5] Thirdly, Hebrews, who had become so poor that they could not support themselves or their families, might sell themselves[6] into servitude; but their servitude would also expire at the end of the sixth year, unless voluntarily renewed.

[1] Exod. xxi. 16.

[2] In the Hebrew Bible, the word used—עֶבֶד—means equally "slave" and "servant."   [3] Exod. xxii. 3.

[4] Exod. xxi. 5, 6.   [5] Exod. xxi. 2.   [6] Lev. xxv. 39.

No unkindness[1] of any sort was permitted towards servants or slaves. A runaway slave might not be captured and restored to his master.[2] If a master struck his servant or slave, and injured him, however slightly, he was obliged to let him go free ;[3] you may, therefore, be sure that no Israelite would risk the loss of his servant by striking him. And when the time of servitude was over, the Hebrew slave or servant did not go out into the wide world empty. He was to have enough to enable him to re-commence his life of freedom. "Thou shalt furnish him liberally out of thy flock and out of thy floor,[4] and out of thy wine-press; of that wherewith the Lord thy God hath blessed thee, thou shalt give unto him : and thou shalt remember that thou wast a bondsman in the land of Egypt, and the Lord thy God redeemed thee, therefore I command thee this thing to-day."[5]

Now you understand why the laws of slavery or servitude were the first of the judgments given to the Israelites. God tells them and us, You have yourselves been bondsmen; remember, when you become masters, not to be tyrants, like the Egyptians, but to be kind and merciful to those who have to serve you.

Protection of Life and Limb.

In treating of the Sixth Commandment—"Thou shalt not kill," I have already told you something about the care shown by the Mosaic code in protecting human life. But, before you will fully under-

---

[1] Lev. xxv. 39, 42, 43.   [2] Deut. xxiii. 15, 16.   [3] Exod. xxi. 26, 27.
[4] Threshing-floor or granary.   [5] Deut. xv. 14, 15.

stand this, you must read for yourselves the laws
relating to personal injury, as detailed in Exod. xxi.
and xxii., and in other parts of the Pentateuch.

If a man killed another intentionally, "with guile,"
it was wilful murder, and he was surely to be put to
death.[1] But if a man killed another by accident,[2]
then he was to be exiled to one of the cities of refuge,
where his life was to be safe from the "avenger of
blood," and he was to remain there till the death of
the high-priest. This exile must have been a terrible
punishment for carelessness, and must have prevented
many of those accidental deaths, which now too com-
monly occur from negligence and want of thought.

But the establishment of "cities of refuge" constituted a further protection to human life, in so far as
it abolished the right of the "avenger of blood" in
cases of accidental killing. In olden times, and even
in modern times among barbarous nations, it was
the custom for the nearest relative of a person killed,
either intentionally or by accident, to be "the avenger
of blood," and to slay him who had caused his
relative's death. The humane Mosaic code permitted
this revenge to be carried out only when the death
was the result of a wilful act, clearly proved; and
the avenger of blood was not allowed to follow to the
city of refuge, and to slay, the man who had been
guilty of manslaughter, or accidental killing.

Even the life of the murderer was not to be sacrificed, without an absolutely certain proof of his guilt.
He could be put to death only on the evidence of at

---

[1] Exod. xxi. 12, 14 ; Numb. xxxv. 16, 18 ; Deut. xix. 11, 12.
[2] Exod. xxi. 13 ; Numb. xxxv. 32 ; Deut. xix 4.

least two witnesses,[1] and these were bound to be eye-witnesses, not merely witnesses bringing circumstantial evidence, or facts tending to criminate the accused, but actual eye-witnesses of the crime.

Other crimes besides murder were punishable by death, such as blasphemy (or speaking disrespectfully of God), worshipping strange gods, Sabbath-breaking, striking a parent, cursing a parent, man-stealing and practising witchcraft; but the punishment of death was so hemmed in by laws of evidence, all in favour of the accused, especially by the law requiring two eye-witnesses of the guilt, that an execution was a very rare occurrence,[2] and the death-punishment might rather be regarded as a preventive—a terror to evil-doers—than a social revenge.

The laws relating to personal injuries, not involving death, have frequently been criticised as barbarously severe. The words used in the Bible are,[3] "Eye for eye; tooth for tooth; hand for hand; foot for foot. Burning for burning; wound for wound; stripe for stripe." If the injury was intentional, the injured party might claim an actual infliction of similar injury: "As he hath done so shall it be done to him."[4] The same law is repeated in Deuteronomy,[5] in connection with the law for the punishment of false witnesses.

It will be readily understood, that this law must have been a terror to evil-doers, and must have prevented many an act of violence. At first sight, it

[1] Numb. xxxv. 30; Deut. xvii. 6.
[2] The Talmud says, not once in seventy years. *Maccoth* 7, a.
[3] Exod. xxi. 24, 25.   [4] Lev. xxiv. 19, 20.   [5] Deut. xix. 21.

seems terribly vindictive, and appears to foster the passion for revenge so natural to injured humanity. But in reality it is conceived in a true spirit of mercy. In an age when strong passions and lawlessness prevailed, no better means could have been adopted than this for curbing the spirit of "might against right," and for protecting the weak against the strong.

It would not be going too far to say that, even in our own times, society would be better for the existence of such a law, if duly hemmed in by laws of evidence sufficient to prevent its abuse. Within quite recent times, the British legislature has adopted the principle of this law, by inflicting flogging upon that class of thieves known as "garotters"—thieves who accompany their theft with acts of violence or assault. The principle might well be carried further. The cowardly trade-outrages known as "rattening," so frequently heard of in the manufacturing districts, and the dastardly assaults on women and children, so common among the lower classes, would soon vanish, if the bully who commits such crimes were led to believe that "as he hath done, so shall it be done to him."

Far from fostering a vindictive and unforgiving spirit, as many have declared, the law has quite the contrary tendency. Before the giving of the Law, it frequently occurred that the man who had suffered an injury, would himself, or through his relatives, inflict the like injury upon the offender. A sort of lynch-law prevailed, such as even now prevails in some parts of Italy, Corsica, and Sicily, where the principle of personal revenge known as "*la vendetta*" exists—a sort of deadly family feud, transmitted from generation to generation, in consequence of some injury done to a remote ancestor centuries ago. The Mosaic law steps in between the injured party and the offender, and declares that the offence must first be proved according to strict rules of evidence, and, if proved, must be regarded as an offence against society, which no longer the individual but the strong arm of the law must avenge. It was to be no longer a case of private revenge, which might overstep the bounds of justice, and mete out a punishment disproportionate to the offence. It was to be a case of calm deliberate decision by the judges, according to strict rules of evidence, and the punishment was to be no greater than the offence.

It is a matter of absolute certainty that the law of "eye for eye" was never practically enforced. The difficulty of awarding a punishment exactly similar to the injury is obvious, especially in cases where an internal injury had been inflicted. It is therefore probable, that the law was intended rather as a threat to prevent crimes of violence, and was also to indicate the extent of the debt due by the perpetrator to his victim. And be it understood, that the law only referred to cases of personal injury intentionally inflicted. The infliction of accidental injury, or even of injuries resulting from a fair fight, was punished differently. The offender was, in such cases, to pay fair compensation, the amount being determined by the judges. We find[1] that if two men fight, and one

[1] Exod. xxi. 18, 19.

injures the other, "and he die not, but keepeth his bed, if he rise again, and walk abroad upon his staff, then shall he that smote him be quit; only he shall pay for the loss of his time, and shall cause him to be thoroughly healed."

The like principle of compensation is enforced in the cases of injuries resulting from negligence. If an ox, known to have been mischievous, gored a man to death, the ox was destroyed, the owner was considered responsible, and deserving of the punishment of death : but he was allowed in this case to do what was not permitted in other capital offences; to "give for the ransom of his life whatsoever is laid upon him;"[1] that is, the judge awarded compensation to the family of the victim, in lieu of inflicting the punishment of death on the careless owner of the ox.[2]

If an ox injured a servant, the owner of the ox was bound to pay compensation to the master for the loss of service, and the ox was to be killed. It must be understood that in all these precepts the ox is to be regarded only as a representative animal, being the beast most likely to inflict injury; and that similar laws were applicable to injuries resulting from the attacks of other animals.

The law of battlements is another representative law, having for its object the protection of human life from possible danger. It is enacted[3] that "when thou

[1] Exod. xxi. 29, 30, 31.

[2] This is not in opposition to the principle enjoined in Numb. xxxv. 31, not to take redemption or ransom ; for that law refers to cases of wilful homicide, not to cases of accidental homicide, or to manslaughter caused by culpable heedlessness.   [3] Deut. xxii. 8.

buildest a new house, then thou shalt make a battle-
ment for thy roof, that thou bring not blood upon thy
house, if any man fall from thence." No modern code
contains laws guarding more jealously the interest of
human life and limb. The law just referred to, doubtless had greater significance in oriental countries,
where most of the roofs are flat, and where people walk
about on the housetops. But the law equally applies
to other places besides roofs, and indicates that any
source of possible danger to life must be carefully and
religiously avoided.

It may be interesting, in connection with this subject, to call attention to the law prescribed in case of
the finding of the body of a person slain by an unknown hand.[1] The solemn procedure was one calculated to ensure the discovery of the murderer, if the
discovery were at all possible. No one can read this
precept, without feeling the strong probability that it
gave rise to the institution of coroner's jury, one of the
oldest legal institutions of this country.

Rights of Property.

In treating of the Eighth Commandment, I told
you that the protection of property was one of the
marks of distinction between savages and civilized
men, and I gave you a few examples of the laws of
the Mosaic Code for the prevention of dishonesty and
for the protection of property. I propose now to tell
you a little more about the same subject.

It was declared unlawful to remove any boundary

[1] Deut. xxi. 1-9.

mark,[1] defining the ancient limits of land; for the removal of such land-mark might rob a neighbour of part of his possessions.

It was declared unlawful to appropriate any lost property; and the finder was bound to search out the owner, and restore the property to him.[2]

The master might not keep back the wages of his servant, but was bound to pay him promptly.[3]

Any injury done by leaving an open pit unprotected had to be paid for by the careless owner of the pit.[4]

If one ox killed another, the owners of the two oxen were to share the dead and living animals;[5] but if the assailing ox was known to have been previously mischievous, and the owner had not tied him up, he had to pay ox for ox, but the dead animal became his property.[6]

Compensation was to be made for any injury, to a field or to a vineyard, caused by straying cattle; and in case of the accidental burning of standing crops, the person who kindled the fire had to make restitution.[7]

If an animal or other property deposited with any-one, was lost or stolen, damaged or destroyed, and the delinquent could not be discovered, he who had taken charge of the property had to be put on trial; and if he satisfied the Judges by a statement on oath that he had not himself been the cause of the loss, theft, or damage, he was absolved.[8] But he had to make good the loss, if the animal or property had been lent to him, the actual owner not being present.

---

[1] Deut. xix. 14.   [2] Deut. xxii. 1-3.   [3] Lev. xix. 13.
[4] Exod. xxi. 34.   [5] Exod. xxi. 35.   [6] Exod xxi. 35, 36.
[7] Exod. xxii. 5, 6.   [8] Exod. xxii. 7, 9.

The rights of property might not be unduly or harshly enforced against the very poor, or against the hungry wayfarer. Those who had occasion to work in, or were passing through, a vineyard, might eat some of the grapes, but might not carry any away with them. And a man passing through a cornfield might pluck a few ears of corn with his hand, and eat them; but he was not allowed to cut any with his sickle, and to remove them in bulk.[1]

Rights of Poverty.

That poverty should have any rights is a proposition that would startle most economists of the present day. They would probably admit the pauper no right but that of a home in a workhouse, or a pauper's grave. But in Palestine there were no workhouses; for the Poor Law of the Mosaic code gave the poor certain rights, whereby they might sustain life, and even recover their lost position.

Charity has always been looked upon by our nation as a cardinal virtue. Even the enemies of our faith and race have always regarded the charity of the Jews as their greatest merit; and the care they have bestowed upon their poor has ever evoked the wonder and admiration of the Gentile world.

However, the charity of our people has probably not been due to mere sentiment, but rather to a habit— the result of the action of our poor-laws—the result, too, of the fact that the poor, in accordance with those laws, occupy a recognised position amongst us. A noble virtue, the effect of noble sentiment, is a sub-

[1] Deut. xxiii. 24, 25.

ject for just pride; but when it is the effect of long-established practice and habit, from generation to generation, becoming part and parcel of the national instinct and character, it is a subject for deep gratitude to the Great God, who taught us that practice and habit in the Code He gave us through His servant Moses.

That Code tells us:—"The poor shall never cease out of the land ; therefore, I command thee, saying, Thou shalt open thine hand wide unto.thy brother, to thy poor and to thy needy in thy land."[1]

These words left much to the liberality of the individual ; but there were certain rights which the poor possessed independently of such liberality.   The gleanings of the field were not to be gathered by the farmer, nor was he permitted to reap the corn standing in the corners of the fields.   These were to be left for the widow, the fatherless, and the stranger. So, too, the forgotten sheaf, the gleanings of the oliveyard and vineyard, and their second crop were to be left for the poor and the stranger.[2]   We are enjoined to lend money to the poor,[3] a loan being less humiliating and less pauperising than a gift; and a loan to any of our own people must invariably be without interest.[4]   "Thou shalt not give him thy money upon interest,[5] nor lend him thy victuals for increase."   Interest was allowed to be charged to a non-Israelite, if the money was borrowed for mer-

---

[1] Deut. xv. 11.

[2] Lev. xix. 9, 10 ; Lev. xxiii. 22 ; Deut. xxiv. 19, 20, 21.

[3] Deut. xv. 8.   [4] Lev. xxv. 36, 37.

[5] נֶשֶׁךְ mistranslated "usury" in the Authorised Version.

cantile purposes; but it was not allowed to be charged, if the debt was incurred by a stranger who had fallen into poverty, or who required help for his subsistence.[1]

At the end of every seven years, every debt was released. "Every creditor that lendeth aught unto his neighbour shall release it; he shall not exact it of his neighbour or of his brother, because it is the Lord's release. Of a foreigner thou mayest exact it again."[2] But even against the foreigner no act of oppression was allowed. "Thou shalt neither vex a stranger nor oppress him, for ye were strangers in the land of Egypt."[3] Nor was the thought of the year of release, and the possible loss of the money to weigh with the lender. "Beware that there be not a wicked thought in thy heart,[4] saying, The seventh year, the year of release is at hand, and thine eye be evil against thy poor brother, and thou givest him nought; and he cry unto the Lord against thee, and it be sin unto thee. Thou shalt surely give him, and thine heart shall not be grieved, when thou givest unto him."[5]

Again it is said, "Thou shalt not harden thine heart, nor shut thine hand from thy poor brother."[6] Nor was the lender, who took security for a loan, to retain the article pledged, if it was an article of necessity: "If thou at all take thy neighbour's raiment to pledge, thou shall deliver it unto him by that the sun goeth down. For that is his covering

---

[1] Lev. xxv. 35. [2] Deut. xv. 2, 3. [3] Exod. xxii. 21.
[4] Wrongly rendered in the Anglican Version, "a thought in thy wicked heart."
[5] Deut. xv. 9, 10. [6] Deut. xv. 7.

only, it is his raiment for his skin : wherein shall he
sleep ?"[1] A widow's raiment might not be taken
in pledge,[2] nor might any implement of daily labour
be accepted as a security.[3]

But the greatest of the rights of poverty was enforced by the law of Tithe. Besides the tithe of all
produce which was annually given to the Levites, the
Israelite was obliged to bring every third year the
tenth part of his increase for the use of the poor.
" At the end of three years, thou shalt bring forth all
the tithes of thine increase the same year, and shalt
lay it up within thy gates : And the Levite (because
he hath no part or inheritance with thee) and the
stranger, and the fatherless, and the widow, which are
within thy gates, shall come and shall eat and be
satisfied ; that the Lord thy God may bless thee in all
the work of thy hand which thou doest."[4]   In every
city, storehouses were established for the reception of
the tithe, and from this reserve the necessitous were
enabled to draw when misfortune befell them. In the
26th chapter of Deuteronomy[5] you may read the
prayer which had to be recited, when each individual
brought his tithe. It began with a solemn declaration
that he had truly given the full tenth of his profit,
withholding nothing, and forgetting nothing ; and it
terminated by imploring the blessing of Heaven on
those who had so obeyed the Divine command.
You may read in the Books of Chronicles and
Nehemiah,[6] how truly and plentifully the tithes were

[1] Exod. xxii. 26, 27.   [2] Deut. xxiv. 17.   [3] Deut. xxiv. 6.
[4] Deut. xiv. 28, 29.   [5] Deut. xxvi. 13, 14, 15.
[6] 2 Chron. xxxi. 5, 6, 12 ; Nehem. xiii. 12.

brought, and you will then readily understand how the tithe liberally supplied the wants of the poor.[1]

But even these were not the only rights of poverty. The year of release was also the sabbatical year, the year in which the land rested. Although during the sabbatical year the farmer was not doomed to idleness (for he could dig water-tanks, erect farm buildings, construct terraces for his vineyards, repair his hedges and boundary walls), the land had to rest, so as to recruit its exhausted strength. No seed was then sown, no vineyard pruned, and no fruit gathered by the owner, the produce of the sixth year being always sufficient for the consumption of three years.[2] But though the land was wholly, and the farmer was partially to rest on the seventh year, the crops still grew, the fruits still ripened. All these crops and fruits belonged to the poor,[3] and this beneficent arrangement probably enabled them to clear themselves of debt by payment, when their sense of honour would not permit the year of release to wipe off their obligation to their creditors.

Thus did our Sacred Code aim at the alleviation of the evils of poverty; but by the laws which it instituted for the holding of land, it did more; it aimed at the prevention of permanent poverty or hereditary pauperism.

The Land Laws.

Every fiftieth year, the year of Jubilee, all land that had been sold reverted to the original owner, or

---

[1] See also " Sabbath Readings," No. 117, " The Tithe."
[2] Lev. xxv. 21. [3] Exod. xxiii. 11.

to his family. So the family of the poor man, who had been compelled to sell his possessions, became again possessed of worldly means ; and thus the institution of the Jubilee, at a time when land was the chief item of wealth, prevented that cardinal evil of civilized life, the concentration of wealth in the few, to the detriment of the many—a circumstance that gives rise to those terrible contrasts of modern society, excessive wealth and excessive poverty.

Except houses in walled cities, which could be sold as a perpetual possession, no landed property could be sold as freehold,[1] "for the land is Mine," saith the Lord. You will find in the Book of Joshua, how, when the Israelites had arrived in the Promised Land and conquered it, the country was divided by lot among the various tribes, and each man had his share. Thus at the outset every one possessed his parcel of land. Now, if a man became poor and sold his land, he or his relatives might, if they had the means, at any time repurchase it, paying for it according to the number of years that had to run to the Jubilee.[2] Even a house in a walled city, which might be sold for ever, could be repurchased at the same price by the original owner at any time within a year of the sale.[3] But, however poor he and his descendants might be, in the year of the Jubilee the land must revert to them, and so their poverty would not be lasting.

All these laws tended to check the greed for acquiring land, seemingly one of the appetites

---

[1] Lev. xxv. 23, 29, 30.   [2] Lev. xxv. 25-27.

[3] Lev. xxv. 29.

of man, which, if inordinately indulged, must tend to the prejudice of his fellow-creatures.

Connected with the land laws, may be mentioned the laws of inheritance. You will find these fully set forth in the twenty-seventh chapter of Numbers. They are particularly interesting ; for one cannot help feeling that these laws of inheritance must have given rise to the Statute of Distributions, which regulates in this country the inheritance of the personal property of those who die without having made a will.

Laws of Government.

I have already pointed out to you that, in its general laws, the Mosaic code deals mainly with principles, and that when it descends to details, those details may be considered as representative examples of the application of those principles. This was necessary for a code which was to be eternal, and whose principles consequently had to be applied to every age, clime, polity, and circumstance.

In the Mosaic laws relating to government, this is clearly seen. They are merely outline laws, which can be applied equally to a monarchy, a republic, or an oligarchy.

No special form of government is prescribed in the Law. But it was ordained, that if the Israelites were to elect a king, he must be one of themselves and not a stranger ; that the king so chosen must not accumulate great wealth or worldly possessions, but that his chief duty was to keep intact the words of the Law. To this end he was bound to write, or to have written for himself, a copy of the Law, which was to be his text-book "all the days of his life." [1]

But though these laws were made for the guidance of the future kings of Israel and Judah, monarchy was not enjoined as a necessary form of government. Provision was made for the Republic which was to succeed the rule of Moses [2]—the Republic over which Joshua was to preside as ruler, general, and judge; and the people were ordered to hearken to his words and obey his mandates. In this commandment, the test of the true prophet [is given, and the nation is warned against the false prophets who might "speak in the name of gods other" than the one true God.

Respect for legally constituted authority and obedience to the law were enjoined early in the code; we find in Exodus (chap. xxii. 28), "Thou shalt not revile the judges,[3] nor curse the ruler of thy people." Social order is the great object of all good government. Hence the law, "Judges and officers shalt thou make thee in all thy gates which the Lord thy God giveth thee in all thy tribes, and they shall judge the people with just judgment."[4]

How the judges and officers were first appointed, you will find described in the eighteenth chapter of Exodus. The law had not yet been given, and Moses was sole judge of Israel. Jethro his father-in-law found him engaged in judicial work from morning till evening, and remonstrated with him, saying, "Why

---

[1] Deut. xvii. 18, 19.   [2] Deut. xviii. 15.
[3] Incorrectly translated in the English Version, "Thou shalt not revile the gods."   [4] Deut. xvi. 18.

sittest thou thyself alone, and all the people stand by
thee from morning unto even ?"   To which Moses mo-
destly replied—" Because the people come unto me to
enquire of God.   When they have a matter, they
come unto me ; and I judge between one and another,
and I do make them know the statutes of God, and
His laws."   Thereupon Jethro tells him that he will
wear himself out with all this toil, and advises him to
" provide out of all the people able men such as fear
God, men of truth, hating covetousness, and place
such over them to be rulers of thousands, rulers of
hundreds, rulers of fifties and rulers of tens, and let
them judge the people at all seasons."   The advice
was followed, and we find that "the hard cases they
brought unto Moses, but every small matter they
judged themselves."

The charge to the judges so appointed we find in
Deut. i. 16, 17, " Hear the causes between your
brethren, and judge righteously between every man
and his brother, and the stranger that is with him.
Ye shall not respect persons in judgment, but ye shall
hear the small as well as the great ; ye shall not be
afraid of the face of man, for the judgment is God's."

The judges were to discharge their duties with
perfect justice, without fear, or favour, or chance of
corruption : " Thou shalt not wrest judgment ; thou
shalt not respect persons, neither take a gift ; for a gift
doth blind the eyes of the wise, and pervert the words
of the righteous."[1]   In Leviticus we read, " Ye shall
do no unrighteousness in judgment ; thou shalt not
respect the person of the poor, nor honour the person

---

[1] Deut. xvi. 19.

of the mighty ; but in righteousness thou shalt judge thy neighbour."[1]

You have already seen that all difficult legal questions were referred to Moses, and you will read in the Pentateuch many examples of reference to him, such as the case of the blasphemer,[2] the punishment of the Sabbath breaker,[3] and the inheritance of the daughters of Zelophchad.[4] But it was necessary to make provision for a Supreme Court of reference for future times ; and hence the following law :—" If there arise a matter too hard for thee in judgment, between blood and blood, between plea and plea, and between stroke and stroke, being matters of controversy within thy gates, then shalt thou arise and get thee up into the place which the Lord thy God shall choose. And thou shalt come to the priests, the Levites, and unto the judge that shall be in those days, and inquire, and they shall show thee the sentence of judgment. And thou shalt do according to the sentence which they of that place which the Lord shall choose shall show thee."[5] It is said that this Law was the origin of the Sanhedrin or Supreme Court of seventy-one members.[6] You may read in Chronicles,[7] how Jehoshaphat, King of Judah, appointed in Jerusalem such a supreme tribunal, having previously placed local judges[8] in every walled city of Judah. You will

---

[1] Lev. xix. 15.   [2] Lev. xxiv. 11.   [3] Numbers xv. 33.
[4] Numb. xxvii. 2.   [5] Deut. xvii. 8, 9, 10.
[6] See Appendix II.   [7] 2 Chron. xix. 8-11.

[8] The local courts consisted of three judges for the trial of civil suits, and twenty-three judges for the trial of criminal suits. The decision of a majority decided ; but though a majority of one was sufficient to acquit a prisoner, a majority of at least two was necessary to convict him. *Sanhedrin*, Chap. I.

read how he charged the judges with the words, " Take heed what ye do ; for ye judge not for man, but for the Lord, who is with you in judgment."

The Court was to be formed of the priests, the Levites, and the judges, the best and most learned "that shall be in those days," and its judgment was to be final and conclusive.

It was a wise provision to establish Courts of this kind to pronounce judgment on matters of difficulty not specially provided for by the Mosaic Code ; for no code, however perfect, could intelligibly provide laws for every possible future change, circumstance, and contingency ; and as times and circumstances change, and human knowledge progresses, the details of the observance of those laws must be adjusted, (but adjusted by competent and recognised authorities), to suit the requirements of those times and circumstances, and the altered condition of human knowledge. And yet they must be so adjusted that neither the principle nor the practice of the Law shall be violated, for " thou shalt not add thereto nor diminish from it."[1] Hence the Israelites were bidden to refer to the living fountain of living knowledge, to the best contemporaneous opinion, "to the priests, the Levites, and unto the judge that shall be *in those days*."

Education.

In these early days of School-boards, when education is for the first time becoming general in this country, and the lowest classes of society are only

[1] Deut. xii. 32.

just emerging from the darkness of ignorance, it is refreshing to turn back to the Mosaic code, and see what provision was there made for the instruction of the young, and especially for their religious education.

The Levites were the appointed instructors of the people: "they shall teach Jacob Thy judgments, and Israel Thy law."[1] From the age of twenty-five to fifty, they performed the service of God in the Tabernacle or Temple, and after the age of fifty "they ceased waiting upon the service," but "ministered with their brethren in the Tabernacle of the congregation to keep the charge."[2]

But though the Levites were thus ordained to be the ministers of religion and the public teachers, the Holy Law established a principle of religious instruction, which was to be by far the most important part of education—the instruction of children by their parents. The laws of God were not to be taught solely by public teachers. "Thou shalt teach them diligently to thy children, and shalt talk of them when thou sittest in thine house, and when thou walkest by the way."[3] It was to be the province of parents to instil religion into their own children, not only for the sake of the children, but for their own sakes. Moses tells the people,[4] "Only take heed to thyself, and keep thy soul diligently, lest thou forget the things which thine eyes have seen, and lest they depart from thy heart all the days of thy life; but teach them thy children, and thy children's children." To

[1] Deut. xxxiii. 10.   [2] Numb. viii. 24—26.   [3] Deut. vi. 7.
[4] Deut. iv. 9.

teach religion to our children is to keep religion alive, both in ourselves and in them. What teaching can be so forcible as a parent's teaching? and what lesson can be so impressive as the lesson given by a father to his children, while walking abroad with them, discoursing of the wonders of Nature and the will of Nature's God?

And so, when God gave ordinances for the guidance of His chosen race, "He established a testimony in Jacob, and appointed a law in Israel, which He commanded our fathers, that they should make them known to their children; That the generation to come might know them, even the children which should be born, who should arise and declare them to their children; That they may set their hope in God, and not forget the works of God, but keep His commandments." [1]

History shows that many branches of knowledge have been lost, and many arts and sciences utterly forgotten, because parents have neglected the natural duty of teaching their own children. This happened with the ancient Egyptians, greatest of all nations of antiquity in the arts of construction, in science and in philosophy; their knowledge became lost to the world, because instruction was in the hands of a privileged and dominant class—the priests—who used their position for their own aggrandizement, keeping their knowledge to themselves, and leaving the multitude in ignorance and superstition. So with the ancient Chinese, conspicuous among Eastern nations for the cultivation of science and literature (traces of which have surprised advanced minds of modern times): nearly all their

[1] Psalm lxxviii. 5, 6, 7.

knowledge was lost to the world in the like manner. But our Code maintains knowledge to be the heritage of the whole human race, and not the monopoly of priest or Levite. It declares that there are to be no priestly mysteries or secrets; that education is a public right of the whole nation as well as a private duty of parent to child; that all revealed knowledge is public property; that though " the secret things belong to the Lord our God, those things which are revealed belong unto us and to our children for ever." [1]

Religious Toleration.

It has been frequently charged against the Mosaic Code that it was wanting in mercy and toleration, inasmuch as it preached the wholesale destruction of certain idolatrous tribes of Canaan. The fact, that the Israelites were entrusted with the duty of utterly exterminating those tribes, must be candidly admitted. They were ordered to " save alive nothing that breatheth;" [2] and the fact is certainly a terrible one. Even the women and children were to be slaughtered.

Why this fearful carnage? The Bible answers the question. The seven idolatrous tribes, the Hittites, Girgashites, Amorites, Canaanites, Perizzites, Hivites, and Jebusites were to be exterminated, " that they teach you not to do after all their abominations, which they have done unto their gods." [3] What those abominations were we know not precisely, for the Pentateuch only hints at certain of these crimes too fearful to mention. " There must have been pollution in everything they touched; for we read that Moses

[1] Deut. xxix. 29.   [2] Deut. xx. 16.   [3] Deut. xx. 18.

ordered all the spoil of Midian to be destroyed, except such things as could pass through the fire, and could thus be purified. There are mental and moral diseases as loathsome and as infectious as any which affect the body. May it not have been even an act of supreme mercy that God, by a terrible act of extermination, prevented the evil from increasing and spreading, till the whole world became a mass of corruption ?" [1]

When, then, we read of these fearful wars of extermination, we must not regard them as evincing anything like a want of forbearance or toleration towards followers of a religion differing from our own ; and we should rather seek in the Pentateuch for the special laws which teach us how we should treat members of an alien faith.

We are told, " Thou shalt not vex a stranger nor oppress him, for ye were strangers in the land of Egypt." [2] Even the Egyptians, by whom the Israelites had been so unmercifully treated, were to be requited with charitable forbearance : " Thou shalt not abhor an Egyptian, because thou wast a stranger in his land." [3] The law knew no difference between Jew and Gentile. " If a stranger sojourn with you in your land, ye shall not vex him. But the stranger that dwelleth with you shall be unto you as one born among you, and thou shalt love him as thyself, for ye were strangers in the land of Egypt." [4] " One law shall be to him that is home-born, and unto the stranger that sojourneth among you." [5]

---

[1] "A Jewish Reply to Dr. Colenso's criticism on the Pentateuch :" p. 146. (Trübner). [2] Exod. xxii. 21.
[3] Deut. xxiii. 7. [4] Lev. xix. 33, 34. [5] Exod. xii. 49.

A stranger was permitted to join in the Divine service of the Tabernacle and Temple, and was even allowed to bring an offering to the altar of God. " If a stranger sojourn with you, or whosoever be among you in your generations, and will offer an offering made by fire of a sweet savour unto the Lord ; as ye do, so shall he do. One ordinance shall be both for you and also for the stranger that sojourneth with you, an ordinance for ever in your generations, as ye are, so shall be the stranger before the Lord."[1] No lesson of religious toleration could be enforced in stronger terms than these. The Bible practically tells us, If God can thus tolerate those who believe not in the true religion, why should not we ? " He loveth the stranger in giving him food and raiment; love ye therefore the stranger."[2]

There is, however, a kind of spurious tolerance which is not the result of true philosophy or true liberality, but rather the effect of religious indifference. It is common enough to hear persons, indifferent to religion, say that one religion is as good as another. Against such indifference the Bible warns us.[3] There may be no lax attachment to our religion. There must be full and complete loyalty to the One and only true God.

That such loyalty need not detract from our tolerance of the religion of others, may be best proved by reference to a prayer—perhaps the most remarkable in the whole Bible—the prayer of King Solomon at the dedication of the Temple. He craves the blessing of Heaven on the building he had raised to the glory of

---

[1] Numb. xv. 14, 15.   [2] Deut. x. 18, 19.   [3] Deut. xiii. 6.

God, and begs that the prayers and supplications, that he and his people may there offer, may be favourably answered; and then he craves the same blessing for those who were not of his own faith : " Moreover concerning the stranger which is not of Thy people Israel, but is come from a far country for Thy great name's sake, and Thy mighty hand and Thy stretched-out arm; if they come and pray in this house ; Then hear Thou from the heavens, even from Thy dwelling-place, and do according to all that the stranger calleth to Thee for." [1]   We know from the Talmudical and other accounts of the Temple (and these accounts are supported by the results of recent investigations) that this prayer was not, as some might suppose, the mere individual expression of the liberality of a wisely liberal king.   For it has been found that, surrounding the *chel*, or raised platform on which the Temple was erected, and lying between the outer portico and the Temple proper, there was a great corridor thirty cubits (forty-five feet) wide, which was known as the " court of Gentiles," destined for the worship of strangers, and that this court, which formed an inner belt encircling the Temple, was many times larger than the " court of the men of Israel." [2]

The prayer of King Solomon, in its application to the Gentile world, was therefore no dead letter.   The liberal spirit which pervades this noble prayer is the spirit of our holy law.   If that spirit had permeated the two creeds which have sprung from our religion, then history would not have had to record, as it

[1] 2 Chron. vi. 32, 33.
[2] Fergusson's " Temples of the Jews."   Murray, 1878.

unfortunately does, so many stories of persecution, so many reigns of terror, so many orgies of fire and sword.

In this century, for the first time in the history of the world, a few Gentile nations have declared the same principle of religious toleration, propounded more than 3,000 years ago by Moses. In some countries the principle has been proclaimed by the civil powers, the spiritual powers still denying the principle. The clergy of most religions other than our own, doubtless actuated by sincere though mistaken motives, still condemn to perdition all who refuse to believe as they do. Living among people, many of whom would hold a close monopoly of God and of eternal happiness, the Jew alone represents, as of old, the true spirit of religious charity and tolerance, proclaiming, as did King David, that God is not a sectarian God, but that "the Lord is good to all, and His tender mercies are over all His works." [1] The Jew, acting in the spirit of the Mosaic code, proclaims all men equal in the sight of God, and believes not that perdition and everlasting torment can be in store for those whose religious belief differs from his own.

The Jew hopes and believes that the day will come when all the world will recognise the one true God. Till then, there may be many religions; there can be but one morality; and so our sages, in the true spirit of toleration, have declared that "the righteous of every faith have their share in the world to come." [2]

[1] Psalm cxlv. 9.
[2] Maimonides, *Hilchoth Teshubah*. Comp. *Sanhedrin*, 105 a.

CHAPTER X.

MORAL DUTIES.

THE laws to which I have referred in the last chapter, I have described under the head of "social duties," because they are the laws which tend to keep society together, and they constitute, in fact, a sort of public law. The laws of which I propose next to treat are also in a great measure social, seeing that they affect every individual, and that society is made up of individuals; but I prefer to set them by themselves, because they relate to private virtue rather than to public law, and also because they appeal to every human being, regardless of race or creed.

It has been truly said that men cannot be made virtuous by Act of Parliament. The restraints of law may prevent men from being criminal, but will not make them virtuous. One constantly meets men who are seemingly good citizens, and who yet are bad, immoral and irreligious men. But such a contradiction the Mosaic Code does not recognise. "Thou shalt be perfect with the Lord thy God,"[1] perfect before God as before the world. It is not sufficient to do one's duty to the country in which we live, to obey its laws, to be patriotic, and to pay our dues to the

[1] Deut. xviii. 13.

State. No one can be a truly good citizen, without
being a virtuous man.

You know already that there are, unfortunately,
a great number of religions in the world besides
your own holy faith. Considering the terrible wars,
strifes and persecutions that have resulted, and still
result, from differences of religious belief, staining
with blood nearly every page of history, it seems a sad
thing that there should ever have been a multitude of
religions ; and one must sincerely long for the time
when, in the fulness of God's wisdom, He may bring
the whole world to adopt that one great and sacred
belief, which you proudly regard as your own.

But terrible as have been the consequences of these
religious differences, there remains one consoling fact
that, with very few exceptions, all religions are agreed
upon the laws of morality, and the principles of right
and wrong. Indeed, curiously enough, many savage
nations, with but little religious sentiment, and no
defined ideas about the nature of God, have yet in
their rude literature recorded laws of morality not
differing greatly from our own, though these laws
may, perhaps, have been but lightly regarded by them.

Love of God.

First among the moral duties which belong to every
religion is the duty to love, fear, and honour God. It
seems so simple a matter to love the Great Being to
whom we owe our existence, our food, our clothing,
our strength, our faculties, and all we possess, that
obedience to this law should be as natural as obedience
to the appetites of hunger and thirst. But our faith,

whatever may be the case with other creeds, does not
permit us to indulge in a piety that costs us nothing,
and that is a mere obedience to a natural instinct ;
for we are told not merely to love God, but to love
Him "with all thine heart, with all thy soul, and with
all thy might."[1]

What does this qualification signify? The history
of Judaism, with its large army of worthies who
have suffered persecution for their faith and yet stead-
fastly adhered to it, and the long array of martyrs
who have sacrificed their lives for the sake of their
religion, will afford the best interpretation of these
words. With all our heart, the centre of our emotions ;
with all our soul, the fountain of our thought, our
reason, and our faith ; with all our bodily powers, with
every nerve and every muscle that makes us beings of
action—we are to show our love and adoration of the
God who made us, and are to be prepared to sacrifice
everything for the love of Him.

But you may reply that this is a vague generality ;
"to sacrifice everything" is a pretty phrase. True,
we Jews are no longer called upon to bear the crown
of martyrdom, to die for our faith; how, then, can we
show our love to the God of Heaven and Earth?
The Bible tells us how to do this : "To keep the commandments of the Lord, and His statutes, which I
command thee this day, for thy good."[2] We have to
keep the Law not only for God's glory or His pleasure,
but for *our* good. Our good and our happiness are
the benign objects of God in giving us the Law. How
can the obedience of a small nation in one of His

[1] Deut. vi. 5.   [2] Deut. x. 13.

little planets profit Him, the Creator of the mighty universe? "Behold the heaven, and the heaven of heavens is the Lord's thy God, the earth also and all that therein is. Only the Lord had a delight in thy fathers to love them, and He chose their seed after them, even you, above all people, as it is this day."[1]

Thus, love of God means obedience to His will; and obedience to His will brings, as its results and reward, our happiness.

And here it may be well to make a digression to indicate one great point of difference between Judaism and other religions. Although our religion undoubtedly requires of us many sacrifices and deprivations, yet Judaism is essentially a happy religion. It is not a religion of long faces, many fasts, much self-mortification, and everlasting seriousness. Our Sabbath, for example, is a rational, not a puritanical Sabbath. We are not to show our love to God by making ourselves miserable : though we are called a "kingdom of priests," we are not to be a nation of monks and nuns. The Nazarite was esteemed a sinner for his asceticism, and had to bring a sin-offering.[2]

We are not to "groan away our lives in a busy contemplation of our sins."[3]   Although several fast-days were instituted in the course of time, to commemorate sad events that had befallen our nation, on one day only in the year does the Law bid us afflict our souls.   We are to "serve the Lord with gladness, enter His presence with singing."[4]   Our religion and our happiness

[1] Deut. x. 14, 15.   [2] Numb. vi. 14.
[3] "Sunny Aspects of Religion."   [4] Psalm c. 2.

arc to go hand in hand. Our love of God and obedience to His laws are to make us happy.

But though the love of God is a duty enjoined by
every religion, there is something special about that
duty as enjoined upon the Jew. For his belief in the
unity of God compels him to give undivided homage
to the Deity he adores. Other creeds have their
secondary deities, or demi-gods, or mediators; but the
God of the Jew is the One sole God, the One Creator
of the universe, who works by His own great power,
and who, nevertheless, may be approached in prayer
and supplication by the humblest of His creatures,
without any mediator. And in these words does He
declare His sole and sovereign power: "See now
that I, even I, am He, and there is no God with Me;
I kill, and I make alive; I wound, and I heal; neither
is there any that can deliver out of My hand."[1]

Herein lies the great comfort of our sacred religion;
and this constitutes another source of happiness for
the Jew. Other faiths have regarded their God as a
Deity who will not forgive without the mediation of a
being, half-God, half-man; or of a priest, who represents himself as the accredited agent of this mediator.
Our religion represents God, as He represents Himself, as a "God, merciful and gracious, long-suffering,
and abundant in goodness and truth, Keeping mercy
for thousands, forgiving iniquity, transgression, and
sin,"[2] so that we need no secondary deity to crave
pardon on our behalf. The priests of other faiths,
anxious to establish their position as mediators, by
playing upon the fears of their credulous flocks, and

---

[1] Deut. xxxii. 39.   [2] Exod. xxxiv. 6, 7.

wishing to make a profit out of the too susceptible
consciences of their congregations, have invented the
terrible idea of hell, with the devil as its presiding
deity; and this hell they represent as a place of eternal
torment for the souls of the wicked and the unbeliever.[1]

Our religion knows no such sacrilegious ideas. It
cannot contemplate the possibility that the same
loving God, who claims our love, and whose universe
teems with proofs of His kindness, can be a vindictive God, capable of giving *eternal* punishment to
a human soul.[2] It cannot conceive that the same
God, who gave us in His code a true message of love,
in which we are enjoined to be kind to our neighbours, our dependents, and even to the helpless
brutes, could inflict everlasting torture on the souls
of those whom He created in His own image; nor
can it admit the possibility that the Almighty God
of good would permit the existence of a devil, or god
of evil, side by side with Himself, to counteract His
goodness and to check His mercy. "There is no
God with Me," is the Divine declaration.

But you will ask, "How about reward and punish-

---

[1] The word *Sheol* (שְׁאוֹל) usually rendered "hell" in the
Anglican version is a mistranslation. It simply means the
grave. (See Gen. xxxvii. 35.)

[2] Some have thought that the prophecy of the future state, in
Daniel xii. 2, 3, necessitates the existence of a place of eternal
punishment. But the words used, דְּרָאוֹן עוֹלָם, which the Anglican
Version translates "everlasting contempt," should rather be
translated "long-lasting contempt;" for the word עוֹלָם does not
necessarily mean eternal. (See Exodus xxi. 6, where the same
word לְעֹלָם denotes duration till the coming Jubilee.)

ment in the future state?" We are taught to believe
this doctrine, and God tells us that He "will not
wholly clear the guilty;"[1] but the idea that the loving
God should inflict on a soul eternal punishment, or
eternal perdition, is too revolting to be even con-
templated. We are told to fear God, to fear His
displeasure, not as we would fear a tyrant king, but
as we would fear to incur the displeasure of a parent,
or to forfeit his love. When, in His Sacred Book,
He speaks of punishing us, it is in the language of a
wise father to an erring child. He does not threaten
us with eternal punishment. "For a small moment
have I forsaken thee, but with great mercies will I
gather thee. In a little wrath I hid My face from
thee for a moment; but with everlasting kindness
will I have mercy on thee, saith the Lord, thy Redeemer."[2]

This is the God we are told to love with all the
emotions of our heart, with all the faith of our soul,
with all the might of our body; and therefore, when
He bids us love Him, He permits us not to couple
with His worship any other god. Our forefathers
were, therefore, ordered not only not to worship any
other gods, but not even to mention their names.
They were to overthrow their altars, to break down
their pillars, burn their groves, and hew down their
graven images.[3] Their love and worship of God was
to be whole and undivided; they were to have no
secondary gods, no intercessors, no mediators.

And when idolatry was ordered to be rooted out,

[1] Exod. xxxiv. 7.   [2] Isaiah liv. 7, 8.
Deut. xii. 3.

another arch-enemy of religion had also to be destroyed —superstition, the offspring of idolatry. Hence there were laws for the prevention of those superstitious practices which had been carried out by the priests of idolatrous nations, who recognised powers other than the Great Power who rules the universe. So we find the command against Moloch-worship, divination, witchcraft, the observing of times, and the other so-called black arts, by means of which the priests of ancient religions were wont to gain ascendancy over the vulgar and the ignorant, by playing upon their fears and exciting their morbid imaginations.

Even in these our times, superstition is not quite dead; for, besides those who cling to the superstitions of other religions, there are people who, under the mistaken title and guise of spiritualism, fancy they believe in some occult supernatural power. But the Jew laughs at such superstitions. Believing in One only God, the First Cause, Sole Ruler of the Universe, he knows and recognises no other Power as divine; and all the wonders he sees, whether he understands their action or not, are wonders of Nature, the work of Nature's One sole God, whom he loves and adores with all his heart and soul and might, and who requites that love and adoration with a mercy enduring for ever.

On the duty of prayer as an outward mode of exhibiting our love of God, I need not here dilate, having treated of that subject elsewhere.[1] It is sufficient to add, that prayer must ever be the spontaneous homage of the heart; not an irksome duty, like a tax unwillingly paid. It must be the voluntary outpouring

[1] Page 103.

of the heart, not alone in the set phrases of the prayer-book, but in the unspoken language of our soul.

For as, in the highest form of love, at the supreme moments of life, soul speaks to soul without word or sound or utterance, so can man, abstracting himself from his surroundings, at all times hold silent communion with his Maker; he can raise his soul upon the wings of wordless prayer, and render silent praise to the One and only God.[1] And this is the meaning of the Psalmist when he exclaims, "Unto thee, O Lord, do I lift up my soul."[2]

Respect for Parents and for the Aged.

In treating of the Fifth Commandment, I have already told you something about the duties we owe to our parents. But it is not only in the Decalogue that those duties are enforced. In the 19th chapter of Leviticus, from which so many ordinances have been quoted, we find, "Ye shall fear every man his mother and his father."[3] In the 21st chapter of Exodus,[4] death is ordained as the punishment of the child who strikes or who curses a parent; and among the terrible imprecations that were pronounced on Mount Gerizim as a warning to the Israelites, we find, "Cursed be he that setteth light by his father or his mother."[5]

First and foremost among the duties that we owe

---

[1] To Thee, even silence is praise." Psalm lxv. 2.—The ancient Egyptians, who, long before the time of Moses, worshipped one chief god, Amun-Ra, whose name they were not allowed to pronounce, always worshipped him in silence. [2] Psalm xxv. 1.
[3] Lev. xix. 3. [4] Exod. xxi. 15, 17. [5] Deut. xxvii. 16.

to our fellow-creatures are those that we owe to our parents. These duties are impressed upon us strongly by nature; for without being taught them, every right-minded child fulfils them by intuition. The Bible, therefore, justly treats the wicked, irreverent son as an unnatural monster not worthy to live. The bad son is certain to be a bad man, and a bad citizen, in every relation of domestic and social life. He is a social pest, and is consequently worthy of death. In the twenty-first chapter of Deuteronomy, you will read about the punishment incurred by the stubborn and rebellious son. The men of his city were to stone him to death. Throughout the Bible, and in our later records, there is no mention of the infliction of capital punishment on a son for an offence against his parents; so we may hope that there was never cause for such punishment, and that the law, severe as it seems, was rather declared as a terror and a warning to those who might be apt to disregard the duties they owed to their parents.

Closely connected with the laws as to filial duties is that which ordains respect to the aged, " Thou shalt rise up before the hoary head, and honour the face of the old man, and fear thy God."[1] For, one aspect of this law, as well as that relating to assaults on parents, must not be forgotten. It was a custom among many barbarous nations to slay old people who were over-whelmed with the infirmities of age; and this act of murder was even committed by sons on their parents.

Although such a custom is shocking to contem-plate, it is perhaps no worse than might be expected

[1] Lev. xix. 32.

from nations with whom brute force and physical strength were the only qualities that were valued. The Mosaic code puts old age on a different basis. The aged are not to be regarded as mere encumbrances, burdening the world with their weaknesses. They are not to be cast aside when their work is over, and their power of work is spent. They are to be treated reverently and respectfully; for though their strength of body may have departed, they have acquired knowledge and accumulated experience as useful to the world as physical prowess. And this is the meaning of King Solomon when he says, "The hoary head is a crown of glory, if it be found in the way of righteousness."[1]   "The glory of young men is their strength, and the beauty of old men is the grey head."[2]

" Thou shalt love thy neighbour as thyself."

The duty involved in this law[3] is one that is included in almost every code of morality and in almost every religious system. There is a well-worn tale told of two learned and rival doctors of the Talmud, Hillel and Shammai, which bears upon this commandment, and indicates the importance attached to it by Judaism. A scoffing heathen applied to Shammai, requesting him to teach him the laws of Judaism in the short space of time that he could stand on one foot. Shammai, in anger, sent the scoffer away. Thus repulsed, he went to Hillel, and made the same request of him. And Hillel replied, "Do thou not unto another what thou wouldst not have another do

---

[1] Prov. xvi. 31.   [2] Prov. xx. 29.   [3] Lev. xix. 18.

unto thee.   This is the whole law; the rest is mere
commentary."

The precept, "Thou shalt love thy neighbour as
thyself," truly embraces every other law of morality.
It is a protest against selfishness—the origin of every
vice, and itself the greatest vice.   If you love your
neighbour as yourself, you will be just to him, you
will not wrong him in any way, you will not hate,
despise or dishonour him ; you will help him in misfortune, and you will judge him charitably.

But perhaps you may think this law to love one's
neighbour as one's self is a little unreasonable—nay,
impossible.   You may ask, How can anyone love his
neighbour as dearly as he loves himself?   Perhaps
you love yourself very dearly, and think a great deal
of yourself, your hopes, your aims and your ambitions.
It is quite natural that you should.   Self-love is
deeply implanted in every human heart.   How then
can you be expected to love your neighbour as yourself ?

In this way.   Your own happiness and welfare
depend on the happiness and welfare of others.   No
king was ever happy whose subjects were unhappy.
No head of a household can be happy, if his family
and servants are in a constant state of discord.   No
employer can be happy, if his workpeople are dis-
contented, sullen in their demeanour, and perpetually
at war with him.   Thus the happiness of every
individual depends on the happiness of those with
whom he comes in daily contact.   If, therefore, you
truly love yourself, and prize your happiness, love
your neighbour as much, and prize his happiness.

The machinery of the social world can only be kept in action, free from friction and disturbance, by recognising the fact that no one can possibly be truly, permanently and honourably happy at the expense of his fellow-creatures. Wealth, with its unequal distribution, will always create different social grades, and on some the burden of work will ever fall more hardly than on others. It does not follow that this heavy burden of work entails unhappiness. On the contrary, those who have to work too hard are not more unhappy than those who lead a lazy, unprofitable life. Still, poverty has its undoubted evils; and it is the duty of the rich to soften down the asperities and hardships that afflict the poor.

Unfortunately, in our artificial state of society, the relations of employer and employed are far from satisfactory, both frequently forgetting the command, "Thou shalt love thy neighbour as thyself." The master is frequently too exacting to his servant, the servant too careless of the employer's interests; and hence arise those unhappy relations between employer and employed, which have so often culminated in ruinous trade-disputes, outrages and strikes. A selfish policy never thrives. There are in this country industries, which have been established and prospered, mainly because masters and men have treated one another as fellow-workers with a common interest, each loving his neighbour as himself, seeking his welfare, and looking for happiness in the happiness of his fellows. But there are other industries which have failed and disappeared, because masters and men have tried to make as much as possible out of each

other, regardless of all considerations but their own
selfish aims.

Nor is it only in the conflict between labour and
capital that this primary law of morality is so often
forgotten. The disputes between individuals which
find their way into the law-courts, and the disputes
between nations which give rise to sanguinary wars,
all have their origin in the neglect of this same law.
The principles of right and wrong are sufficiently
clear, so that no man need wrong his neighbour in
ignorance. If he loved his neighbour as himself, he
would not wrong him, and would no more think of
damaging the interests of his neighbour than of
endangering his own.

But as regards nations, the law has greater force.
War, that dread curse, which has converted many of
the fairest gardens of the earth into huge cemeteries;
which has changed friends into fiends, human beings
into brutes, and aroused passions which only the chill
hand of death could subdue—war would have no
existence, if every nation, instead of envying, despising,
or hating, would love its neighbour as itself. Patriotism
becomes the worst of vices when, forgetful of that
duty, a nation wages a war of aggression against a
neighbour whose land it covets.

War is, in sober truth, a hideous thing; and so men
strive to clothe its hideousness in decent garb. They
hide the blood beneath the crimson uniform, and
stifle the groans of wounded men with music jubilant
and gay. They drown the sobs and sighs of orphans
and of widows with songs of victory, and call the
murderous work of battle a work of glory.

But if the truth be told, whispered or thought, war is at best but wholesale homicide, the aggressors but wholesale murderers ; aggressive war, at best, but wholesale robbery ; the nation longing for its neighbour's lands, but wholesale plunderers and thieves.

And of the wars waged or pretended to be waged for a principle of honour, none would exist if honour meant but honesty, and glory meant God's glory and not man's. His glory is to " make the whole world kin," to make this world a world of peace and happiness, to make man's life "like days of heaven upon earth." Therefore He gave to man this law of love— "to love his neighbour as himself"—to widen the sphere of human sympathies, to bridge the rivers, seas and oceans with one broad span of wide philanthropy, to make the earth one nation, and all mankind fellow-citizens.

Honesty and Truth.

The duty of truthful, honest dealing has been already enforced in treating of the Third and Eighth Commandments. The command is again repeated in Leviticus, " Ye shall not steal, neither deal falsely, neither lie one to another." [1] " Thou shalt not defraud thy neighbour." [2] " Just balances, just weights, a just ephah, a just hin, shall ye have." [3]

The arm of the law, in all civilized countries, protects the weak against the strong, and prevents direct robbery by the highwayman. But there is an

[1] Lev. xix. 11.　　　[2] Lev. xix. 13.　　　[3] Lev. xix. 36.

indirect robbery which too often evades the law, and is unfortunately very prevalent in most commercial countries. To deal falsely, to misrepresent wares and merchandise to be what they are not, to lie to a purchaser as to the value or cost of a commodity, to give short weight, are all forms of commercial immorality which sap the foundations of society, and yet by some are regarded almost as matters of course and mere incidents of business. The evils engendered by such loose principles of dealing are incalculable. A general distrust and suspicion take the place of confidence. The purchaser is bound to waste his time in a vigilant examination of what he buys, lest he may be defrauded; and, notwithstanding his vigilance, he may yet be cheated. Goods have to be weighed and measured, over and over again, lest, at some point of transfer or transit, something may have been abstracted. Nor must it be imagined that acts of dishonesty exist only among small traders. Recent experience has shown that merchants of the highest reputation have been guilty of gigantic frauds; and when those frauds were discovered, their plea was simply that they were quite the usual thing, and that most people did as they did.

Distrust, suspicion, and loss of time are not the only evils resulting from commercial dishonesty. Dishonesty breeds dishonesty. The honest trader finds that he cannot compete successfully with the dishonest one, and becomes dishonest like his neighbour; and so the standard of morality becomes generally degraded. Many think this condition of things harmless, because every man of the world is prepared for it, and believes nothing but the evidence of his senses. But, in truth, the results are very serious, and, most serious of all, not to the intended victim, but to the dishonest trader himself. His notion of honour becomes vitiated and blunted. He acquires loose ideas regarding honesty and truth.

But God has declared that "all that do such things and all that do unrighteously are an abomination unto the Lord thy God;"[1] and it is surely not difficult to imagine that He, who is the Essence of Truth and Justice, must abominate those who steal, or deal falsely with, or lie one to another.

Truth is the basis of all morality. "A righteous man hateth lying," said King Solomon.[2] He who adheres to truth will be righteous in all things. Nor must the truthfulness consist merely in abstaining from a direct lie. Equivocation, flattery, misrepresentation, and duplicity are all forms of lying as hateful as the bold and direct lie, perhaps more so. "Deliver my soul from lying lips and a deceitful tongue," is the prayer of King David.[3] "Guard my tongue from evil, and my lips from uttering deceit," is our own thrice-repeated daily prayer. Truth is the guardian of the soul. If it retain truth, it will retain innocence; and contact with the world will leave it unharmed and unstained.

"Who," asks King David, "shall ascend unto the mountain of the Lord? or who shall stand in His holy place? He that hath clean hands, and a pure heart; who hath not lifted up his soul unto vanity, nor

---

[1] Deut. xxv. 16.   [2] Prov. xiii. 5.   [3] Psalm cxx. 2.

sworn deceitfully; He shall receive the blessing from the Lord, and righteousness from the God of his salvation."[1]

Avoidance of Slander and False Report.

When treating of the Third and Ninth Commandments, I told you something about the frightful sin of speaking falsely of others. Our concern is now with a group of laws all closely connected with the law against false evidence.

"Thou shalt not raise a false report,"[2] applies not alone to individuals, but to things and circumstances. Great injury may be done by publishing false reports or rumours, though they be not intended to injure any one. The law just quoted is directed against exaggeration, misrepresentation of facts, and misstatement of events. The love of the marvellous is strongly implanted in the human mind. It is curious to notice how easily people believe what they are told, regardless of the goodness or badness of the authority; and the more marvellous a tale is, the more ready people are to believe it. "It does no one any harm," is the common reply to the censure of such false reports. But, both to the individual and to society, it does much harm, though the reputation of the individual who may be the subject of the report may remain untouched.

History has been frequently falsified, whole nations libelled, religion perverted, by the raising of false reports. The lies that have been told in the name of religion have been truly frightful in number, and

[1] Psalm xxiv. 3-5.   [2] Exod. xxiii. 1.

magnitude, and results. It is not too much to say that the true interests of religion have, in all ages, greatly suffered through the raising of reports of false miracles by the over-zealous priests of religions other than our own. The priest bids the layman believe all he tells him with complete and unquestioning faith. The intelligent layman cannot believe what seems to him nonsense; and from being asked to believe too much, ends in believing nothing. "Truth, above everything," should be the motto of priest, preacher and teacher. "As for Truth, it endureth and is always strong; it liveth and conquereth for evermore."[1] It is common enough to hear men in authority say, this or that is dangerous doctrine. No doctrine can be dangerous if it be true. The interests of religion are always identical with the interests of truth. The great God of Truth does not want a lie to be told in His service. He declares, "The prophet which shall presume to speak a word in My name, which I have not commanded him to speak . . . . shall die."[2]

The law, "Thou shalt not curse the deaf, nor put a stumbling-block before the blind,"[3] may be considered to belong to the same group as the law last referred to; for no one can imagine it possible that any human being could be so diabolically wicked, as actually to curse a deaf man, or actually to put an obstacle in the path of a blind man. "Cursing the deaf" must assuredly mean, speaking slander of those who, being absent, are deaf to what we say of them; and putting a stumbling-block before the blind must mean, laying

[1] Esdras.   [2] Deut. xviii. 20.   [3] Lev. xix. 14.

a trap for the unwary, who are blindly ignorant of what is being done to their prejudice.

"Thou shalt not go up and down as a tale-bearer among thy people"[1] is another and more direct law against slander. No matter if even the tale be true, and though your neighbour be worthy of blame, you are not to be a tale-bearer. However blameworthy he may be, the fact is no excuse for your hating him. "Thou shalt not hate thy brother in thy heart; thou shalt in any wise rebuke thy neighbour, and not suffer sin to rest upon him."[2] This law represents the true principle of religious charity, and is at the same time a caution to those self-righteous people, who take delight in reviling their less religious, or perhaps less outwardly observant neighbours. Such people, who are "righteous overmuch," as King Solomon calls them, are directed to show their piety, not by looking down with supercilious glance upon their less pious neighbours, but by remonstrating with them privately, and by gently winning them over to the path of virtue.

The Duty of Purity.

I have already quoted at the commencement of this chapter the Commandment "Thou shalt be perfect with the Lord thy God,"[3] and though there are very many ordinances which relate to the subject of moral purity, this one comprehends all the rest. For it enjoins us to be modest, chaste, and pure; it bids husband and wife to be faithful to each other; it

[1] Lev. xix. 16.   [2] Lev. xix. 17.   [3] Deut. xviii. 13.

bids us to be decent in our conduct, demeanour, and conversation, and even in our thoughts, and so to " be perfect with the Lord."

It is just in such points as these that the virtue of the Jewish race has always been pre-eminent ; for the true Jew ever remembers that an All-seeing Eye is watching him, and carefully noting his every deed, word, and thought.

The Duty of Forgiveness.

Most difficult of all private duties is the duty of forgiveness ; for forgiveness is not always within our control. Still God commands us : " Thou shalt not avenge nor bear any grudge against the children of thy people, but thou shalt love thy neighbour as thyself : I am the Lord ; " [1] and a little consideration will show that forgiveness of an enemy is a duty that we owe equally to God, to ourselves, and to our fellow-creature.

To God, because He who is Omnipotent can avenge our cause if He will ; and if we ourselves retaliate, we seem to doubt His justice, His power, or His will to defend us. " Say not thou, I will recompense evil, but wait on the Lord, and He shall save thee." [2] To ourselves it is a duty to forgive ; for the sooner an injury is forgotten, the better for our own peace of mind ; moreover, by forgiving others, we make ourselves worthy of forgiveness by the Almighty. " To the merciful, God will show Himself merciful." [3] To our enemy it is also a duty ; for we give him the oppotunity of making us amends, and so enable him

[1] Lev. xix. 18.   [2] Prov. xx. 22.   [3] Psalm xviii. 25.

to blot out his sin against us; for enemy though he be, he is our neighbour, and we have been taught " thou shalt love thy neighbour as thyself."

This act of forgiveness is the highest charity, the greatest kindness of man to his fellow. To give alms to the poor, to help the distressed, to be kind to the stranger are all easy and pleasant duties; but to so far love our enemy as to forego vengeance and bear him no grudge, is the highest form of virtue, because it is so much at variance with our strongest impulses.[1]

Kindness to Animals.

God gave man "dominion over the fish of the sea, and over the fowl of the air, and over the cattle, and over every creeping thing that creepeth upon the earth."[2]

But in assigning to him this proud position, he imposed upon him certain duties and restrictions, intended to confine his power within reasonable limits. Man was to have control over the animal creation, but he was to remember that all birds and beasts and fishes and creeping things were yet God's creatures, all alike objects of His loving care.

Accordingly when God gave us the Law, He impressed upon us the duty of kindness to animals. For

---

[1] The Founder of Christianity, in a certain address to his disciples, is reported to have said, " Ye have heard that it hath been said, Thou shalt love thy neighbour and hate thine enemy. But I say unto you, Love your enemies." It will be seen that this was a gross misrepresentation; for nowhere in our Bible are we enjoined to hate our enemies; on the contrary, we are ordered to forgive them. (See Prov. xxv. 21.)   [2] Gen. i. 26.

seven days after birth, no animal was permitted to be
taken away from its mother.[1] If an animal had to be
slaughtered, it might not be killed on the same day as
one of its young,[2] lest perchance the one might see
the suffering of the other. An ox was not permitted
to be muzzled while treading out the corn,[3] lest it
might be irritated at being prevented, in the presence
of plenty, from satisfying its hunger. Nor was an
ox permitted to be yoked with an ass at the plough,[4]
lest the pace or tension of one animal might overtax
the strength of the other. No animal might be worked
on the Sabbath-day, so that even the poor dumb
brute shared with man the blessing of rest. It was
commanded that any one seeing an animal fall beneath its burden must render help to raise it.[5] Even
" if thou see the ass of him that hateth thee lying
under his burden and wouldest forbear to help him,
thou shalt surely help with him."[6] It is pronounced
to be a duty to lead back an animal that has strayed,[7]
even if it be owned by an enemy.[8]

During the wanderings of the Israelites in the wilderness, all animals that were slaughtered for food had
to be brought for that purpose to the door of the
tabernacle, and it was unlawful to slay an animal elsewhere. The blood of the slaughtered animal was
sprinkled on the altar, and the fat was burnt.[9] In
this manner the act of slaying an animal for food was
dignified and promoted to a religious act, and there
was no chance of any wanton cruelty. When the

[1] Lev. xxii. 27.   [2] Lev. xxii. 28.   [3] Deut. xxv. 4.
[4] Deut. xxii. 10.   [5] Deut. xxii. 4.   [6] Exod. xxiii. 5.
[7] Deut. xxii. 1.   [8] Exod. xxiii. 4.   [9] Lev. xvii. 2-6.

Israelites reached the Promised Land, this restriction was removed, and they were allowed to slay animals anywhere.

The law, which thus first gave to the priests the province of slayers of the cattle, probably gave rise to the custom always prevalent among the Jews, even down to the present time, of appointing men of high religious character as slaughterers of animals used for food. The best guarantee was thus afforded that the prescribed rules should be conscientiously observed, and also that the animal should be slain with the least possible pain.

The Jew consequently does not indulge in that kind of sport which consists of killing. He does not shoot pigeons, grouse, and pheasants for the mere pleasure of taking deadly aim at them. The animals he requires for food he has slain by the most expert, thus avoiding all needless torture.

If we are asked why God made so many laws for the protection of animals from cruelty, we may reply that the laws enjoining kindness to dumb animals form only part of the great Law of Love which the Pentateuch inculcates.[1] If man be taught by these laws to be kind to dumb animals, will he not all the more be kind to his fellow-men? Will not he who spares pain to his ox, spare pain also to his servant, and treat his dependants with kindness and with brotherly love?

---

[1] The same humane teaching is to be found in the Book of Proverbs: "A righteous man regardeth the life of his beast." (Prov. xii. 10.)

CHAPTER XI.

SANITARY LAWS.

THE laws relating to health are too numerous to mention in detail ; and it will be sufficient to treat of them in their broad outlines only.

The main principles of the laws of purification, as laid down in Leviticus and Numbers, appear to be that as infectious diseases are mostly communicated by contact, all cases of infection are to be isolated ; that all contact with any centre of infection is to be avoided; that when-such contact has been unavoidable, there must be, first, segregation, to prevent the spread of infection, and finally purification, before the infected person is re-admitted into society.

Every corpse was considered a possible centre of infection. Hence, those who touched a corpse,[1] or who were under the same roof as a corpse,[2] or who touched a grave,[3] had to purify themselves on the third day, and it was not till the seventh day that they were declared clean, after having again purified themselves, washed their clothes, and bathed themselves in water.

In quite recent time, medical men have come to the conclusion, that infectious diseases can only be stamped out by the most careful system of isolation. Nevertheless, it will be seen that the sanitary laws of the Pentateuch clearly enforce this principle,

[1] Numb. xix. 11, 12.   [2] Numb. xix. 14.   [3] Numb. xix. 16.

and point to isolation as the first duty incumbent on a patient suffering from communicable disease, or on a person bearing the germs, or even the possible germs, of infection ; and it is declared that he who "purifieth not himself defileth the tabernacle of the Lord ; and that soul shall be cut off from Israel." [1]

The great scourge of the East was, and in many places still is, leprosy ; and in the thirteenth chapter of Leviticus will be found the most exact and stringent rules for the prevention of the spread of this malady by contagion or infection.   Infected clothing was burnt ; [2] an infected house had to be first emptied, the infected parts of the building removed, and the walls scraped. Then, if the infection proved chronic, the whole house had to be razed to the ground, and the materials removed to an unclean place never to be used again. [3] The priest acted as physician.   It was he who had to declare the patient, the garment, or the house clean or unclean.   Before the re-admission of the leper into society, certain sacrificial rites had to be performed ; but above all certain ablutions had to be made by the patient, and his hair had to be shaved off.

In these times, when cleanliness is known to be an essential condition of health, it will not be a subject of surprise to find the washing of the clothes and the bathing of the flesh with water ordained as material acts of purification. [4]   If these simple remedies alone

---

[1] Numb. xix. 13.   [2] Lev. xiii. 55, 57.   [3] Lev. xiv. 33-45.

[4] It is worthy of note that the English adage, "Cleanliness is next to godliness," has its origin in the Mishnah, where we find precisely the same sentiment in the proverb, נְקִיּוּת מְבִיאָה לִידֵי טְהֲרָה, "Outward cleanliness leads to inward purity." *Sotah*, ix. 15.

had been prescribed for the prevention of infection, they would doubtless have been disregarded and neglected ; for there is a tendency of the uneducated mind to respect a remedy of a complex, and to disregard one of a simple kind ; just as we find that Naaman[1] doubted the efficacy of the seven simple ablutions in the Jordan, prescribed by Elisha as a cure for his leprosy, because the cure was not accompanied by any incantation or ceremonial.

But probably this was not the only reason why the ablutions were accompanied by priestly rites. It must be remembered that many diseases take their origin in intemperance, excess, and other infractions of the moral law. So it was a salutary act to bring the influences of religion to bear upon the patient, not only with the object of impressing upon him the need of an amended life, but of reminding him that, though God delegates His healing powers to man, the Great Physician is God Himself, to whom we owe life and health and every blessing.

The law for the disposal of excremental matter[2] by burial in the earth is truly a remarkable one, and the most enlightened researches of modern science have proved its wisdom. The modern system which permits such matter to discharge into and pollute our rivers, though it has been scientifically carried out by a complex arrangement of drainage, and at an enormous cost, is now acknowledged to be a gigantic blunder ; and the best authorities are now of opinion that, though storm-waters should be led into the rivers, sewage should be led into the earth, to enrich

[1] 2 Kings v. 11. [2] Deut. xxiii. 12, 13.

the soil, and reproduce the food whence it takes
its origin—a recognition of the wisdom of the Mosaic
ordinance last cited.

We have already referred to the law, which declared
unclean all who touched a corpse, or a grave, or who
happened to be under the same roof as a corpse, and
which required their purification before they could be
re-admitted into society.   But the law was much more
stringent as regards the priests.   These were not
permitted to come near a corpse under any condition,
except on the death of a near relative, namely, a
parent, wife, child, brother, or unmarried sister;[1] and,
even in these exceptional circumstances, they had to
be purified, and to remain apart for seven days.[2]

The sanitary importance of this rule must be clear,
seeing that in the East the diseases most prevalent
are contagious ; that a corpse, which in warm climates
decomposes rapidly, is a highly probable source of
infection ; and that the priests, being also the physicians,
if allowed to touch the dead, might communicate
mortal disease from the dead to the living.   But these
laws, which seem to regard the human corpse as a
subject of uncleanness, (a point of view rather
repugnant to modern ideas,) have a further meaning,
far beyond their sanitary significance.

Our people have always regarded their dead with
the greatest respect and veneration.   The careful
watching of the corpse from the moment of death till
the funeral hour, the reverent ablution of the dead, the
following of the remains to the grave with all marks
of respect, regardless of the rank or station of the

---

[1] Lev. xxi. 1-3.   [2] Ezek. xliv. 26.

deceased, and the rule which assigns to each corpse,
even to that of a pauper, a separate grave as an
everlasting possession — all these customs, indicating
an affectionate tenderness for the dead, seem strangely
at variance with those Mosaic laws, which treat the
human corpse as a thing defiling him that touches
it. What, then, can be the object of these laws, apart
from their sanitary purpose?

A glance at the history of certain ancient nations,
and even at the customs of some religions of our own
day, will furnish us with a reply. In ancient Egypt,
the country where the Israelites had so long dwelt,
the treatment of the dead was the great absorbing
thought of the living. To build a grand tomb for
himself was the first thought of every Egyptian. The
greatest pains were taken to preserve the bodies of
the dead. The more perishable parts were removed,
and the body embalmed, wrapped tightly in bands
of linen to prevent the access of air ; and the preser-
vation of the body from decay was considered
essential to the happiness of the departed soul.
The chief books in the Egyptian literature were
those relating to the funeral ritual. Before the
tombs of the Egyptians, altars were erected, and
on these altars their relatives offered sacrifices. In
times of difficulty or danger they would consult the
dead, and pray for their intervention, or for their
advice. The privilege of burial was not allowed to
all. According to Champollion, those who were declared by the forty-two judges, upon good evidence,
unworthy of interment in the City of the Dead,
were refused burial, and had to be kept for ever by

their families, standing upright in closed coffins against a wall inside their houses, a lasting disgrace to their relatives. Poor people who died in debt were refused burial; and, at one time, a creditor could make his debtor give as security the mummy of his father.[1] The City of the Dead was under the control of the priests of Egypt, who had high privileges, and possessed one-third of the land. Their influence over the people was enormous, chiefly derived from their power either to award honours or to offer indignities to the dead. At one period of Egyptian history they assumed to themselves the rank and rights of gods. The huge burial-places erected in Upper Egypt for the kings and priests (and the kings were always priests) contained temples where the worship of secondary gods took the place of the worship of the God of gods—the primitive Egyptian religion; and thus we see the evil resulting from the gigantic corpse-traffic, which became at last the aim and end of religion in Egypt.

No wonder that Jacob, fearful that his body might become an object of worship for future generations, exclaimed as a last request to his son, "Bury me not, I pray thee, in Egypt;"[2] or that Joseph, with like apprehension, made the children of Israel swear that they would carry his remains from Egypt to Canaan.[3]

But you need not go back three thousand years to learn to what "base uses" the dead human body may be applied. In our own days there are superstitions as bad, and perhaps more mischievous. In the churches of Catholic countries will be found bones of

[1] Herodotus II., 136.   [2] Gen. xlvii. 29.   [3] Gen. l. 25.

so-called saints, who lived centuries ago, reverently preserved as relics, and kept as objects of idolatry. Many of these are alleged by the priests to be capable of working miraculous cures even now ; and as the priests hold aloft these human relics—perhaps a fleshless skull, or perhaps a shrunken human hand, or perhaps only a single bone—with great pomp and ceremony, the assembled multitude bend the knee, and accord to these remains of frail mortality a worship which should belong to the Supreme God alone.

No wonder, then, that God should bid His people regard human remains and the graves of the dead as unclean. No wonder that He should forbid His priests even to go near a dead body. If the priests might not go near a corpse, how much less might they consult the dead, or offer a spurious worship at their tombs, or present sacrifices at their graves, or carry bits of old mortality before the eyes of an ignorant multitude, or work pretended miracles with the fragment of a corpse?

When one calls to mind the fearful struggles, that have taken place to obtain possession of the bodies of so-called saints, and to hold domination over certain sepulchres called by some " holy," one cannot but admire with rapt wonder the Divine foresight whereby *all* sepulchres were declared unholy and unclean, and whereby, when our great legislator, Moses, died, his burial was so arranged that " no man knoweth of his sepulchre unto this day."[1]

Not of the dead, as dead, are we to think. Not upon the body, mouldering in corruption, are we to

[1] Deut. xxxiv. 6.

ponder ; for even the mummy, embalmed with costly
care, and wrapped in richest cerements, must pass to
dust ; but on the *spirit* of the departed are we to
bestow our thoughts ; on their example and their
influence ; on their worth and on their work ;[1] and if
we would think of our beloved dead as they are,
let us think of them as disembodied spirits, rejoicing
in the presence of their Maker, working His will in
the better world, as they worked His will in this.

The laws relating to food (although to some extent
also laws of outward distinction,) may be all classed
under the head of sanitary laws; for they may be
fairly considered to have been ordained in the
interests of health, moral and physical.

When God blessed Noah and his sons after the
flood, He delivered into their hand the whole animal
world, and told them, "Every moving thing that
liveth shall be meat for you, even as the green herb,
have I given you all things. But flesh with the life
thereof, which is the blood thereof, shall ye not eat."[2]
In those early days, there were no dietary restrictions
but these two :—a living animal might not be muti-
lated to afford food,[3] and the blood of an animal
might not be eaten.

These laws were repeated by Moses, but with far

[1] In the words of the Talmud, אֵין עוֹשִׂין נְפָשׁוֹת לַצַּדִּיקִים מַעֲשֵׂיהֶם
הֵן הֵן זִכְרוֹנֵיהֶם, "The righteous need no monument: their deeds
are their best monuments." *Talm. Jerus. Shekalim*, 6.

[2] Gen. ix. 3, 4.

[3] Travellers relate that it is not uncommon for savage wandering tribes, reduced to hunger during a march, to cut out and eat
slices of their beasts of burden. Even the Abyssinian Chris-
tians still follow this odious practice.

greater detail and circumstance. We find in Leviticus,[1] "Moreover, ye shall eat no manner of blood,
whether it be of fowl or of beast, in any of your
dwellings. Whatsoever soul it be that eateth any
manner of blood, even that soul shall be cut off from
his people." With even greater stringency is the law
repeated later: "Whatsoever man there be of the
house of Israel, or of the strangers that sojourn
among you, that eateth any manner of blood, I will
even set my face against that soul that eateth blood,
and will cut him off from among his people. For the
life of the flesh is in the blood; and I have given it to
you upon the altar to make an atonement for your
souls; for it is the blood that maketh an atonement
for the soul. Therefore I said unto the children of
Israel, No soul of you shall eat blood, neither shall
any stranger that sojourneth among you eat blood."[2]
In Deuteronomy the same injunction is repeated:
"Only ye shall not eat the blood; ye shall pour it
upon the earth as water."[3] And further in the same
chapter[4] we are told, "Only be sure that thou eat
not the blood, for the blood is the life, and thou mayest
not eat the life with the flesh. Thou shalt not eat it;
thou shalt pour it on the earth as water. Thou shalt
not eat it, that it may go well with thee, and with thy
children after thee."

What can be the object of this prohibition, so
stringently and so frequently repeated? The Bible
gives us as one reason that the blood was used
upon the altar as an atonement sacrifice; but this

---

[1] Chap. vii. 26, 27.   [2] Lev. xvii. 10, 11, 12.
[3] Deut. xii. 16.   [4] Deut. xii. 23, 24.

cannot be the sole, or even the chief, reason; for with
regard to the bulk of the bloodshed in the slaughter
of beasts for food, namely, the blood of animals not
killed at the door of the Tabernacle,[1] the Israelites
were told to pour it on the earth as water.

The full, and absolutely certain, reason must remain
a mystery, until the great problem of life is solved.
We know nothing of the mystery of vital action; but
we know that the blood is the vehicle of life to the
animal frame—the circulating medium, maintaining
vitality in every organ of the body, and feeding the
brain, the fountain of thought and action. We know,
from the ascertained influence of certain narcotics,
that what passes into the blood after the processes of
digestion, affects the brain; sometimes acting on the
intellectual, and sometimes on the moral, qualities of
man; sometimes weakening and sometimes stimulating
those powers; sometimes depriving him of volition
and converting him into a sort of sentient feather, the
sport of the slightest impulse, without a will or a
wish of his own. How the brain is acted upon, we
know not; but we know enough to feel sure that what
we eat and drink does affect the mental and spiritual
part of man. What then is more probable than that,
if the blood of a brute animal—that blood which
is its life—enters our frame, some of the qualities of
that animal may become communicated to us through
its blood, and that part of the nature of the animal may
thus enter our nature, and debase and brutalise us?

Experience lends a strong probability to this view;
and, if the view be correct, the precepts so strongly
prohibiting blood are easily understood.

[1] Deut. xii. 15, 16.

Our traditional mode of slaughtering cattle, by cutting the throat, was evidently ordained for the purpose of draining from the body of the animal the greatest possible quantity of blood; and the custom adopted in all Jewish households, of steeping meat in water for half-an-hour and keeping it afterwards strewn with salt for an hour before cooking it, has, doubtless, for its object the extraction of any blood still remaining.

When we further examine the laws prohibiting the use of certain animals for food, the leading principle of those laws seems to be that all animals which themselves feed on blood are pronounced unclean, and are prohibited. No quadruped might be eaten except such as had cloven feet, and also chewed the cud. Such animals as had only one of these characteristics, (such as the camel, the *shaphan*,[1] the hare, and the swine), were regarded as unclean; their carcases might not even be touched, much less might they be used for food. The law, limiting the eatable animals to cloven-footed ruminants only, excluded the whole range of carnivora, or animals that eat flesh. Flesh-eating animals are, of necessity, blood-eating animals; so it is not difficult to see why they are prohibited.

No fish might be eaten except such as had fins and scales.[2] Twenty species of birds are also enumerated[3] as unclean, and forbidden as food. All worms and creeping things, and all insects, with the few ex-

---

[1] Probably the jerboa; mistranslated "coney" in the Authorised Version.

[2] Lev. xi. 9, 10.   [3] Lev. xi. 13-19.

ceptions enumerated,[1] are also prohibited; and it is quite possible, although not absolutely capable of proof, that nearly all those prohibited animals are, in some degree, carnivorous, and consequently sanguinivorous, or blood-eating.

It would be impossible, apart from this last consideration, and with our present limited knowledge, to assign a special sanitary reason for the prohibition of each one of these animals. We know but little of the habits of most animals, and we know absolutely nothing of their inner life. But, inasmuch as all the prohibited animals are described as unclean, there must doubtless be something in their structure and habits rendering them unwholesome as objects of human food. The filthy habits of the swine, and the shocking diseases to which it is liable, and which it engenders in those who feed on it, are very well known; and in modern times it has been thoroughly recognised by scientific medical men that swine's flesh is unwholesome food, even if the animal itself may have been healthy when slain. Swine will eat any garbage, however decomposed, and they have even been known to devour their own young. The forbidden birds include several which are known to live on carrion of the filthiest kind, and to delight in blood. Judging the unknown from the known, all the forbidden animals may be considered as unwholesome; and the Law wisely describes them as abominations, not even to be touched, when dead, much less eaten.

Certain kinds of fat (חֵלֶב), specified by tradition,

---

[1] Lev. xi. 22.

and including the particular fat used for sacrifice,[1] were forbidden to be eaten ; as was also the flesh of any animal that was accidentally wounded, or that died of disease.[2] This last precept has given rise· to the excellent traditional practice among the Jewish people, that all animals slain for food must be "searched "—the vitals being examined by skilled persons, with the object of ascertaining whether the animal was free from disease. In case of disease being discovered, the animal is pronounced unfit for food (טְרֵפָה).

The law also forbids us to "seethe a kid in its mother's milk." The word גְּדִי (gedi), translated "kid," here means the young of any mammal. The command seems at first sight a strange one ; and its meaning has been questioned by many of the most learned commentators. It is repeated three times in the Pentateuch;[3] in the first two places in connection with the offerings, and only in the last in connection with the dietary laws. It is not found among the dietary laws of Leviticus; whence it has been supposed by some to have principally reference to a sacrificial rite. The great Maimonides (himself a physician of eminence) considers the prohibition to be solely a sanitary one, as he regards the mixture of flesh and milk too indigestible a food ;[4] but the more probable reason is that given by Abarbanel,[5] who represents that there is something cruel and repugnant to natural sentiment in boiling a young animal in the

---

[1] Lev. iii. 17 ; vii. 23.   [2] Exod. xxii. 31 ; Deut. xiv. 21.
[3] Exod. xxiii. 19 ; Exod. xxxiv. 26 ; and Deut. xiv. 21.
[4] *Moreh Nebuchim*, iii. 48.   [5] Commentary on Exod. xxiii. 19.

milk that was destined for its own nourishment; and he sees an analogy between this precept and that which forbade the killing of any animal and its progeny on the same day.

Strange as it may appear, it is certain that even now it is a custom among the Arabs of the desert to eat kid boiled in goat's milk; and the Rev. Mr. Porter relates, in his book of travels among the giant cities of Bashan, how this dish is offered to travellers as a great delicacy. It is also equally certain that the Jews have always abstained from such an unnatural mixture of food. According to traditional interpretation, the precept forbids the eating of meat or any preparation of meat with milk or anything prepared from milk.

Apart from the sanitary considerations, which most probably lie at the root of all the dietary restrictions of our people, there is another consideration—the moral influence which such laws exercise, by reason of the restraints which they place on our appetites. That the Jews are distinguished for temperance, is universally acknowledged. As social and convivial in their habits as any of their fellow-citizens, our people are yet moderate in their enjoyments; and drunkenness, the great and overwhelming curse of this country, finds no place among the vices of the Jews. For this immunity from the evil of intemperance, freedom from many of those diseases which affect other races, and a remarkable longevity, we may well regard ourselves as indebted to our dietary laws; which, while they permit us to enjoy in moderation the good things of life, place a curb on our appetites so habitually as to render moderation our second nature.

In conclusion, it must be observed that, though we cannot know with absolute certainty the object and intention of every one of the dietary laws, it is yet our duty, remembering the Source whence these precepts have come to us, to obey them, be their object apparent or not.

CHAPTER XII.

The Historical Fasts and Feasts.[1]

Every nation that has a history has certain anniversaries which are marked as red-letter days in its calendar. But most nations willingly or wilfully forget their past misfortunes ; their self-love and vanity prompting them to hold in remembrance only their glories.

With us it is different. Not that our self-love and vanity are less than our neighbours. But our history is different. For since we lost the land of our inheritance, our history has been, with few and comparatively short exceptions, one long tale of persecution and humiliation. Now and then, indeed, the black clouds have broken, and the sun has burst resplendent through the mists, driving away for a little while the dark shadows which enveloped us ; but too soon the bright orb was hidden from view, and "a horror of great darkness," blacker than ever, fell upon us.

And now again, thanks to God, we Jews, in this happy country, and in most parts of the civilized world, luxuriate in the sunshine of fortune. We live

---

[1] Although these fasts and feasts do not properly come under the head of either Natural or Revealed Religion, yet they fill so important a place in our religious ritual and in Jewish domestic life, that, in a work like the present, it would not be right to omit reference to them.

in peace and liberty, our lives and property secure, and we begin to regard our past sad history almost as a frightful nightmare, scarcely as a series of real facts.

But in good and in evil times, it has been the custom of our people, as each anniversary came round, to praise God for good and evil alike,[1] to celebrate our past glories with heartfelt gratitude, and to call to mind our past sufferings with lamentations indeed, but equally with a voice of thanksgiving. For in darkness or in light, in sorrow or in joy, the Jew still felt himself the surviving heir to a precious heritage, and, confident in the future of his race, was grateful if he only lived—no matter how—lived to transmit to unborn generations that heritage in all its purity.

Four of these sad anniversaries are not only historical but biblical. They are mentioned as fasts in the Book of Zechariah[2]—the 17th day of *Tamuz* (שִׁבְעָה עָשָׂר בְּתַמּוּז),[3] the 9th day of *Ab* (תִּשְׁעָה בְּאָב), the 3rd day of *Tishri* (צוֹם גְּדַלְיָהוּ), and the 10th day of *Tebeth* (עֲשָׂרָה בְּטֵבֵת).

The fast of *Tamuz* commemorates the taking of Jerusalem by Nebuchadnezzar, King of Babylon ; the fast of *Ab*—the saddest anniversary of all—the destruction of the First Temple by Nebuchadnezzar, and

---

[1] חַיָּב אָדָם לְבָרֵךְ עַל הָרָעָה כְּשֵׁם שֶׁמְבָרֵךְ עַל הַטּוֹבָה : "It is our duty to praise God equally for the evil and for the good."—(*Berachot*, 54, a.)   [2] Zech. viii. 19.

[3] Although, according to Jeremiah (chap. xxxix. 2), the conquest of Jerusalem, prior to the destruction of the First Temple, took place on the ninth day of the fourth month, yet the fast is kept on the seventeenth, because on that day Jerusalem was taken by the Romans, just before the destruction of the Second Temple.

the destruction of the Second Temple by Titus, the
Roman General.   The fast of Gedaliah on the 3rd
day of *Tishri* is the anniversary of the murder of
Gedaliah, chief of the remnant of our people, who
clung to Judea after the destruction of the First
Temple.[1]   From that date, the independence of the
Jews ceased, until the restoration in the days of Cyrus.
The fast of *Tebeth* commemorates the commencement
of the siege of Jerusalem by Nebuchadnezzar.

Reading these dry details, which seem a mere cata-
logue of misfortunes, it is difficult to realise their full
import.   But if you will read for yourselves the narrative of the destruction of the First Temple, as detailed
in the last chapter of the second Book of Kings, and
in the last chapter of the second Book of Chronicles,
and the history of the siege of Jerusalem by Titus, as
described by Josephus, you may form some idea of
the horrors attending these national calamities, when
the city was consumed with famine, so that "there
was no bread for the people of the land," when the
besiegers ruthlessly slew everyone in the fated city,
"and had no compassion upon young man or maiden,
old man, or him that stooped for age."

Never in the world's history has such a siege taken
place as that which finally overthrew the sacred
city; never has a city been so completely destroyed
as was Jerusalem—destroyed so that scarcely a vestige
of its ancient glory now remains, save a few cyclopean
masses of masonry, the foundations of its outer walls,
and a few underground vaults, cisterns and aqueducts,
beneath or near the site of the sacred Temple-enclo-
sure.

[1] 2 Kings xxv. 25.

Perhaps human nature is so constituted, that we may find it hard to lament the loss of what we, personally, never possessed; and thus many thoughtless people may smile when they are told to mourn for the loss of Jerusalem. But if you read in the Bible and in works of history and antiquities what Jerusalem was; if you read descriptions of her glorious Temple, and call to mind that that Temple was *the* place on all the earth chosen by God as His Holy House, the abode of the Divine *Shechinah*, the religious centre of the chosen people, the envy of surrounding nations, "beautiful for situation, the joy of the whole earth;"[1] when you remember that all this would now be ours, but for the sins of our forefathers and the tardiness of our own repentance; when you call to mind that, instead of that glorious heritage, we have nothing left to us but the Written Word—no land of our own, no Temple of our own—and that on and near the site of the glorious Temple, church, chapel and mosque rear their proud heads, but no House of God where the Jew can worship the One and only God—then, perhaps, if you are a fervent Jew, you may realise what you have lost. And the fasts which recall that loss may seem to you wisely ordained commemorations, inviting us to con-sider how best we may regain the City, and the Temple, and the glory that has departed from us; inviting us to consider how best we may contribute to the fulfil-ment of our prophesied restoration, speedily and in our days, by meriting that fulfilment. "For in Mount Zion and in Jerusalem shall be deliverance, as the Lord hath said, and in the remnant whom the Lord shall call."[2]

[1] Psalm xlviii. 2.   [2] Joel ii. 32.

Still our past history is not all gloom. Our history is, indeed, too much a history of persecutions, but it is also a history full of providential escapes.   Two of these marvellous escapes from dangers, which might have utterly exterminated us, but for the protecting hand of Providence, we celebrate by festivals of joy and gladness—the feast of *Purim*, and the feast of *Hanucah*.

Who can read the Book of Esther, without discerning, in the wonderful chain of events therein related, the guiding hand of an all-directing Providence ? Mordecai, who, presumably, compiled the book in the days of his political greatness,[1] studiously avoided inserting anywhere in his narrative the name of God ; for he wrote the chronicle equally for Jews and Persians; and the latter, who worshipped the sun-god Mithras, and paid allegiance to the secondary divinities of good and evil, Ormuzd and Ahriman, knew not the God of the Hebrews. But, though the Great Name is absent, we see everywhere in this marvellous chronicle the directing Hand of Him who is the Guardian of Israel.

Of late there has sprung up a school of thinkers and writers—men who think little and write much—who, vainly seeking to erect history into a science, would make every event, small or great, an inevitable fact produced as a necessary consequence of an unerring law, independent of the will of man or the control of a governing Providence.

But no one can read such a stirring history as the Book of Esther presents, without feeling that this hard

---

[1] Esther ix. 30-32.

necessarian doctrine is at fault here, and that the ordinary sequence of events could never have produced the
startling, and almost romantic, incidents to be found
in the chronicle of Mordecai—incidents which crowd
one on the other, till the climax at length brings the
doomed children of Israel out of the depth of despair,
and places them on the pinnacle of salvation and
triumph.   Many historians have remarked, that the
unexpected always occurs.   Perhaps the "always" is
an exaggeration; but the aphorism, which is not so
very far from the truth, shows the falsity of the necessarian doctrine, and points to the existence of a controlling Power, who shapes the destinies of men and
nations, and who reigns superior to that "reign of
law," which He created, and can therefore vary or
suspend.

When, then, we celebrate the Feast of Purim, as
did our rescued forefathers in Shushan, "with light
and gladness, and joy and honour," we must keep
foremost in our mind the recognition of God's
government of the world; and when we read the
Book of Esther, and pass from the contemplation
of the Divine intervention therein displayed to the
consideration of the personages, who were the chief
instruments and agents of that intervention, we must
note with wonder and admiration, how a despised
Jew and Jewess became, by rare acts of courage and
self-devotion, the saviours of their nation; how, when
they had reached the summit of earthly fame and
power, their great anxiety was to place on record an
imperishable memorial of their marvellous escape;
and how, finally, the Jew Mordecai, raised to the post

of first minister to the king of one hundred and twenty-seven provinces, though "next to the king" yet remained steadfast to his faith and race, "great among the Jews" and "seeking the welfare of his people."[1]

The events that gave rise to the Feast of *Hanucah,* or Dedication, are described in full detail in the Books of the Maccabees, which will be found in the Apocrypha. About the facts contained in the Books of the Maccabees there can be no doubt, as they receive ample confirmation from other historical sources.

About two centuries before the Romans destroyed the Second Temple, Judea was ravaged by the army of Antiochus Epiphanes, King of Syria, who penetrated to Jerusalem, and even took possession of the sanctuary. Resistance seemed useless. The priests fled from the Temple, and the Syrians there set up their idolatrous worship, with all its foul abominations. They then tried to convert the Jews to their own shameful religion. The ordinances of Judaism were proscribed, the worship of God was forbidden, and all were ordered, upon pain of death, to bow down before the idols of the Syrians. Thousands of Jews died the death of martyrs, because they persisted in clinging to their own religion. Many, weakened by privations and torture, became, or pretended to become, converts to heathenism, and many fled to distant parts of Judea, taking refuge in the mountain caverns.

All seemed hopeless, and it appeared as if Jews and Judaism were about to vanish for ever from

[1] Esther x. 3.

the face of the earth, when suddenly there arose a family of priests, who took upon themselves the apparently impossible task of resisting the idolatrous invaders. These heroes, consisting of an old man, named Mattathias and his five sons, were the Maccabees,[1] or Hasmoneans; and they commenced their work of salvation for Israel by bidding defiance to the Syrians, when they invaded Modin, their village home. For at Modin the invaders had set up altars for the worship of their idols, and these the Maccabees, jealous for the True God, indignantly swept away.

The Syrians, accustomed everywhere to receive submission, were amazed at this boldness, and tried to bribe Mattathias and his sons, by promises of honours and riches, to yield to the king's commands, and to embrace the idolatrous religion. But the Maccabees indignantly refused; and rallying around them a handful of villagers, whom they had inspired with a patriotism and religious fervour like their own, they engaged in battle with the hosts of Syria, and, though outnumbered to an enormous extent, conquered.

No sooner had they thus gained their first victory, than the Maccabees re-established the worship of the True God, and then proceeded to organise a small army with which to liberate their country. But the old priest, Mattathias, did not live to see the end of

---

[1] The name Maccabee is said to have been derived from the initial letters of the words, מִי כָּמֹכָה בָּאֵלִים יְיָ, "Who is like unto Thee among the mighty, O Lord?"—the inscription on the banner of Judas, the son of Mattathias.

the conflict. He died, leaving his sons to continue the task he had commenced, and inciting them by his last words to the work of regenerating and reviving the nation and the religion he loved so well. The sons fought like lions. Everywhere the little handful of Jewish patriots conquered. Legion after legion of the Syrians, led by the most renowned generals of King Antiochus, fell in battle, struck down by the small band of Maccabee soldiers. Nothing could withstand the prowess of these Jewish heroes ; and, after a succession of victories, unbroken by a single reverse, they marched to Jerusalem, determined to crown their glories by rescuing the Holy City from the pagan hands that had desecrated the Sanctuary. Here again they were victorious; for they drove out the Syrians from Jerusalem, once more regained possession of the Sacred Temple; and the remnants of the hosts of Antiochus gradually retired from Palestine.

Then, the soldiers' work over, the priests' work, the purification of the desecrated Temple, began. Every vestige of the idolatrous worship was removed; new altars were built, new holy vessels were set up, the lights on the sacred candlestick were once more kindled, and the ancient worship of the Most High was re-established. Then was celebrated the first "Feast of Dedication" with great rejoicing. It lasted eight days ; and it was ordained that, for ever after, the Jews should celebrate as a festival this wonderful escape and the religious revival that followed it.

How it is celebrated, you all know. You know how for eight nights we illumine our homes with festive lights ; commencing with one, and adding one daily till eight lights are reached ; and how, when these lights are kindled, joyful hymns of thanksgiving are sung to celebrate the salvation of Israel by the hands of the Maccabees.

The lesson taught by *Hanucah* is similar to that taught by *Purim*—the recognition of the Hand of God in human history and human destiny. One can well imagine the worldly-wise of the Maccabee age laughing at the temerity of Judas and his brothers, when they, with their handful of villagers, ill-clad, un-practised in the arts of war, and deficient in the im-plements of battle, went to fight the hosts of Syrian soldiers; just as Goliath laughed at the stripling David, and just as, in our own time, the worldly-wise of many nations predicted failure to the small band of Italian patriots, who undertook the liberation of their country.

But Providence is superior to earthly force, and skill, and numbers—Providence, whose guiding Hand we see in every page of History. This Providence rules the world—

> " with good
> Still overcoming evil, and by small
> Accomplishing great things ; by things deemed weak
> Subverting worldly strong and worldly wise."
>
> *Milton.*

And thus, this wonderful episode of our deliverance from the Syrian yoke shows us how Providence selects as instruments, not always the powerful and strong, but sometimes even the weakest, humblest, and poorest, to work His Will.   To regenerate an expiring nation, to revive the fast-dying embers of a glorious religion, and to restore its influence, He selects the poor, weak, old priest, and his five sons—inhabitants of an obscure village of Palestine.   These were to be the saviours of their people.   These were to inspire their followers with the courage of lions to meet and conquer an enemy many times stronger than they. These were to rekindle the fire of religious zeal among their fellow-Jews.   These were to drive out the idolater and to restore the true religion.   "Not by might, nor by power, but by my spirit, saith the Lord of Hosts."[1]

[1] Zech. iv. 6.

CHAPTER XIII.

THE FUTURE LIFE.

No question concerns man more than the question of the future life. Life is so short, Eternity so long, that the one absorbing thought of life might well be, How shall we pass Eternity?

And yet, happily for ourselves, this is not the one absorbing thought. To every one, even to those on the brink of the grave, life has many interests; and the *present moment* is ever paramount in importance. When God made man of the dust of the earth, He meant him to have earthly interests, so that he might fulfil his mission as part of the work of creation.[1] If all men were to pass their lives like monks or fakirs, spending all their time in penance, prayer, and contemplation, neglectful of their duties as members of the human family, there would soon be an end to the human race, and the Divine project of creation would, so far as humanity is concerned, be frustrated.

Therefore, God endowed man with strong appetites, and tastes, and ambitions, that (held in proper restraint) they might serve as a spur to healthy action of heart and brain, giving a zest to life, and making life a thing to be enjoyed. An ever-present thought of death and futurity, would spoil that zest; and

[1] גַּם אֶת הָעֹלָם נָתַן בְּלִבָּם "Also he hath set the world in their heart." (Eccl. iii. 11.)

hence, happily for man, God has so constituted the
human mind that the prevailing thought of life is
life itself—life here on earth, with its needs, its duties,
and its enjoyments.

But, deeply implanted as is the love of life in every
healthy human heart, it is not more deeply implanted
than the hope and expectation of a future state.
Hence, though eternity is not an ever-present subject
for contemplation, it is one that crops up very frequently and persistently in every thinking mind; and
no religious person should suffer a day to depart without bestowing much more than a passing thought
on the future of his soul.

What does Religion tell you about the immortality
of the soul ?   What Natural Religion teaches you, you
already know.[1]   But what does Revealed Religion,
what does the Bible tell you, about this all-important
subject ?

Upon the future of the soul, the Pentateuch gives
us no *direct* information.   But it tells us at the outset
that "God created man in His own image;"[2] that
"He breathed into his nostrils the spirit of life ; and
man became a living soul."[3]   Of no other being but
man is it declared that "God breathed into his
nostrils the spirit of life."   These very words indicate
the kinship of the human soul to the Divine Spirit.
. Again, when we are told that God created man
in His own image, it cannot mean that man's
bodily form is in the image of God; for we are
repeatedly warned that God has no bodily form or
similitude.   It can therefore only mean that the soul

[1] Part I., Chaps. V. and VI.   [2] Gen. i. 27.   [3] Gen. ii. 7.

of man is a reflection of the Deity Himself, who is an eternal and spiritual Being.

But, vague and indistinct as may be this indication of the soul's immortality, as derived from the Mosaic account of Creation,[1] the Pentateuch tells us enough to show that Moses must have been well versed in the doctrine, and that the silence of the early books of the Pentateuch upon the topic was due only to the fact that the doctrine was thoroughly established as an axiom or postulate. Indeed, if one reads any work treating of ancient Egypt, it is clear that at the time of the Exodus, and even long before, the doctrine of a future state was known to the Egyptians, and played no small part in the inner and domestic life of that nation. It is therefore absolutely impossible that Moses, who was trained at the court of Pharaoh (and every Pharaoh was a learned priest), could have been, as some have maintained, ignorant of the idea of the soul's immortality.

An investigation of a few passages in the Pentateuch will clear up all doubt on this subject, and will show that, in many cases, the Law refers, although not directly, yet pointedly enough, to an after-life.

Quite early in the Bible we are told that " Enoch walked with God, and he was not, for God took him."[2] If God took him, surely it could not have been for the destruction of his soul, but that his soul might live in a better and happier world to enjoy the reward of godliness.

[1] The vagueness is increased by the ambiguity of the Hebrew word for soul נֶפֶשׁ (*Nephesh*), which also means " person," and sometimes " life."   [2] Gen. v. 24.

We find another hint at the soul's immortality in
the history of the patriarchs. God promised Abraham, " Thou shalt go to thy fathers in peace." [1] Now
this could not imply that he was to be buried with
his fathers in peace; for, as a matter of fact, he was
buried in Canaan, at a great distance from the home
and the graves of his ancestors at Haran. The promise could, therefore, only imply a reunion of the soul
of Abraham with the souls of his relatives who had
preceded him. A like phrase is adopted by the
Bible historian in relating the death of Jacob. The
patriarch charged his sons, "and said unto them, I
am to be gathered unto my people;" [2] and then he
proceeds to tell them how they are to bury him with
his fathers in the field of Machpelah; and his death
is described thus : " He gathered up his feet into his
bed, and yielded up the ghost, and was gathered unto
his people." [3] Now, the " being gathered to his
people" could not imply his burial ; for the subsequent
chapter contains a narrative of several events which
preceded the actual burial; namely, the embalming
of the body, the forty days' mourning, the petition
to Pharaoh for the removal of the remains to Canaan,
the march of the funeral cavalcade, and the seven
days' mourning at Atad ; and if it did not mean the
burial, surely it must have meant the consummation
of the hope of the righteous for the righteous soul—
the reunion of that soul with the souls of those who
had gone before.

In the narrative of the deaths of Aaron and of Moses
the same phrase is used : "And die in the Mount whither

[1] Gen. xv. 15.   [2] Gen. xlix. 29.   [3] Gen. xlix. 33.

thou goest up, and be gathered unto thy people; as Aaron thy brother died in Mount Hor, and was gathered unto his people."[1] Now both these great men had unknown, lonely, and separate burial-places in the wilderness, certainly far removed from the resting-places of their fathers; and we are, therefore, irresistibly led to the conclusion that the phrase "to be gathered to their fathers" expressed the fact, or at least the belief of the historian, that the dead are re-united to their forefathers in a spiritual existence beyond the grave.

In many places in the Pentateuch God decrees the punishment of excision (כָּרֵת, *koreth*) for the infringement of certain important laws, in these terms: "That soul shall be cut off from among his people." Now, it can be clearly proved that these words do not simply imply a shortening of life here, but some punishment in a future state. For, in the case of the Moloch-worshipper, the Bible says, "The people of the land shall stone him with stones. And I will set my face against that man, and I will cut him off from among his people."[2] It is evident that if the Moloch-worshipper was to suffer death by stoning, there was no possibility of further shortening his existence by cutting him off from among his people—a punishment which must, therefore, be one having reference to the future state of his soul.[3]

But it may be argued, Why did not God, through

---

[1] Deut. xxxii. 50.

[2] Lev. xx. 3.

[3] These and other Biblical references to the same effect will be found in the "Immortality of the Soul."—"Sabbath Readings," No. 62, by Rev. Dr. Hermann Adler.

His servant Moses, clearly and distinctly propound
the important doctrine of Immortality, promising
undying happiness in a future existence as a reward
of piety, and giving indications of the nature of those
spiritual rewards, instead of promising long life and
wealth, and all worldly blessings as the recompense
of virtue?

"Truly a difficult question. But we may probably
find a solution of the problem by imagining a converse
state of things.

" Suppose that the Bible told us, without the slightest
ambiguity, that there was an after-life, that the soul
was an immortal part of man, which, released from
its earthly bonds, would enjoy happiness or be doomed
to misery in accordance with its deserts. What would
be the result?

" In the first place not a single disinterested action
would be left to be performed, even by the best of
men. Every prudent man would calculate the effect
of each good deed he performed, or of each temptation he resisted, and would, as it were, keep a debit and
credit account with his Creator. Even as it is, there
is not too much disinterestedness in the world. Inter-
twined with patriotism we see ambition; intermixed
with honesty we find' policy—the fear of the law;
interwoven with religion we often find submission to
fashion. The sterling good deed, the act of duty
which is contrary to interest, to sentiment, to impulse, to fashion, and to inclination—this is the act
which deserves eternal reward. But what act would
be disinterested, if the promise of heavenly reward
were unmistakeably clear and distinct? The cool,

calculating man would be the best man. But he would
not be a good man in the sense in which we now understand the term. He would be commercially good ;
his good deeds would simply be good investments—
investments of which the profit, though deferred,
was certain—not only certain, but when attained,
eternal.

" But there would be no merit in this kind of goodness. The object for which it would seem we are
placed upon earth would be annulled. This world
would be no test, no place of trial, to ascertain our
worth. It might be a test of our sordid prudence—
not of our moral worth. The aim and object of our
existence in this world would be frustrated.

" Next, let us ask what end would have been served
by a direct promise of immortality ? It would not
have sufficed to have merely given the promise of a
state of being which the mind cannot fully grasp.
The mere promise of eternal happiness would have
been to the majority the promise of a phrase—a mere
vision—not a tangible, comprehensible reward. Our
ideas of happiness are chiefly, if not entirely, derived from the physical world by which we are sur-
rounded. What would have been the use of describ-
ing, as the recompense for goodness, a condition of
spiritual happiness, which the soul, wrapt in its
mortal garb, could not have understood? We could
not appreciate a promise of pleasures which belong
wholly and solely to a spiritual state of existence. But
we can understand the pleasures of earth, because they
are pleasures experienced by the agency of the senses.
Every one can appreciate such pleasures; and there-

fore it is that we find, in the Bible, material blessings held out as the recompense of well-doing. It would not have served to preach to the untutored people of ancient times, that Virtue is its own reward."[1]

Our ancestors, just delivered from the slavery of Egypt, were not a people with strong spiritual cravings. The Bible represents them, while yet living amid miracles, as lamenting the flesh-pots of Egypt, looking back with fond regret to the time when they "did eat bread to the full,"[2] calling to mind, with greedy thoughts, "the fish which we did eat in Egypt freely, the cucumbers, and the melons, and the leeks, and the onions, and the garlick."[3] Men such as these would not have been attracted by promises of a spiritual happiness, long deferred. A different incentive had to be offered. They were therefore promised rich harvests and overflowing granaries, length of days and multitudinous progeny.

Lessing, the great philosopher-poet, who, through his intimate friendship with Moses Mendelssohn, had acquired a keen appreciation of Judaism, explains, in language of remarkable force, the reticence of the Pentateuch on the topic of the Soul's Immortality. He writes—"The Hebrews were a rude, unruly people, who had everything to learn. Only gradually could they rise from the conception of a patriarchal, national deity to the knowledge of the One God. So, too, could their moral education only be conducted on the plan of rewards and punishments, addressed to

---

[1] "The Bible and Immortality." "Sabbath Readings," No. 71 ; By the Author of this work.
[2] Exod. xvi. 3.   [3] Numb. xi. 5.

the senses. Their regards went no further than this earth; they yearned for no life to come. To have revealed this to them, before their reason was ripe to grasp it, would have been the fault of the school-master who urges on his pupil too rapidly."[1]

But though the Pentateuch contains unmistak-able hints as to the immortality of the soul, the later Scriptures contain much more than hints; sufficiently showing that the doctrine was not first learnt in the Babylonish exile, but that it was accepted, if not by the masses, at least by cultivated minds.

King David, in many of his psalms, uses expres-sions which show, that to him the Soul's Immortality was no unfamiliar doctrine. In the *Michtam*, that beautiful psalm which is read in houses of mourning, he says, "My heart is glad and my glory rejoiceth; my flesh also shall rest in hope. For Thou wilt not leave my soul in the grave,[2] neither wilt Thou suffer Thine holy one to see corruption. Thou wilt show me the path of life; in Thy presence is fulness of joys; at Thy right hand there are pleasures for ever-more."[3]

Again, in the 17th Psalm, called the "Prayer of David," after speaking with disdain of the prosperity of "men of the world which have their portion in this life,"[4] he closes with the words, "As for me, I will

---

[1] *Die Erziehung des Menschengeschlechts.* Maimonides uses a similar argument in the Introduction to his Commentary on the 10th chapter of *Sanhedrin.*

[2] Wrongly translated "hell" in the Authorised English Ver-sion.   [3] Psalm xvi. 9, 10, 11.

[4] Psalm xvii. 14.

behold thy face by righteousness. I shall be satisfied, when I awake, with thy likeness." [1]

In the 49th Psalm, which contains so powerful a homily on the vanity of wealth and fortune, the Psalmist thus declares his belief in a future state: "But God shall redeem my soul from the power of the grave; for He shall receive me." [2]

In the 103rd Psalm, he thus exhorts his soul to bless the Lord who had endowed it with Immortality. "Bless the Lord, O my soul; and all that is within me, bless His holy name. Bless the Lord, O my soul, and forget not all His benefits; Who forgiveth all thine iniquities; who healeth all thy diseases; Who redeemeth thy life from destruction; who crowneth thee with loving kindness and tender mercies." [3]

And in the 73rd Psalm, in which the Psalmist seeks to solve the problem of the prosperity of the wicked and the trials of the righteous, and finds the solution when he "went into the sanctuary of God," and "understood their end," he exclaims, "Thou shalt guide me with Thy counsel, and afterward receive me to glory. Whom have I in heaven but Thee? and there is none upon earth that I desire beside Thee. My flesh and my heart faileth, but God is the strength of my heart, and my portion for ever." [4]

---

[1] Psalm xvii. 15. It is almost superfluous to state that such phrases as "Thy face" and "Thy likeness" are not intended to assign bodily similitude or form to the Deity. They are mere anthropomorphisms, or figurative phrases adapted to the common notions and language of man. To use a well known maxim of the Rabbis, דִּבְּרָה תּוֹרָה כִּלְשׁוֹן בְּנֵי אָדָם, "The language of the Bible is the language of man."

[2] Psalm xlix. 15.   [3] Psalm ciii. 1-4.   [4] Psalm lxxiii. 24-26.

The prophet Isaiah declares the unknown glories of the future state in these words, " Since the beginning of the world men have not heard, nor perceived by the ear, neither hath the eye seen, O God, beside Thee, what He hath prepared for him that waiteth for Him." [1]

The last chapter of the Book of Ecclesiastes, which seems to be a reply to the worldliness and scepticism of the preceding chapters, contains the most pointed assertion of the doctrine of the Soul's Immortality in the well-known words, " Then shall the dust return to the earth as it was ; and the spirit shall return unto God who gave it." [2]

With such expressions as these in Holy Writ, who can, with any approach to truth, assert, as has been so repeatedly asserted, that the doctrine of Immortality was unknown to the ancient Hebrews, and that the Jews, at quite a late period of their history, derived their knowledge of that doctrine from heathen and Christian sources ? The doctrine must have been not only known to our people in primæval times, but must have been so far recognised as a self-evident fact, and so far interwoven in their natural belief, as to have required no enforcement by the authority of Divine Revelation.

" And if we would have a revelation of Immortality, what other need we have, what stronger can we have, than the inner voice (stronger than written or spoken words), which tells us of an eternal destiny? 'The inward horror of falling into nought,' is the true revelation to the soul of the soul's eternity. Our

[1] Isaiah lxiv. 4.　　　　　[2] Eccl. xii. 7.

own consciousness proclaims the great truth; and if the Bible hints at it faintly and incidentally, instead of firmly, plainly, and dogmatically, it is because the object of the Bible is not to reveal the happiness of eternal life, but to teach us how to deserve and achieve that happiness." [1]

And who, with a gleam of reason, can talk of anni- hilation of the soul?—who conceive its possibility? Who?—especially in these days, when philosophers declare even matter to be indestructible, and force, by the conservation of energy, eternal in its effects. Shall physical force be everlasting, and the Soul which, by the power of Will, gives life to force, itself lack immortality? It cannot be.

Then with the natural revelation of the Soul's Immortality, and the Bible's strong hints of a future state, how should the Jew regard Life and Death? He should regard *Life as a mere incident in Eternity, and Death a mere incident in Life*—the opening of the door of Immortal Life.

Lord Bacon says, "Men fear death, as children fear to go in the dark ; and as that natural fear in children is increased by tales, so is the other." [2]

And truly those superstitious tales of hell and its torments, the inventions of the priests of other religions, who have traded on the fears of men, have

---

[1] "The Bible and Immortality," before quoted.

[2] "Bacon's Essays," II., *On Death.* Lucretius (Book III. 78.) makes a similar remark—" For even as children dread all things in the thick darkness, thus we in the daylight fear at times things not a whit more to be dreaded than what children shud- der at in the dark." .

done the greatest mischief to Religion, and have, by painting Death as a hideous monster, robbed life of what should be one of its purest joys, the placid contemplation of our earthly end, the happy anticipation of reunion with those we love, and with the loving God from whom our spirit came. For who, believing in the boundless goodness of God, can look upon death, despite the sufferings which precede it, as anything but a blessing—the last and final blessing which He bestows upon man on earth ?[1] We hail as a sweet blessing the repose of sleep. Why fear the sleep which hushes to eternal rest the weary, aching heart and brain, and awakens to a life of freedom the imprisoned soul? It is conscience that makes us cowards. It is a sense of unworthiness, that makes us lend a ready ear to those who disseminate the vile idea of utter perdition and eternal punishment.

But though conscience may make us cowards, it need not make us unbelievers. Mindful of the endless goodness of Him who made us, conscience may tell us that we are unworthy of God's loving countenance in the world to come; but conscience should not place a limit to God's loving kindness, forgiveness, and tolerance of His erring creatures. In the words of the philosopher last quoted : "It were better to have no opinion of God at all, than such an

---

[1] A Rabbi made the striking remark on the words of Scripture וְהִנֵּה טוֹב מְאֹד זֶה מָוֶת, "'And God saw everything that He had made, and behold it was very good'—aye even Death;' *Midrash, Bereshith Rabbah*, ch. ix. And similarly Seneca classes Death among the great boons of Nature, "*inter munera naturæ.*"

opinion as is unworthy of Him; for though the one is unbelief, the other is contumely."[1]   Judging from all our past experience, we can only think of God as infinite, unlimited Mercy.   The *Midrash*[2] tell us that when the Supreme Being, asked by Moses to show him His glory, caused all His goodness to pass before him,[3] He opened to his astonished gaze the treasure-houses of Heaven, pointing out to him, one after the other, the rewards in store for the righteous; but that when at length He exposed to view one treasure-house larger than all the rest, piled up with precious things beyond number, and Moses, in rapt astonishment, exclaimed, " Lord, what is this great storehouse ?" God answered him, " This is the storehouse of happiness for those who have no merit of their own."

Such is the Jewish view of God's mercy to the undeserving.   And surely it is no extravagant idea, when we call to mind man's career on earth.   He enters the world helpless and naked.   Loving hands receive him, tend him, clothe him, and feed him; loving hearts educate him; and however great the struggle of life, there is evidence, at every step and stage, of a Providence that guides him, unworthy though he be.   Unworthy, indeed; for since none are free from sin, if God were a vindictive Being as some religions would represent Him, even the best of us would be struck dead long before we attained manhood.   But He has no vindictiveness.   He has declared that His ways are not as our ways; that as the heavens are higher than the earth, His ways are

[1] " Bacon's Essays," XVII., *On Superstition.*

[2] *Midrash, Shemoth Rabbah*, ch. 45.

[3] Exod. xxxiii. 18, 19.

higher than our ways, and His thoughts higher than our thoughts.[1] And He has declared Himself "merciful and gracious, long-suffering, and abundant in goodness and truth, keeping mercy for thousands, forgiving iniquity, transgression and sin." Surely He who provided gentle hands and hearts to receive us on entering this world, will provide a loving welcome for the soul, released from its earthly envelope, whether it be the soul of the sinner trembling for its future, or the soul of the pious, yearning for that perfection which the earth forbade.

Think not that such mercy, infinite and universal, is inconsistent with justice. He who fashioned the heavens, and balanced the countless suns and planets in boundless space, can surely adjust rewards according to our deserts. "The great, the mighty God, the Lord of Hosts is His name. Great in counsel and mighty in work; for Thine eyes are upon all the ways of the sons of men; to give every one according to his ways, and according to the fruit of his doings."[2] But Justice does not require annihilation, perdition, or eternal punishment. Justice to weak, faulty, erring, and imperfect man, rather requires mercy—mercy illimitable from the Perfect Being who created us. And so when the time will come—as come it must to all—when death approaches, though the parting from loved ones may be with tears, and the severance of earthly ties may be with lamentations, yet let there be no fear in the soul as it enters the presence of its Maker; for, merited or not, the loving mercy of God is the sure passport of every soul to heaven and happiness.

[1] Isaiah lv. 8, 9. [2] Jer. xxxii. 18, 19.

And yet the good will have the reward of their goodness; and yet the wicked will be requited for their wickedness; for God will by no means wholly clear the guilty.[1] Man cannot be saved from the natural consequences of his sin. Of the reward in a future state we know nothing here; and still we may, perhaps, gain some slight foretaste of its nature from the sense of spiritual delight we experience after the performance of a truly good, unselfish act, involving heavy sacrifice. Of the punishment in a future state we can know nothing here; and still we may, perhaps, have some slight foreshadowing of its nature from the sense of remorse, which follows the commission of a sin. Just as the grown man looks back on the foibles of his childhood and youth with contempt, and perhaps disgust, so may we well imagine the soul, released from its earthly envelope, burdened with remorse at the sins of its worldly career, until the Great "God of the spirits of all flesh" shall have purified it from its earthly stains.

And as to the shares and proportions of reward meted out to each, though there will be Heaven for all, immortality for all, happiness for all, through the boundless mercy of God, the happiness will, perhaps, be greater or less, not according to the measure in which it is *bestowed*, but according to the measure in which it is *deserved*.

Perchance that happiness, whatever it be, will be the purer, because God, in His Book, has not made it a matter of bargain with man;[2] because the pro-

[1] Exod. xxxiv. 7.

[2] Antigonus, of Socho used to say, "Be not like servants who

mised guerdon is vague and indistinct; because the acme of happiness comes as the consequence of virtue, not as the reward of virtue. For it is the un-selfish, disinterested work that is truly godly—satis-fying God and satisfying the soul, by its purity and lack of motive—the labour done without hope of profit, fame, or reward, the work wrought for the glory of God and the good of man.

---

serve their master in consideration of receiving a reward ; but be like servants who serve their master without any hope of receiving a reward ; and let the fear of Heaven be upon you."— *Aboth* i. 3.

CHAPTER XIV.

PROPHECY AND ISRAEL'S HOPE.

WHAT do we mean by Prophecy? Why are we to believe in the prophets? What do the prophets teach us?

You all know that the Bible is divided into three great sections—the Law, the Prophets, and the Sacred Writings. Now, the Prophets contain much that is by no means prophetic, and that is distinctly historical. Indeed there are many of the so-called prophets who never prophesied, in the common sense of the word—that is, who never foretold coming events. It has been well shown by the learned Dr. Benisch,[1] that the so-called prophets (נְבִיאִים) and their disciples, the sons of the prophets (בְּנֵי הַנְּבִיאִים), were not, of necessity, men who foretold the secrets of the future, but that they were the scholars, sages, and statesmen of the people; that they excelled in poetry, oratory, and music; that they were the guardians of the Law, the interpreters of God's will, the chroniclers, moralists and preachers of biblical times.

Those who attained the faculty of foretelling future events were but few in number. Withdrawing them-

[1] "The Sons of the Prophets" ("Miscellany of Hebrew Literature").

selves from the occupations and pleasures of the world ; sanctifying themselves to the service of God, whose works and ways they were ever studying with awe and reverence; possessed of the highest spiritual longings ; and looking down upon the earth and earthly things from an eminence far above, and, as it were, outside this world, these few select men became the messengers of God to man.

Theirs was not merely the insight acquired by the astute historian, who reads the future by the light of the past, and who, making History a science, traces a faint outline of coming events from the parallel records of bygone times. Theirs was not the mere warning voice of worldly wisdom, nor the sage counsel of human genius, nor the sad foreboding of the anxious patriot. Their prophecies were messages from God, delivered in His name, and bearing all the tokens of Divine authority.

Nor were these prophecies mere presages of future history. Interspersed with their predictions of good and evil, were golden words of wisdom, joyous songs of prayer and praise, stirring exhortations to duty, mournful dirges for glory lost and gone, glowing thoughts of the Divine Majesty, visions of heavenly hosts, dreams of celestial bliss ; and all pourtrayed in the winged words of sweetest poetry. But interwoven with the main fabric of prophecy, we find the Divine Word, as promulgated on Sinai; its teachings are never lost sight of; no contradictions, no inconsistencies, no new covenants superseding the old ; but a unity of thought, design, and feeling, a consistency of principle, showing that One Mind inspired all the Prophets—the Mind Divine that gave us our Law.

We, living in these days of materialism, when many doubt the possibility of miracles, because such miracles as the Bible relates do not now happen, may perhaps feel, if not doubt, at least wonder, that the Great Maker of the Universe should choose a few obscure men in one of the tiniest of His planets, (a planet however large to us, yet infinitely small compared with any of the countless suns that bespangle the wide heavens,) and should make those men the exponents of His Will to their fellow mortals on that little planet. The mind with its finite ideas, cannot grasp the notion of a Being infinitely great condescending to the infinitely small; and this is the cause of the difficulty experienced by some. But once admit the Divine Government of the World, which all Religion teaches, once admit that God in His mercy does concern Himself with the welfare of His creatures, infinitely small though they may be compared with Himself—and the difficulty vanishes. Why should not God, who witnesses every act of our lives, single out His own agents to work or to proclaim His Will on earth? Why should not He who breathes the spirit of genius into one, the spirit of poetry into another, the spirit of invention and discovery into a third, inspire others with the spirit of prophecy, as a warning to the wicked, and a hope and encouragement to the righteous? He makes all the forces of Nature His servants; He "makes the winds His messengers." Where, then, is the improbability in His choosing the best of men to declare His Will to the creatures whom He loves?

Chief and first among the prophets was Moses, unlike all others in his direct communication with God.[1] You know well how first he proved his Divine mission by working miracles, at first personal miracles, but afterwards miracles that affected a whole people. You know well the part he took in the Divine Revelation, how he became the Teacher, Judge, and Leader of his nation during the forty years' wanderings. Before his death, he gave his people a prophetic insight into their future, first in that remarkable chapter of blessings and curses,[2] then in his dying song, full of fervid eloquence,[3] and lastly in his parting blessing to the tribes.[4]

The prophets who came after Moses could never hope to vie with him in position and influence. Yet they, too, were to have their credentials; and the people were not to listen to their voice before those credentials had been produced. For Moses commanded his people[5] not to listen to every one who pretended to be the bearer of a message from God. Still, they were told that prophecy was not to cease; that a prophet, one of themselves, would be raised up, in whose mouth God would put His words; who should speak all that God would command him; and to this prophet they were to hearken.[6]

And what was to be the test of a true prophet? It was to be two-fold. "When a prophet speaketh in the name of the Lord, if the thing follow not, nor come to pass, that is the thing which the Lord

[1] Deut. xxxiv. 10.
[2] Deut. xxviii.
[3] Deut. xxxii. 1-43.
[4] Deut. xxxiii.
[5] Deut. xviii. 14.
[6] Deut. xviii. 18, 19.

hath not spoken, but the prophet hath spoken it presumptuously ; thou shalt not be afraid of him."[1] The test of true prophecy is, thus, first, the common-sense test—fulfilment. There is no demand for blind belief, no call upon credulity, a credulity so often mis-termed faith ; but the test was to be the evidence of the senses. Next, the word of the prophet, if it is to be believed, must be consistent with the revealed Word of God. "The prophet which shall presume to speak a word in My name which I have not commanded him to speak, or that shall speak in the name of other gods, even that prophet shall die."[2]

We read in the 28th chapter of Jeremiah of the false prophecies of Hananiah the son of Azur, and how he died for his sin ; and in the subsequent chapter we read of the false prophets of the Captivity—Ahab the son of Kolaiah, Zedekiah the son of Maaseiah, and Shemaiah the Nehelamite—and of their punishment. The Jews in Babylon gladly listened to the prophets who brought them pleasant tidings of freedom, contradicting the true prophets who had foretold a captivity of seventy years. But the prophets of peace and joy were false prophets. They had no divine credentials. They had not even the credentials of a pure, unsullied life ; for they had "committed villany in Israel."[3]

But, after all, the chief test of prophecy must always be—fulfilment. Certainly the fulfilment may be due, as was the case with many of Jeremiah's pro-

---

[1] Deut. xviii. 22.   [2] Deut. xviii. 20.

[3] Jer. xxix. 23 ; xxiii. 14. This argument and its illustrations are further developed in Appendix IV.

phecies, many years after the prediction ; and time
only would duly verify such a prediction.   But
Jeremiah had foretold the fall of Jerusalem years
before the event, when, humanly speaking, such an
event would have been thought impossible ; so that,
his previous predictions having been verified, his prophecy of the restoration was entitled to belief.

If we go back to the early history of Samuel,[1] we
shall find the like practical test of prophecy applied.
God had foretold to Eli the impending downfall
of his priestly house, in consequence of the wickedness of his two sons, Hophni and Phinehas.   The
same terrible fact was revealed to Samuel, who
"feared to show Eli the vision."   But when the old
priest pressed him, "and Samuel told him every whit
and hid nothing from him," he saw how Samuel's
vision corresponded with the revelation he had himself received, and he exclaimed, "It is the Lord, let
Him do what seemeth Him good."   Immediately
afterwards we read that "Samuel grew, and the Lord
was with him, and did let none of his words fall to
the ground ;" that is, his predictions came true ;
"and all Israel, from Dan even to Beersheba,[2] knew
that Samuel was established to be a prophet of the
Lord."

In the Book of Kings,[3] we shall find similar, and
perhaps more conspicuous, evidence that the prophet
had to prove his miraculous power before he could be

---

[1] 1 Samuel ii. and iii.

[2] That is, from the extreme north to the extreme south of
Palestine.

[3] 1 Kings xiii. 1-5.

regarded as a true prophet. King Jeroboam had set
up two calves of gold in Bethel and in Dan; had
wickedly declared them to be the gods of Israel; had
appointed a mock priesthood, drawn from the lowest of
the people; had ordained a feast at Bethel, built an altar
there, and offered sacrifices on the altar to the golden
calf. "And, behold, there came a man of God out of
Judah, by the word of the Lord, unto Bethel; and
Jeroboam stood by the altar to burn incense. And
he cried against the altar in the word of the Lord,
and said, O altar, altar, thus saith the Lord : Behold
a child shall be born unto the house of David, Josiah
by name; and upon thee shall he offer the priests of
the high places that burn incense upon thee, and
men's bones shall be burnt upon thee. And he gave
a sign the same day, saying : This is the sign which
the Lord hath spoken. Behold the altar shall be
rent, and the ashes that are upon it shall be poured
out." The "sign" immediately came to pass ; and
thus the bystanders knew that the prophet was foretelling the truth. It is hardly necessary to add that
the prediction was fulfilled to the letter two hundred
and fifty years later. [1]

The first prophecy of Elijah,[2] that which foretold
the three years' drought, took effect from the moment
of its prediction ; so no further credential was needed.
Elisha's credential was the miraculous passage of
the Jordan in the presence of the sons of the
prophets ; and when they saw him, they exclaimed,
"The spirit of Elijah doth rest on Elisha." [3]

[1] 2 Kings xxiii. 15, 16.   [2] 1 Kings xvii. 1.

[3] 2 Kings ii. 14, 15.

When, therefore, we read in the Bible the words of the prophets, we may rest assured that those who regarded them as prophets, in their own times, had good and valid reasons for so regarding them, and that they did not blindly accept their statements on trust, without previous evidence of their prophetic gift.

But we, living in an age far distant from the time when these prophetic warnings and promises were uttered, have the best evidence of their truth ; for time has verified nearly all of them in so wondrous a fashion, that we sometimes stand amazed at the coincidence of prophecy, in all its smallest details, with accomplished facts. The prophecies relating to Palestine, Assyria, Babylon, and Egypt, have been all fulfilled, not only in their broad outlines, but even to the minutest particulars. Yet some prophecies remain unfulfilled ; and what shall we say to them ? If nine out of ten prophecies of one prophet have been realised, shall we discredit the tenth ? Shall we not rather say, that the tenth is not yet ripe for fulfilment ? And when we find the same unfulfilled prophecy foretold equally by several other prophets, the majority of whose predictions have also come true, is it not reasonable to conclude that, in the fulness of time, the as yet unrealised prediction in which so many prophets concur, will also come to pass ?

To us Jews, the question is a momentous one; for the unfulfilled prediction, to which I refer, is the prophecy of the restoration of Israel. We Jews, who love our religion, have hopes apart from the hopes of worldly suc-

cess. Wherever the Jew is domiciled, he lives two lives
—his life as a citizen, and his life as a Jew. He loves
with tender love the land of his adoption, whose laws
protect him and his property, and shield him from
persecution. He is a patriot to the land which gave
him birth, and gladly bears the burdens of citizenship,
faithfully obeys the laws, and shares in his nation's
joys and tribulation. But the fervent Jew has another country that he loves without detriment to
his love for the land of his birth. He loves that land
which was the cradle of his Faith, the home of
the patriarchs, the glory of his nation ; the land which
contains Zion and Jerusalem. He thinks of it, not as
it is, desolate, barren, and forsaken, its towns ruinous,
its fields un-tilled, its holy places in Gentile hands; he
thinks of it, as it was in the days of its pristine glory,
and as it will be when all the prophecies regarding it
shall have been fulfilled.

Nor is his hope for the restoration of his people
a mere insensate longing to re-possess the land of his
inheritance; for this world has fairer homes than
Palestine ; more fertile fields than its stubborn
plains ; more verdant slopes than its rocky hills ;
but the hope of Israel is for a spiritual restoration,
which shall make Palestine once again the religious
focus of the world, Jerusalem again the Holy City of
the earth, Zion once more the mount of God—a
spiritual restoration, which shall make the essence of
his Faith—the belief in the One and only God, and
submission to His will—*the religion of the world.*

Let us hear what the prophets tell us concerning
the future of Israel, and Israel's land.

First of all, Moses foretells to repentant Israel a happy return to the Land of Promise, in clear language, free from doubt or oracular ambiguity, in these words: "And it shall come to pass when all these things shall come upon thee, the blessing and the curse, which I have set before thee, and thou shalt call them to mind among all the nations, whither the Lord thy God hath driven thee, And shalt return unto the Lord thy God, and shalt obey His voice according to all that I command thee this day, thou and thy children, with all thine heart, and with all thy soul; That then the Lord thy God will turn thy captivity, and have compassion upon thee, and will return and gather thee from all the nations whither the Lord thy God hath scattered thee. If any of thine be driven out unto the utmost parts of heaven, from thence will the Lord thy God gather thee, and from thence will He fetch thee. And the Lord thy God will bring thee unto the land which thy fathers possessed, and thou shalt possess it; and He will do thee good, and multiply thee above thy fathers."[1]

This prophecy is as yet unfulfilled. It did not come to pass at the close of the Babylonish captivity; for the ten tribes of the kingdom of Israel were not included in the restoration under Ezra and Nehemiah. It must, therefore, have reference to a restoration yet to come.

Next, let us hear what Isaiah reveals to us on the same subject. Isaiah, though his thoughts are mostly clad in the resplendent garb of brilliant imagery, or in the fiery mantle of impassioned poetry, when he

[1] Deut. xxx. 1-5.

prophecies the second restoration, is perfectly clear
and circumstantial: "And it shall come to pass in
that day, that the Lord shall set His hand again the
second time to recover the remnant of His people,
which shall be left, from Assyria, and from Egypt,
and from Pathros, and from Cush, and from Elam, and
from Shinar, and from Hamath, and from the islands
of the sea. And He shall set up an ensign for the
nations, and shall assemble the outcasts of Israel, and
gather together the dispersed of Judah from the four
corners of the earth."[1]

Israel, whose lost ten tribes are yet undiscovered,
is to join with Judah in the happy restoration. And
when is this marvellous event to take place? The
restoration is to be heralded by the previous advent
of him whom we style the Messiah, or the Anointed,
not a god, but a man, a descendant of David, a man
filled with the spirit of God, worthy of being the har-
binger of a glorious restoration ; and thus does Isaiah
describe him :—"And there shall come forth a rod
out of the stem of Jesse, and a branch shall grow out
of his roots. And the spirit of the Lord shall rest
upon him, the spirit of wisdom and understanding,
the spirit of counsel and might, the spirit of knowledge and of the fear of the Lord : And shall make
him of quick understanding in the fear of the Lord;
and he shall not judge after the sight of his eyes,
neither reprove after the hearing of his ears : But
with righteousness shall he judge the poor, and
reprove with equity for the meek of the earth ; and
he shall smite the earth with the rod of his mouth,

[1] Isaiah xi. 11, 12.

and with the breath of his lips shall he slay the wicked. And righteousness shall be the girdle of his loins, and faithfulness the girdle of his reins."[1] . . . In those days, "The earth shall be full of the knowledge of the Lord, as the waters cover the sea."[2] For this restoration will not affect Israel and Judah alone; it will affect the whole world. At the advent of the Messiah, there will be a time not only of knowledge, but of peace: "And it shall come to pass in the last days, that the mountain of the Lord's house shall be established in the top of the mountains, and shall be exalted above the hills, and all nations shall flow unto it. And many people shall go and say, Come ye, and let us go up to the mountain of the Lord, to the house of the God of Jacob; and He will teach us of His ways, and we will walk in His paths; for out of Zion shall go forth the law, and the word of the Lord from Jerusalem. And He shall judge among the nations, and shall rebuke many people, and they shall beat their swords into ploughshares, and their spears into pruning-hooks; nation shall not lift up sword against nation, neither shall they learn war any more."[3]

At this epoch the oppression of tyrants will come to an end, and the pride of kings will be humbled. *Religions* will be abolished, and *Religion* will reign supreme. "And the loftiness of man shall be bowed down, and the haughtiness of man shall be made low, and the Lord alone shall be exalted in that day. And the idols he shall utterly abolish."[4]

[1] Isaiah xi. 1-5.   [2] Isaiah xi. 9.   [3] Isaiah ii. 2-4.
[4] Isaiah ii. 17, 18.

But though the whole world will thus profit by the restoration of Israel, our people are still to remain the depositaries of God's Holy Law, and through them the earth is to be enlightened. "And the Redeemer shall come unto Zion, and unto them that turn from transgression in Jacob, saith the Lord. As for Me, this is My covenant with them, saith the Lord: My spirit that is upon thee, and My words which I have put in thy mouth shall not depart out of thy mouth, nor out of the mouth of thy seed, nor out of the mouth of thy seed's seed, saith the Lord, from henceforth and for ever."[1] "And the Gentiles shall come to thy light, and kings to the brightness of thy rising."[2]

Jeremiah, the priest, who had prophesied in several successive reigns the downfall of Jerusalem and Judah, and who became himself a witness of, and sufferer by, that terrible calamity; whose wail over the captivity of his people finds utterance in those Lamentations, which seem written in scalding tears—Jeremiah, too, foretells the coming of the Messiah, and the happy restoration of his race: "Behold the days come, saith the Lord, that I will raise unto David a righteous Branch, and a King shall reign and prosper, and shall execute judgment and justice in the earth. In his days Judah shall be saved, and Israel shall dwell safely."[3] . . . . "And they shall dwell in their own land."[4]

Even out of the darkness of the dungeon, where the wicked king Zedekiah had imprisoned him, thinking to stifle his prophetic utterances, there came to

[1] Isaiah lix. 20-21.   [2] Isaiah lx. 3.   [3] Jerem. xxiii. 5, 6.
[4] Jer. xxiii. 8.

Jeremiah, coupled with the presage of immediate evil, the promise of the great and permanent restoration of his people in distant days: "Behold, I will gather them out of all countries, whither I have driven them in Mine anger, and in My fury, and in great wrath: and I will bring them again to this place, and I will cause them to dwell safely. And they shall be My people, and I will be their God: and I will give them one heart and one way, that they may fear Me for ever, for the good of them and of their children after them: and I will make an everlasting covenant with them, that I will not turn away from them to do them good; but I will put My fear in their hearts, that they shall not depart from Me." [1]

Ezekiel, whose spirit of prophecy seems to have sprung out of the miseries of the captivity, but who, more than any other prophet, gives us, as it were, a glimpse of the transcendent glories of heaven, prophesies in like terms the return of his nation from their long exile, their renewed obedience to their Divine Ruler, and the permanency of Israel's settlement in the Holy Land. "Thus saith the Lord God: Behold, I will take the children of Israel from among the heathen, whither they be gone, and will gather them on every side, and bring them into their own land. And I will make them one nation in the land upon the mountains of Israel, and one king shall be king to them all; and they shall be no more two nations, neither shall they be divided into two kingdoms any more at all. And David My servant shall be king over them; and they shall all

[1] Jer. xxxii. 37-40.

have one shepherd ; they shall also walk in My judgments, and observe My statutes, and do them.   And they shall dwell in the land that I have given unto Jacob My servant, wherein your fathers have dwelt ; and they shall dwell therein, even they and their children, and their children's children for ever, and My servant David shall be their prince for ever. Moreover, I will make a covenant of peace with them ; it shall be an everlasting covenant with them ; and I will place them and multiply them, and will set My sanctuary in the midst of them for evermore." [1]

And thus does Ezekiel address the desolate hills of Palestine, so as to show that our return will not be to a parched and arid waste, but to a land abounding in riches, and smiling under the blessings of peace and plenty : " But ye, O mountains of Israel, ye shall shoot forth your branches, and yield your fruit to My people of Israel ; for they are at hand to come.   For behold I am for you, and I will turn unto you, and ye shall be tilled and sown.   And I will multiply men upon you, all the house of Israel, even all of it ; and the cities shall be inhabited, and the wastes shall be builded.   And I will multiply upon you man and beast, and they shall increase and bring fruit, and I will settle you after your old estates, and will do better unto you than at your beginnings, and ye shall know that I am the Lord." [2]

The Minor Prophets[3] join in these good tidings of

---

[1] Ezek. xxxvii. 21, 22, 24, 25, 26.   [2] Ezek. xxxvi. 8-11.

[3] The Minor Prophets are so called by Biblical scholars, not because these prophets were inferior in prophetic gift to Isaiah, Jeremiah or Ezekiel, nor because their predictions

our future restoration, and there is a remarkable coincidence everywhere in the terms of their prophecies. The prophet Zechariah, who delivered to the captives of Babylon the message of their speedy return, and who encouraged them to proceed with the rebuilding of the Temple in spite of their adversaries,[1] foretells the concourse of the nations to Jerusalem to join in the true worship : " Thus saith the Lord of Hosts ; it shall yet come to pass that there shall come people and the inhabitants of many cities. And the inhabitants of one city shall go to another, saying, Let us go speedily to pray before the Lord, and to seek the Lord of Hosts; I will go also. Yea, many people and strong nations shall come to seek the Lord of Hosts in Jerusalem, and to pray before the Lord."[2]

And in these times, when we see how the world is gradually recognising the marvellous wisdom of our Law in all its bearings, and acknowledging its debt to the Jew who has observed, and, by observing, preserved that code through ages of persecution ; when we see the honoured position which our people are everywhere achieving, it seems as if this prophecy, too, is not far from fulfilment :—" In those days it shall come to pass that ten men shall take hold out of all languages of the nations, even shall take hold of the skirt of him that is a Jew, saying, We will go with you ; for we have heard that God is with you."[3] In

---

were of minor value ; but because their writings are smaller in bulk and quantity. In the Hebrew Version they are called תְּרֵי עָשָׂר "the Twelve."

[1] Ezra v. 1.		[2] Zech. viii. 20-22.		[3] Zech. viii. 23.

those days the mythologies of now dominant religions will have become curiosities of human history, and will give place to the pure monotheism of Israel. "The Lord shall be king over all the earth; in that day shall there be one Lord, and His name ONE."[1]

To us, living in a free and happy country, not only tolerated but respected by our fellow-citizens of other creeds, and admitted to the honours and dignities of the State; to us enjoying full liberty, religious and civil, the question may fairly suggest itself, why should we long for a restoration of our ancient kingdom, why should we wish to return to Jerusalem? Why pray for the termination of a captivity in which we are free men? Why repine at a misfortune nearly 2,000 years old, which lost to us our own country, but which, after long and bitter misfortunes honorably borne by our ancestors, has given to us another country which we have reason to love so dearly?

But to the Jew who understands the mission of Judaism, Palestine, his mother-country, is not dead—is but in a trance. She will surely awake, and yet claim him as her own. To the Jew, the restoration of the Holy Land is no empty phrase, and his prayers for the renewed glory of Zion are no unmeaning utterances; for with these hopes he associates the promised glories of the Messianic era and the regeneration of the entire human race; and thus prays not in selfish prayer for his own good, or even for the good of the chosen people alone, but, in the broadest spirit of philanthropy, prays for a condition

[1] Zech. xiv. 9.

of things which will embrace the happiness of all mankind—an era of one religion, One God.

For he reads the dismal page of History, and there sees how, though Religion was given to man as the greatest blessing, Religions have proved the greatest curse. He reads of wars waged for centuries between Mahometan and Christian, hatred between these two creeds surviving even now, and causing the latest of European wars. He reads of the persecutions of Christian by Christian, feuds between Greek Church and Latin Church, between Protestants and Catholics, the *autos-da-fé* of the Inquisition, the burnings of Smithfield and of Oxford. He reads of creeds split up into every possible form of dissent, its priests quarrelling about candles and vestments and postures and other like trifles, till he feels inclined to exclaim with the Psalmist, " He that sitteth in the Heavens shall laugh ; the Lord shall have them in derision." [1]

And then he turns to his own glorious History, and finds his Religion outliving all the rest, unchanged, unsullied, evergreen through the long lapse of ages, existing still in all its pristine vigour, surviving still with all the most important forms, prayers, ceremonies, and beliefs of ancient Bible-times. He asks himself : Wherefore this sempiternal life of Israel's Creed ? Why this ever-renewed youth of his Religion, in spite of persecution and oppression, in spite of the law of change and decay, whose influence is to be traced in all things else ? And he thinks it must be the fulfilment of the Divine

[1] Psalm ii. 4.

law of Nature, "the survival of the fittest"—the survival of that creed destined to be the Creed of the World.

For the Jew alone remains as he was, in spite of his lost nationality. Other nations springing from obscurity, rose, achieved greatness, became dictators of the world, then fell into decay and perished utterly, their grandeur and their monuments mingling with the dust. But the Jew survives them all.

He sees, in the history of the past, his people exiled, plundered, tortured, massacred ; but he sees also how Judaism outlived its persecutors, and even derived from persecution new vitality. Driven hither and thither about the world, first tolerated, then banished, then recalled, then driven again into exile, the Jew left his trace everywhere, like the wandering thistle-down, blown about from field to field, the sport of the winds, the plaything of the gales. In commerce, in literature, and in general knowledge, the Jew has achieved a high position. But his greatest achievement has been that everywhere in his exile, through ages of persecution, he has held aloft the pure, unalloyed Word of God as the standard of morality, and his pure belief in One sole God, to whom man is responsible, as the standard of Religion.

This last has been his mission in bygone days, and it is his mission yet. For now, standing on his lofty eminence, he witnesses the battles of the creeds, and pities the combatants. He sees them fighting about the shadows of which he proudly holds the substance—shadows of the Bible-creed prolonged in irrecognisable distortion, as the bright sun of truth advances, directing men to believe only the credible.

Standing on his lofty eminence of credible belief, he thinks he sees the world in time to come, wiser with age, turning to the One True Faith to which he, as custodian, has so long clung; and amid the ruins of exploded superstitions, amid the ashes of burnt-out beliefs, amid the wreck of irreligion, amid the crash of creeds, he thinks he sees his own emerge triumphant—THE RELIGION OF THE WORLD.

APPENDIX I.

EVOLUTION AND DESIGN.

MANY have expressed the opinion, that the "Argument from Design" in proof of the Existence of a God, which Paley was the first to popularise, and which I have here[1] attempted by familiar examples to adapt to the comprehension of the young, has become weakened, if not wholly invalidated, by the recent theory of Evolution.

According to this theory, now accepted by some of the greatest philosophers of the age, and which, it must be admitted, is largely, indeed powerfully, supported (though far from proved) by well-established facts of science, the Earth and its contents did not come into their present state of existence by a series of separate and distinct, or, so to speak, arbitrary acts of creation, by so many fits and starts of creative energy, but are the results of certain natural forces, acting upon matter according to fixed laws, causing gradual changes and developments in living things, and, by slow degrees, during the course of countless ages, transforming the simplest into the most complex and varying forms of life, till the present climax was reached ; and that climax itself no final climax, but itself, like many that preceded it, a starting point for a gradual decline of some, and for an equally gradual higher development of other forms of life.

If this theory be true, "every organic being has a place in a chain of events. It is not an isolated, a capricious fact, but an unavoidable phenomenon. It has its place in that vast, orderly concourse which has successively risen in the past, has introduced the present, and is preparing the

---

[1] Part I., Chap. I.

S

way for a predestined future. From point to point in this vast progression, there has been a gradual, a definite, a continuous unfolding, a resistless order of evolution. But in the midst of these mighty changes stand forth immutable the laws that are dominating over all."[1]

But if this theory of Evolution be true, if a slow and gradual transformation from one living form to another—a transformation obedient to fixed law—is in our belief or mental vision, to take the place of that sudden calling forth of life, which we have hitherto associated with the idea of Creation, what, it is asked, becomes of the "Argument from Design?" Can a living thing be said to have been designed, if it arose in the ordinary course of events, if its coming into life was not only not specially designed, but was even an unavoidable event?

I would answer, that the "Argument from Design" is vastly intensified in force, if the theory of Evolution be true. For if it be true, as the Evolutionists tell us, that all living creatures have gradually descended from a low organic form known as protoplasm, acted upon by forces, which have ever remained subject to the same invariable laws, what must be said of the Origin of such protoplasm, such force, and such law, as could produce such results as the living creatures which people our world? Are not the marks of design all the more striking, if, with a foresight which the human mind can scarcely grasp or realise to the faintest degree, the matter, force, and law were so ordained, countless ages ago, as to produce, *without intervention in the interval* (as the Evolutionists would have us believe), a world teeming with all forms of life, as we see it now?

I would maintain, that if the doctrine of Evolution be true, (and much yet remains to be proved before it can be regarded in any other light than that of a highly probable theory,) the scheme of primal creation is thereby immeasurably ennobled, that the presence of Design is *ipso facto* proved—design of a kind so far-sighted, so multifarious, so full of numberless nascent and unborn conditions of life, each productive of countless forms of life, actual and potential, that the mind, contemplating the huge gap between the protoplasmic form and the complex vertebrates

[1] Prof. Draper's "Conflict between Religion and Science."

of to-day, quails beneath the burden of the developmental idea ; and we feel that language is poor and weak, nay, powerless, since DESIGN is the strongest word we have to cover the far-sighted Creative Intention, which started into life a world of germs, that, after countless ages, could produce the wondrous world of life now surrounding us ![1]

[1] It is remarked by Sir John B. Byles (*Foundations of Religion*, page 26) that, in the latter part of Voltaire's life, the argument from design was that which most impressed the philosopher, and seems to have removed from his mind not only all doubt, but all fear of ever doubting again :—"J'admets cette Intelligence Suprême, sans craindre que jamais on puisse me faire changer d'opinion. Rien n'ebranle en moi cet axiome, tout ouvrage démontre un ouvrier."

APPENDIX II.

THE SANHEDRIN, AND THE ORIGIN OF THE TALMUD.

WE have already seen[1] how, at the instance of Jethro, the first local Israelitish courts of justice were established by the appointment of "rulers of thousands, rulers of hundreds, rulers of fifties, and rulers of tens," who "judged the people at all seasons." But the Supreme Court, which, later in Jewish history, acquired the Greek name *Sanhedrin*, is said to have had its origin in the events related in the eleventh chapter of Numbers.

"And the Lord said unto Moses, Gather unto Me seventy men of the elders of Israel, whom thou knowest to be the elders of the people, and officers over them; and bring them unto the tabernacle of the congregation, that they may stand there with thee. And I will come down, and talk with thee there; and I will take of the spirit which is upon thee, and will put it upon them; and they shall bear the burden of the people with thee, that thou bear it not thyself alone."[2]

Moses found the task of governing and controlling the people too burdensome for him. The Lord accordingly directs him to associate with him seventy elders, to share with him the burden of the people. The Bible does not tell us clearly how the selection was made; but tradition tells us that it was made in this fashion: Six candidates, known for their prudence and worth, were selected from each tribe, thus making seventy-two, or two in excess of the required number. Seventy pieces of parchment were marked with a certain sign, and two pieces were left blank. The seventy-two then drew lots. Eldad and Medad are

¹ Page 158.   ² Numb. xi. 16, 17.

supposed to have been the two who drew blanks, and their peculiar position is described in a later part of the same chapter.[1] The remaining seventy were duly installed, " and when the spirit rested upon them, they prophesied."

The functions of the august assembly thus constituted were, the maintenance of order and the instruction of the people, more especially the solution of difficult points of law, beyond the powers of the tribal or local courts; and thus appears to have originated an institution which, in later times, exercised the greatest influence upon the development of Judaism—the Sanhedrin.

In post-biblical history, the great Sanhedrin is constantly mentioned as a body which constituted a common centre of religious authority to all the children of Israel, throughout their dispersion. Much has been written on the subject. An Englishman, John Selden, who lived in the reign of Charles I., wrote a Dissertation in Latin, entitled, " De Synedriis et Præfecturis Juridicis veterum Ebræorum." An elaborate Treatise on the subject has just been published by Dr. Hoffmann, entitled " Der oberste Gerichtshof in der Stadt des Heiligthums." Some scholars suppose that this great council did not arise until the days of Ezra, and that it was a new institution devised by this sage. But the weight of probability is against this view. It is not likely that the council of seventy elders, established by Moses by express command of God, should have been merely a temporary tribunal. There had been previously a temporary appointment of elders, who, together with Aaron and Hur, were to rule the people, while Moses was absent for forty days on the mount of God,[2] but, judging from the sequel—the history of the worship of the golden calf—these delegates could have had little influence over the people. The spirit of Moses was not upon them.

But with the tribunal of Seventy ordained in the Eleventh chapter of Numbers it was far different. Moses had been so wearied by the strain of his burden, that he had begged God to take his life rather than permit him to continue in his wretchedness.[3] No temporary appointment would have

[1] Numb. xi. 26-29. [2] Exod. xxiv. 1-14.
[3] Numb. xi. 15.

given to Moses the necessary relief. It is not credible
that the transfer of the spirit of the great Legislator to the
Seventy Elders would have been effected as a mere
temporary expedient, and the Bible does not mention any
special exigency needing the special and temporary work of
the Elders. Indeed, the whole language of the text indicates
the permanency of the institution. " When the spirit
rested upon them, they prophesied, and did not cease." [1]

It is true that we do not find the Tribunal of Seventy
again referred to in the Pentateuch in distinct terms ; but
such an omission would be quite in accordance with the
Biblical style of narrative, which, while most explicit in
some passages, contents itself with mere hints and allusions
in others. Thus, when we find in the narrative of the
rebellion of Korah, that the elders of Israel followed Moses,[2]
there can be no doubt that reference is made to the
Council of Seventy, who aided him in communicating to
the people the Divine behest. Again, in the 27th chapter
of Deuteronomy, where we find[3] that Moses with the
Elders of Israel charged the people to keep the commandments, it was doubtless again the Council of Seventy who
acted as assessors to the great Legislator. We again meet
with allusions to the Elders in the time of Joshua and the
Judges, and we may readily understand that if Moses had
needed the support of a tribunal to share with him the
duties and responsibilities of government, his successors
would still more urgently need such aid.

It is probable that the Tribunal of Seventy fell into
abeyance during the reign of some of the Kings, who
desired to rule despotically, unchecked by representatives
of legally constituted authority. But there can be no doubt
that King Jehoshaphat strove to re-organise it, for we
are told,[4] " Moreover in Jerusalem did Jehoshaphat set of
the Levites and of the priests and of the chief of the
fathers of Israel, for the judgment of the Lord, and for
controversies," and he appears to have imparted to the
tribunal a two-fold character, by appointing two presidents,
one, the high priest, for religious matters, and the other the
ruler of the house of Judah for civil causes.

When our fathers returned from the Babylonian captivity,

[1] Numb. xi. 25.   [2] Numb. xvi. 25.   [3] Verse 1.   [4] 2 Chron. xix. 8.

the Institution was revived by Ezra, the Seventy Elders in all probability forming a part of the "men of the Great Synagogue."[1] But it is at the time of the Maccabees that we find the Tribunal of Seventy flourishing in all its vigour, as the Supreme Council of State. It is mentioned in all the most important State documents. Thus, when Jonathan makes a league with the Lacedæmonians, he writes : "Jonathan the High Priest and the Elders of the nation, and the priests and the other people of the Jews unto the Lacedæmonians, their brethren, send greeting."[2]

The Talmud gives full particulars of the mode in which members of the Sanhedrin were appointed, and as to the functions the tribunal had to fulfil. The tribunal was originally called *Beth Din Haggadol* (בֵּית דִּין הַגָּדוֹל), "the Great House of Judgment," but it acquired the name Sanhedrin (סַנְהֶדְרִין) from the Greek συνέδριον, which simply means "assembly," at the time of the Macedonian supremacy, the senators of that state being called συνέδροι or assembly-men.

The Sanhedrin consisted of seventy members, besides the president, *Nassi* (נָשִׂיא), prince or patriarch; and thus it exactly corresponded with the Assembly in the Wilderness, which consisted of seventy Elders, with Moses as president. Each member of the Great Sanhedrin was called to his high office by ordination (סְמִיכָה) or imposition of hands, and this ceremony connected him, through a long chain of prophets and judges, with Joshua, whom Moses himself had ordained by Divine command.

The members were selected, not from the privileged or wealthy classes, but exclusively from those who were distinguished for their personal worth and high attainments. The king was not eligible, lest his opinion, backed by his lofty authority, might carry too much weight. It is stated that the moral qualifications necessary for admission to the august assembly were wisdom, modesty, the fear of God, disinterestedness, the love of truth, humanity, and an

---

[1] These were 120 in number, and were the first compilers of a Jewish liturgy, on which our present prayer book is based.

[2] I Macc. xii. 6.

unstained reputation. Moreover, the Israelite admitted to a seat in the Great Council was required to be profoundly versed in the Law, and was also obliged to show himself well acquainted with a wide range of studies not theological, such as astronomy, physics and medicine. He had likewise to be a good linguist, so as to be able to understand evidence in foreign tongues without the aid of an interpreter, and he was also expected to be acquainted with the philosophies, opinions, practices, and superstitions of the heathens. The High Priest himself could not *claim* to be a member of the Sanhedrin; but preference was given to him, as well as to the ordinary priests, if they possessed the necessary qualifications.

The *Nassi*, or president, was chosen entirely on account of his pre-eminent worth and wisdom. The senior member of the Seventy, called the *Ab Beth Din* (אָב בֵּית דִּין), "father of the house of judgment," sat at the right hand of the president, and the rest of the Seventy sat before them in the form of a semi-circle.

The place where the sessions of the Sanhedrin were ordinarily held, was the *Lishchath Hagazith* (לִשְׁכַּת הַגָּזִית), a hall in one of the courts of the Temple.

The functions of the Tribunal were two-fold, executive and legislative. It constituted the Supreme Court of Judicature, which tried all cases of national importance, such as cases of false prophets, a traitor high-priest, an idolatrous tribe or city, and, generally, all capital cases. It should be added that the Talmud distinctly asserts, that the power of inflicting capital punishment was taken away from the Tribunal by the Romans forty years before the destruction of the Second Temple, and that it was only the Roman procurator who could confirm and execute the sentence of the Sanhedrin. This fact is an important one, as it rebuts the charge, which has been the cause of so much persecution, that the Jews crucified Jesus. He was certainly arraigned before the Sanhedrin as a false prophet, but the punishment was executed not by Jews, but by Romans, and according to Roman custom; for crucifixion was not one of the Jewish modes of capital punishment.

The legislative function of the Sanhedrin was derived

from its judicial function. Like all supreme courts of appeal, it gradually built up a system of "case law" upon the broad substructure of statute law; the statute law being, in the present instance, the Mosaic code with its traditional interpretation. Deriving its authority from the precept in Deut. xvii. 8-10, to which we have already referred,[1] the Sanhedrin did not permit its system of "case law" to drift gradually into chaotic confusion, as is the custom in many modern communities, and notably in England; but, sitting permanently, it collected and collated ancient traditions, judgments, and decisions, gave coherence and system to them, and thus enabled many enactments of the Pentateuch, otherwise obscure, to be carried out in practical life.

These decisions were voluntarily accepted by the people. At first they were traditional, handed down from Sanhedrin to Sanhedrin, from teacher to pupil by word of mouth, codified, but not allowed to be reduced to writing, lest the traditional law which, in certain circumstances, could be modified by subsequent decisions, should be confounded with the immutable written law promulgated on Sinai. But later on, about 150 years after the destruction of the Second Temple, when the nation was dispersed in many countries, Rabbi Judah, the Prince, or the Holy, fearing that the traditions might be lost or forgotten amid the many trials to which our people were subjected, determined to reduce to writing the entire bulk of the traditional law, a work already commenced a century back by the disciples of the renowned Hillel. Aided by his sons Simon and Gamliel, and by other sages and scholars of his time, he accomplished this work, condensing the tradition into six divisions, which he styled the *Mishna* (מִשְׁנָה) (Learning).

The traditions once codified and reduced to writing, no new laws or decisions were permitted to be added to them. But, as time went on, the Mishna itself became a starting point and basis for further development and commentary; and the two centuries succeeding its codification being a period of great mental activity among the remnant of our nation, an enormous mass of commentary was at length

[1] Page 160, "Laws of Government."

accumulated, which was, in course of time, collected by Rabina and Rab Ashi, and formed the work now known as the *Gemara* (גְּמָרָא), *i.e.*, Tradition. The *Mishna* was completed about the year 200, the *Gemara* about the year 500 of the common era. These two works together constitute the *Talmud* (תַּלְמוּד), or Study of the Law.

There are two recensions of the Talmud—the Jerusalemean and the Babylonian; the latter being the more comprehensive work, and that generally referred to when the term "Talmud" is used.

APPENDIX III.

MIRACLES AND REVELATION.[1]

THE present age is not distinguished for faith. Education, which has done much to improve the reasoning powers, has unconsciously and incidentally been the means of unsettling men's minds in matters of religion.

The mind, when untutored, is ready to receive any statement with blind credulity; but when it is fortified by training and education, it is inclined to test facts with the touchstone of logic, and it rejects as unworthy of belief allegations which will not bear that test.

It is possible that religion may have flourished most in those times when the people were most ignorant, and that unbelief may have been rampant amongst those who were most highly educated. We do not stop to ask whether an education which leads to such results is a proper, wise, and beneficent education. We merely state the fact as we find it—that education, which ought to have been the handmaid of religion, has too often proved its enemy.

A sad and bitter conclusion. For are we to close our schools, lest our children should be unbelievers? or are we to forbid the study of logic, and clip the wings of Reason, lest our young should eventually lose faith? Truly a momentous question,—a question which concerns every one of us as individuals and as members of a community.

Moreover, the question is one which does not concern

---

[1] This and the following paper are (with slight variations) reprinted from the "Sabbath Readings," published by the Jewish Association for the Diffusion of Religious Knowledge.

Judaism alone. It concerns the whole world—our community, indeed, less than any other: for our religion makes fewer demands upon faith than any other. Yet the question concerns all in some degree. For every religion claims to be founded upon some kind of revelation; and it is revelation which the highly cultivated sometimes doubt, sometimes half believe, sometimes deride, sometimes discredit altogether.

And, let us be frank. How few there are amongst us, in whose mind doubts have not at some time arisen as to the truth of some one or more points of revelation, the truth of some miracle or another! Some suppress their doubts, imagining them to be wicked; others smother them, fearful lest the flame of unbelief should spread and devour their faith; but most who doubt are too indifferent to pursue the subject, lest they be made uncomfortable.

Believing this to be the present state of things, we set ourselves in this chapter the task of showing that the Mosaic revelation demands not credulity, that our faith demands no sacrifice of reason. We further propose to venture in a future chapter on a definition of those limits, on the one hand, beyond which no religion should claim our belief; and on the other hand, of those limits beyond which no logic should dare to tread. Conscious of the difficulty of the task, we venture on it, though hopefully and confidently, yet with all humility.

Every religion claims to be based on some kind of revelation—our religion, perhaps, on the simplest of all. The Mosaic revelation embraces a series of miracles all wonderful and yet not incongruous—a series of separate miracles, chief among which were the delivery of a nation from bondage, and the presentation of a code of laws spoken by God in the presence of thousands of witnesses.

Simple as this revelation is, free as it is from incongruity or contradictory circumstances, it cannot be denied that on reading the narrative of all the miracles which compose it, the question must arise in many thinking minds, "Can all this be true?" And when we speak of thinking minds, we do not allude to such as are ready to credit any statement, however incongruous, that may be presented in the name of religion, and who make a virtue of their so-called faith—

which is, after all, the cheapest virtue in the world;—nor do we allude to the opposite extreme, the sceptical mind which believes or chooses to believe nothing; but we speak of such minds as are reasonable and thoughtful, minds which have already satisfied themselves by the reasonings of natural theology, irrespective of revelation, of the great fact of the existence of a God.

This, the foundation of all religion, the belief in the existence of God, is by itself *no* religion. History has shown that religion requires something more. Nature, which amply and in many ways proves that there is a God, has shown observant man hundreds of physical laws, but has given him no moral law. True, every man is endowed with an inner voice, a conscience, capable to some extent of directing and advising him in matters of morality; but this conscience is not a complete nor an infallible guide; for the standard of right and wrong fixed by man differs in different individuals, places, and times, and is dependent on different circumstances, inclinations, or interests. In many parts of the East, it is considered no sin to lie, and truth is regarded as almost a weakness. In some parts of the world, to deceive in commerce is not deemed roguery, but is dignified by the name of smartness, and the "smart" man becomes an object of admiration.

Neither nature nor conscience would teach us how to worship God, or what are our duties towards our fellow-men; they would not tell us how frequently we should keep a sabbath, what proportion of our means we should give to the poor, what should be the punishment of the murderer, and a multitude of other important points of information, which revelation alone teaches us, and which not only are absolutely necessary for us to know, but which must be conveyed to us with the force of an authoritative injunction. A standard of morality was indispensable, and this could only be supplied from a source which was far above the bias and prejudice of humanity;—it could only be supplied by the Creator Himself.

But when God had determined to reveal His will to the world, and to establish that standard of morality which we now call the Mosaic Code, how was He to make Himself known? How was He to make even a section of the human race understand that He was indeed and alone their Creator, whom it was their duty to obey; that He was indeed the Great God and Universal Father, whose attributes were Justice, Mercy, and Love; that He was the God whose worship was to displace and supersede all forms of worship and all phases of superstition, to which mankind had been hitherto inclined or accustomed?

Only by supernatural manifestations, or miracles, could this be accomplished. If Moses had come before the Israelites with the simple declaration, that the great Creator "I AM," the God of their forefathers, had sent him, no one would have been likely to believe or trust him; but when he showed them the signs and miracles with the performance or revelation of which he was entrusted, they saw that he indeed possessed Divine credentials, and they believed him.

But miracles, such as they saw at first, might have appeared to many of them mere jugglery; for did not the magicians of Egypt, learned in the mysteries of Nature, work like wonders by their enchantments? Therefore, in order to prove that Moses was the messenger of God, and that the God by whose power the miracle was wrought was the One True Lord, the Creator of Heaven and Earth, a succession of miracles was necessary, such as were impossible to be even in appearance imitated by the enchanters of Egypt—signs and wonders which involved the great mystery of life and death; one miracle, above all, which decimated the land of the oppressor by the death of all the firstborn, and finally the crowning miracle, which led the nation of Israel through the Red Sea on dry land, and drowned the hosts of their pursuing foes. And, when the Israelites saw themselves rescued from slavery and beheld their oppressors dead on the shores of the Sea, then, only then, for the first time, did they truly and sincerely "believe in the Lord and in His servant Moses."

Prepared by this marvellous deliverance, their minds were ready to receive the revelation of Sinai. Amid the thunder and the lightning, the voice of Heaven was heard, proclaiming the behests of the Creator, and declaring the will of the Lord God, who had brought out His people from Egypt, from the house of bondage. Well can we understand how a nation, which had been so miraculously saved from slavery and from the jaws of impending death, must have been ready listeners to that voice which declared itself to be the voice of their Saviour; well can we understand how with one accord the whole nation exclaimed, " All that the Lord hath said will we do and obey." [1]

But it is one thing to hear and believe, and another thing to act upon that belief. The religion of Sinai was not to be a mere faith, a mere religious sentiment. It was to be the Religion of Action. It was not to remain simply an abstract scheme of morals. The words spoken on Sinai were not to be an unpractical Sermon on the Mount. They were to be carried into practice by the Israelites, so that their religion might pervade and dignify every act of their every-day life.

But this was a hard task, and the young religion had to be nursed. We wonder at and censure our forefathers when we read how they (a stiff-necked people as they were rightly called) failed again and again in their allegiance to the God who had saved them ; but who can tell what struggles they must have had to encounter in subduing long-cherished tendencies and forsaking long-practised habits, the superstitions of a life-time, the habits of thought which had become part of their being? Therefore, the new religion had to be nursed. And how? By continued heavenly interpositions; by the performance of miracles again and again; by the constant assurance of the Actual Divine Presence among them. A continuity of miracles was necessary. It was necessary to show the nation of wanderers, that the God who had led them from Egypt still regarded them, and watched over them. Hence the series of divine interpositions which made the forty years' journey through the wilderness one long, forty-years' miracle. When the journey's end was attained, a new generation, born and reared amid miracles, had reached their prime, a nation had in fact grown up with a full sense of the Divine Power, and a knowledge of its own mission. The new religion was safe so far as regarded its own professors. Miracles were thenceforth required only to assure the position of Israel among the surrounding nations.

[1] Exod. xxiv. 7.

So far we have endeavoured to show that a Divine revelation, as a foundation of true religion, was indispensable for the welfare of man, and that miracles were necessary as the credentials of such revelation. Turn we now to the task of showing the possibility and credibility of miracles.

And here let it be distinctly understood that we are not called upon to prove that miracles are *probable;* for improbability is one element of a miracle. The Israelite, who believes in the story of the passage of the Red Sea, may and should consider the story improbable in the ordinary acceptation of the word, and contrary to the ordinary course of nature. If he does not so consider it, if he tries to make the story a probable one, by seeking, as some German critics have done, to reduce it to the level of a natural phenomenon, he runs the risk of ceasing to regard it as a miracle.

What is a miracle? A seeming departure from the usual and natural order of things. Such a departure is of itself, under ordinary circumstances, highly improbable. But however improbable, however difficult to credit, no one who believes in a Creator can say that a miracle is impossible. Surely He who made and furnished and arrayed the world can, if He so will, reverse, suspend, or alter exceptionally, and for a wise purpose, the order and arrangement which He has established as the course of nature. Surely to Him who sustains all the world, who provides all its inhabitants with food, shelter, and raiment, by what we call the natural order of things, it must have been an easy matter to have provided the band of wandering Israelites with manna and clothing in the wilderness by an unseen agency, by a direct operation of His own, or at least by an unknown instrumentality, instead of by the intervention of the arts of man. Surely to Him who created the Sun, with its wondrous radiating powers of Heat and Light, who made the atmosphere and endowed it with its marvellous power of refraction, it must have been an easy matter to have momentarily so varied that refractive power as to make the sun appear to stand still while Joshua was fighting His battle. He who permanently holds myriads of enormous orbs suspended in the firmament, and regulates their courses through space with infallible precision; He who converts a minute grain of seed into a gigantic tree; could He not as easily, and for a special purpose, arrest or reverse the course of waters, or produce manna in a desert?

To Him who in the ordinary course of nature performs acts gigantic in their magnitude and effects—acts wonderfully great—the performance of such incidental miracles as these must indeed be but a trivial exertion of His power. We do not say that miracles are possible because God is Omnipotent—for no human mind can soar to the dizzy heights or fathom the mighty depths of Omnipotence—we simply say that the miracles of the Bible are possible, because they are so inconsiderable in magnitude when compared with the every-day work of the Great Creator. Indeed, nature as it is, is a miracle far greater, far more wondrous than all the miracles of the Bible taken together.

But here we must face another difficulty, which may possibly present itself to some minds. Is it likely, it may be asked, that God who is so great, should concern Himself in the trivial affairs of this little world, reversing or modifying the ordinary order of things, and suspending the operation of the natural laws which He has framed, and so act in order that one nation may be victorious and that another nation may fall? But why do we ask ourselves this question? Because we are human, and wrongly judge of God by a human standard. Because we know that we ourselves, if absorbed in one great piece of business, often neglect or overlook the smaller; and we fancy, forsooth, that God must do the same, and can scarcely imagine a Great God, the Creator of Heaven and Earth, occupying Himself with the destinies of nations, and even of individuals.

Now let us look to the works of Creation and be corrected. The God who made the giant elephant and the sturdy oak, made also the little ant and the humble lichen, —nay, more, He has created myriads of unseen organisms which float about the air, and which only the microscope can reveal to our senses, and into every one of these He has breathed the breath of Life, and every one of these He has endowed with some beauty or peculiarity of form.

T

We would say, then, that He who concerns Himself with the creation, and the life and the death of (to us) invisible creatures, may and would, nay, must inevitably concern Himself with the affairs of man, the crown of His great creation.

And does it appear strange that God, the Creator of Heaven and Earth, should condescend to make known His will to man, and, for such purpose, should, amid thunder and lightning, speak in human language from the summit of Sinai? Does it seem impossible that the Great Creator should deliver to man a code of laws to guide him in his journey on earth, and to lead him to Heaven? Surely, for God who created man for man's happiness, it would not be a work beneath His dignity to teach him to attain the happiness for which He destined him.

Is it not rather more natural and more consistent with His attributes of justice, mercy, and love, that God should, at an early age of mankind, instruct one man, and through him one nation, and through that nation all humanity, in the ways best calculated to lead to their moral perfection and happiness? Surely if man's creation had an object— and who can deny this?—that object could be attained only through that direct instruction which we call Revelation.

And shall it be said that it seems strange, that such a miracle as a Divine revelation should have taken place only in olden times, thousands of years ago? shall it be said that it seems strange, that God spoke to men only in days when the world was young, when it was dark with ignorance, and full of violence, oppression and wickedness? Why, for these very reasons, that age was the most appropriate for such a revelation. The heavenly interposition could not have been vouchsafed in a more opportune season. But, further, is there not constantly a voice of revelation in every human mind, heart, and soul, a voice which confirms the revealed Divine will in words almost as plain as those wherein " the Lord spake unto Moses "? Is not that voice—the conscience—as great a miracle as that which thundered the Divine behest from Sinai? Truly this voice of conscience is as wondrous a pheno-.menon as the voice which spake from Sinai !

And whence comes the spirit of genius which raises man above his fellow-man ? Whence comes the new conception, the power of adaptation which we call design, the overflowing of the soul which we call poetry? What are all these marvels but revelations? and we know no more how these came into the mind than we know how the soul came into the body. The miracle of revelation is not a bygone wonder, though the voice which spake from Horeb is hushed and still.

Miracles, then, are possible, because He who made can unmake ; they are possible, because He who disposed the order of things can modify and suspend that arrangement. The miracles of old are possible, because we see their parallels even in our own time, though we have ceased to wonder at them through their habitual recurrence.

Why, then, does it require so great an effort of faith to believe in the miracles of the Bible? Is it because we do not see marvels of the same kind in these present days? "This is not an age of miracles," some say. We do not hear now-a-days of showers of manna, nor of the dividing of a sea which stands erect like two walls, while a host of men passes between them. It is the absence of such miracles at the present time, it would appear, which makes the miracle so incredible, so improbable.

But it must be observed that it is not a marvellous or unaccountable deed which constitutes a miracle. Every day we see hundreds of such wonderful or unaccountable facts, and these would doubtlessly be regarded as miracles, if we did not witness them constantly, and regard them as matters of course. We see, for example, a hen's egg, after exposure to heat, burst into life and become a living creature. Anyone who saw this phenomenon for the first time would consider it to be a miracle, and even we, who have an opportunity of witnessing it every day, cannot but marvel at the wonderful metamorphosis. The same may be said of a thousand phenomena which we see daily, and which, because we see them daily, we regard as matters of course, and as part of the usual order of nature.

But what is the order of nature? An Israelite, born during the wanderings in the wilderness, accustomed to see daily the pillars of fire and cloud, which showed the way in the trackless desert, must have come at length to regard them as portions of the usual order of nature, and must have felt astonished at their disappearance at the end of the forty years' wandering. Probably he may have considered their disappearance a miracle; certainly he must have regarded it as a departure from the (to him) natural order of things.

Now we witness, at the present day, a phenomenon some-what analogous to the pillars of fire and cloud. By means of a magnetic needle, the mariner can guide his ship across the pathless ocean by day and by night. No one has yet discovered the secret of the magnet's power. A savage, who might happen to see a mariner's compass for the first time, would think it a miracle. We who can see its action daily, regard it as part of the natural order of things. To us it is no miracle. But suppose that one day the needle in every mariner's compass were found to have lost the property of turning northward; suppose that the power of the magnet were to cease suddenly, and never to be again recovered, we should not only deplore the loss; we should also marvel at it. The loss would appear almost a miracle. But in course of time, and gradually, the habit of thought would change. Little by little, an idea might come into the minds of thinking men that perhaps the power of the magnet, which never was understood (even when it was most effective) was miraculous; and after the lapse of ages, sagacious, sceptical people would perhaps begin to doubt whether there ever was such a thing as a mariner's compass endowed with the wonderful powers which books attributed to it, or whether the whole history of it was not a fable. At last, the pillars of fire and cloud, which were alleged to have led the Israelites through the desert, and the compass which was alleged to have led navigators across the seas, would be regarded alike by the sceptic as doubtful facts. Not accustomed to see such things in his day, he would regard the report of their former existence as incredible.

But, suppose that there were evidences of the former existence of this miraculous magnetic power; suppose that not only books of science but the literature of every nation contained incidental allusions to magnets and magnetic phenomena, what would our sceptic say? Perhaps he might urge that he did not believe books, and that authors copied one another's lies. Of course this would be unfair, and yet one could scarcely answer such an aspersion on literature. Suppose, however, the sceptic found that every sailor, all the world over, once a year and on the same day of the year fasted and prayed in memory of the great loss navigation had sustained hundreds of years back, when the power of the compass came to an end, what would he say then? He would, we think, begin to doubt his doubts, and distrust his unbelief. He would say "books may be false, but such a universal custom as this must have had its origin in some such event as the cessation of the magnetic miracle. No doubt the alleged miracle did exist."

Now we have taken this imaginary case in order to illustrate an actual condition of facts. The sceptic may discredit the Bible and the miracles which it registers. He may disbelieve all history, sacred and profane. He may doubt the truth of all those incidental allusions to the Scriptural miracles contained in the records of almost every ancient nation. But he cannot ignore the existence of the Jews. The Jews stand in the position of the hypothetical sailors to whom we have referred. The Jews, all over the globe, celebrate, year after year, at the same time and with uniformity of practice, the same customs.

Let us give examples. On the 14th day of Nissan, all over the world, the first-born male of every Jewish family recognises, by a fast, the great miracle which exempted the Israelites from the most terrible of the plagues of Egypt—the slaying of the first-born. On the 21st day of Nissan in every year, and all over the world, the Jews joyously sing in their synagogues the triumphal song of Moses to celebrate the miraculous passage of the Red Sea. On the 6th day of Sivan in every year, and all over the world, the Jews celebrate the Sinaitic revelation, by reading in their places of worship, with all solemnity, the soul-stirring words of the Decalogue. On the 15th day of Tishri, in every year, wherever Jews congregate, they dwell or eat in tabernacles, in order to celebrate, with more or less rigour of observance, the marvellous sojourn in the wilderness, when all our forefathers lived in booths for forty years, fed, clad, and sustained by a miraculous Providence.

"Can we imagine a system of observances, such as those of the Passover, as now celebrated, to be based upon a mere myth? Or can we imagine a festival like the Feast of Tabernacles, as always observed among the Jews, founded upon a mere fable? If there had been no real Passover, no real exodus from Egypt, no real dwelling in booths in the wilderness, when or how could these commemorative observances have been instituted? And, if gratuitously instituted, how would they have been so implicitly and persistently observed, involving, as they undoubtedly do, considerable personal trouble and inconvenience? Can we imagine such a state of things, as an entire nation assembling, for the first time, by common consent, to perform the passover observances, as the celebration of an event of which they had just heard for the first time, or had just found written in a book? Such a state of things would be impossible. Such observances, distinguished by absolute uniformity of practice, could only have originated in one way—viz., *in the event itself*."[1]

"Ye are my witnesses,"[2] said the Creator to His people, thousands of years ago; and truly we and our observances are living and speaking witnesses of the Divine revelation. Our customs are the links which bind the present to the past. The links may be scattered here and there over the face of the earth. Here and there they may be tangled; but far, far back into the misty realms of remote antiquity they can be traced—traced home to the great events, the wondrous miracles which formed their origin.

Herein lies one of the most marked differences between the miracles of our revelation and the alleged miracles of other religions. And were we not averse to a discussion which might wound the feelings or disturb the minds of our neighbours, we could easily show how all the miracles alleged by the creeds born long after the Sinaitic dispensation differ in circumstances, in objects, in results, and in evidence from those of our Revelation, and how cogent have been and are the reasons for their rejection by Judaism. But such a controversy would be foreign to our present object.

[1] A Jewish Reply to Dr. Colenso's Criticism on the Pentateuch, p. 17.   [2] Isaiah xliii. 10.

Revelation, then—our revelation—is not a matter of faith. It is a matter of evidence. Nature shows that there is a God. Sacred history, proved true by our observances, teaches us that God revealed Himself to our forefathers, proclaiming His will to the world, and giving to man a code, which was to be a guide for all ages and for all conditions and circumstances. The miracles wrought when God so revealed Himself were marvellous indeed. Apparently improbable when detached from the consideration of circumstances, yet they were probable, nay, they were necessary. All this we have shown, and we have shown, too, how we Jews, scattered exiles though we be, are witnesses of revelation and of miracles 3,000 years old—witnesses of those facts which form the foundation of *all* religion.

O, glorious mission of the Jewish race! to be not only custodians of God's law, not only a kingdom of priests, but living witnesses of the Divine Will and Word; at every festival breathing the breath of life into a history, which would otherwise have been to the world long ago a dead, a mythic tale; proving by observances, institutions, and customs the truth of the Divine revelation, and the heavenly origin of the Book of books!

Jews, be proud of your mission! cherish your institutions, maintain the customs of your religion, and so verify the words which constitute the patent of your nobility, "Ye are my witnesses!"

APPENDIX IV.

LIMITS OF FAITH AND ENQUIRY.

IN the last chapter, we ventured to show that the history of the Mosaic revelation can be believed without taxing our credulity; that that history is not a matter of faith, but a matter of evidence ; that that evidence is of the clearest and most unimpeachable character; that the witnesses to the great Truth are none other than ourselves, our institutions, and our observances.

We showed, too, how the miracles which attended the Divine revelation—marvellous though they were—could be believed without requiring of us any sacrifice of reason ; that they were necessary adjuncts of revelation ; that to believe them required faith, but not credulity.

Faith, but not credulity. Where shall we draw the line between the two? Where does faith leave off and credulity begin? What shall he that has faith believe, and what shall he discredit? When shall Reason bend its head to Faith, and how shall it, without abdicating its sway? These are questions which affect every religion, and ours perhaps more closely than any, because our religion can afford enquiry.

Let us, then, attempt in the present chapter to define the limits on the one hand, beyond which no religion should claim our belief; and, on the other hand, the limits beyond which no logic should dare to tread.

No religion should tax our faith to such an extent as to ask us to believe in an incongruity. A miracle, which is something contrary to our experiences, may be believed ;

but a miracle which involves a contradiction in terms, a moral impossibility, a logical contradiction, should not be believed. Let us illustrate our meaning by a well-known story:—

A lady, who prided herself on her great faith, was asked whether she believed the story of Jonah having been swallowed by a whale. "Yes," was her reply, "of course I do; and if the Bible had said that Jonah swallowed the whale, I would also have believed it."

Now, the story of Jonah being swallowed and then disgorged by a sea-monster is certainly very startling; it is quite contrary to all our experiences, and it requires a great effort of faith to believe it; still, it involves no incongruity and no contradiction. But if the Bible had stated that Jonah had swallowed the sea-monster, the story would have been incongruous and wholly incredible; for we know that a small object cannot contain an object larger than itself, and that no miracle could make it do so.

Any religion that would tell us that, by one of its miracles, a part became greater than the whole, or that two and two made five, or that a thing was right and wrong at the same time, or that past time would come back again, would be wholly unworthy of belief; for such statements would involve moral impossibilities, incongruities, contradictions in terms.

But perhaps the reader may ask why we take such pains to demonstrate what every rational person must see to be a truism. We shall show that we are not contending with a mere shadow.

There is a religion—rather a wide-spread religion—which represents that there is a Deity, consisting of three distinct personages acting independently of each other, but yet forming one Deity, one and indivisible. Of course, any rational man would say that a being cannot be *one* being and *three* beings at the same time; that if a being be indivisible, it cannot consist of three independent parts; that the whole theory is a contradiction in terms.

But those who profess the creed which propounds this remarkable doctrine tell us in reply, that we cannot reason upon such a matter, and that men only require faith to believe in it.

We answer that though credulity can make a man believe nonsense, faith cannot; faith is the credit which the mind lends willingly *to that which has been tested and found trustworthy;* while credulity is the blind surrender of mind and reason to the untried scheme, or dreamy phantasy, or senseless theory, or cloudy mystery.

Why does the child have faith in his parents, and believe what they tell him? Because he has had experience of their kindness and of their love. He trusts them because he always finds them true to him. Childlike faith is not a blind faith, as some would maintain. It is a faith born of experience; and it is the stronger, the stronger its origin.

When Abraham left his native land, his kindred, and his father's house, at the bidding of God, was it blind faith that dictated obedience? Was it not rather the strong belief in the mission that was before him, the strong abhorrence of the idolatry of Haran, the strong confidence in the God who had saved him from the flames of the fire-worshippers, that made him believe in the Lord, so that " it was accounted to him for righteousness"? His faith was not blind credulity. It was *belief,* the offspring of experience. It had fed on the broad pastures of reason, and drunk from the deep wells of thought.

And even with Abraham, the father of the faithful, faith required to be fed and nursed by supernatural manifestations. " Lord God," he exclaimed, when he had been told that his seed would possess the land of Canaan, "whereby shall I know that I shall inherit it?" and God solved his doubts in a vision. Later yet, when a son was promised to him in his old age, he fell upon his face and laughed, and his wife exclaimed, " Shall I of a surety bear a child?" scarcely believing such an improbable event. God asks him, " Is anything too hard for the Lord?" And, still later, when he feared lest with the sinners of Sodom his kinsman Lot might be destroyed, and seemed to question the Divine justice in the words, " Shall not the Judge of all the earth do right?" he shows that his faith even then was not quite complete.

But when the promise is fulfilled, and in his old age the longed-for son is born, and the prospect of a multitudinous progeny dawns upon him, we see a change. His faith is complete. Steadfast in that faith, he binds his son on Mount Moriah, for he knows that the command of the All-just, the All-merciful Ruler of the Universe must have been prompted by some wise and holy purpose.

Later yet, when he sends away his servant to seek a wife for his son from amongst his own kindred, he is confident that God will favour his mission; and, addressing the trusty Eleazar, he says, "The Lord God of Heaven, who took me from my father's house, and from the land of my kindred, and who spake unto me and sware unto me, saying, Unto thy seed will I give this land, He shall send His angel before thee." Abraham's faith is perfect. It had grown with a natural growth; experience had strengthened it; and, in his old age, his faith in God was ripe.

Let us now turn from the early Pentateuch history to the Mosaic code itself, and we shall there see that the same standard of experience is set up as the only trustworthy basis of belief. Moses points out to the people in the following words the test whereby the false prophet may be detected:—"When a prophet speaketh in the name of the Lord, if the thing follow not, nor come to pass, that is the thing which the Lord hath not spoken, but the prophet hath spoken it presumptuously."[1] Belief in a prophet was not to be that mere mental effort which some call faith; it was to be founded upon some fact within the experience of the believer.

In the book of Jeremiah[2] we find this principle actually carried into practice. Hananiah, the son of Azur, prophesies falsely the speedy return of Israel from the captivity; and Jeremiah, knowing the prophecy to be false, thus challenges Hananiah in the presence of the priests and the people:— "The prophet which prophesieth of peace, when the word of the prophet shall come to pass, then shall the prophet be known that the Lord hath truly sent him. . . . Then said the prophet Jeremiah unto Hananiah the prophet, Hear now, Hananiah, the Lord hath not sent thee, but thou makest the people to trust in a lie. . . . Therefore thus saith the Lord, Behold, I will cast thee from off the face of the earth: this year thou shalt die;" and the

[1] Deut. xviii. 22.   [2] Jer. xxviii.

chapter concludes with the words, "So Hananiah the prophet died the same year in the seventh month."

But though the revelations of prophecy are to be thus tested by evidence and experience, we are not to allow ourselves to be led away to believe in that which is repugnant to reason, and at variance with the express command of God. We are told[1] "If there arise among you a prophet or a dreamer of dreams, and he giveth thee a sign or a wonder, and the sign or the wonder come to pass whereof he spake unto thee saying, Let us go after other gods which thou hast not known, and let us serve them, thou shalt not hearken unto the words of that prophet or that dreamer of dreams, for the Lord your God proveth you to know whether ye love the Lord your God with all your heart and with all your soul."[2]

The fulfilment of the prophecy or portent, then, is not to be the only test. There may be jugglery or chicanery; even the prophecy may verily be fulfilled, or the sign and the wonder may truly take place; but if the prophet bring a strange religion "which thou hast not known," a religion full of mystery and incongruity, a religion inconsistent with the behests of God as revealed directly to His people on Mount Sinai, such a prophet is not to be believed.

No matter, then, if at the foundation of a new creed its exponent or prophet gave signs and wonders which came to pass. Even assuming (which we do not grant) that those alleged miracles were historically true, we should not be justified in obeying him, when he bids us "follow after other gods," whom we neither know nor comprehend.

That God, who is unchangeable, did not in one day make a covenant with His people, and through that people with the whole earth, revealing His will, His behests, and His attributes, to abrogate and repeal that covenant on another day; substituting for a clear, simple, and comprehensible religion, a religion which is all mystery, all incongruity, credible only by excessive credulity. The revelation of Sinai was not given to be revoked by a new

---

[1] Deut. xiii. 1-3.
[2] The line of argument and Biblical illustrations here given are to a certain extent coincident with those in Chapter xiv. But it is thought desirable not to omit them in this reprint.

covenant at a future epoch of the world's history. True, it did not reveal everything to our finite senses. It did not solve at once every problem in nature, for "the secret things belong to the Lord our God;"[1] but those things which it did reveal are the eternal heritage of our race ; they are clear, credible, comprehensible, even to our children ; they "belong to us and to our children for ever, that we may do all the words of God's Law."[1]

Thus far we have endeavoured to define the limits beyond which no religion should claim our belief. Let us now seek to discover the limits beyond which no reasoning should dare to tread.

When and where is Reason to stand still, and hand us over to the guardianship of Faith? Logic must not travel alone into the regions of the unseen, the illimitable, the eternal. ·In matters of religion, logic may deal only with what we see, and feel, and know, founding all its reasonings upon axioms known and indisputable. Nor may we in our thoughts and reasonings about God, His ways and works, judge of Him and them by our own petty human standard; "for My thoughts are not your thoughts, neither are your ways My ways, saith the Lord."[2]

Nor may we waste our mental energies in vain attempts to reconcile conflicting points, which in this life never will be reconciled. What is the use, or where our right, to seek to reconcile Geology with Genesis—the foreknowledge of God with the freewill of man—or any other such conflicting questions? What right have we to institute a suit between the two, and then to seek in vain to reconcile the suitors?

Geology and Genesis! How do we know that we do not wrongly read the stony book of nature, or do not misconceive some words at least upon the page of Revelation? The languages of both are dead ; the one we read by the faint glimmer of analogy, the other by the flickering flame of old tradition.

Predestination and freewill! Freewill we *think* we understand; but when we trace volition to the brain, and ask how freewill acts, all certain knowledge ends. We know the brain gives impulse to the nerves and muscles; but how, in what manner, no mind can comprehend. We

Deut. xxix. 29.   [2] Isa. lv. 8.

think we have freewill; but find volition modified by circumstance of time and place, weather, health, and fancy, and a thousand trifles which we would scarcely own.

Predestination! What mind can fathom to its depth the meaning of Divine foreknowledge, defining that one word Omniscience? Omniscience! knowledge of all events to all eternity, knowledge, too, extending back, and back, and back to that eternity, which is past and gone! Whose mind can grasp this one idea, even the shadow of omniscience? And yet men talk so glibly of predestination and freewill, and seek to reconcile the two!

On the fatal rock of attempted reconciliation, many have wrecked their faith. The busy brains of shallow reasoners work hard to reconcile. They twist and turn the facts, distorting truth, till truth appears a falsehood. To their shallow minds all is beautifully reconciled and deftly fitted; but thoughtful men are not so satisfied. They see religionists build up religion on shifty quicksands of specious quibbles. "Is this religion?" they ask: and their questions end in doubts, their doubts in unbelief.

A sad result. Not that we must therefore suppress reason and under-rate its powers. But reason must not proudly rear its head, and deem itself antagonist to faith. It is in truth a marvel. In all nature, reason has no parallel; and yet the mightiest effort of the greatest human mind must be of petty insignificance in the sight of Him who rules all mind and matter. Perhaps the infant's soul in heaven knows more than Newton ever knew on earth; perchance, transplanted to the realms above, the idiot's soul set free, may look down upon the master-work of master-minds on earth; and in its high pre-eminence of thought, may scorn to laugh at those small minds which laughed to scorn his own.

Such thoughts as these should check our small conceits, our overweening pride of reason which would weigh all things in the balance of logic, and seek to make religion, virtue, and futurity demonstrable like Euclid's elements. There must be a point where reason must bend its head to faith, and bid it take up the thread of a half-finished argument.

Reason shows us not infallibly the aim and end of life

and living things.   The great problem—why do we live and die?—reason will never solve with certainty.   All it can do is to lead us to surmises from known facts and ascertained analogies; to prove to us what we all feel true without such proof: that there is a God, and that that God is good and works for our good.   Then faith, not credulous and blind belief, but faith built upon the sure foundation of experience of God's mercies, tells us all the rest; tells us of the future we all hope to gain, and of the immortality we all hope to inherit.

Here Reason bends its head to Faith without abdicating its sway.   It says, "So far, no farther can I guide you. Those dizzy heights of future, that dark abyss of past, no human mind can penetrate.   Eternity, infinity, omnipotence, are only *words* to men.   Through those broad plains of the illimitable ask me not to lead you.   But you may read the future from the past.   The sun which rose to-day will rise again to-morrow; and so the God, who always has been good, tender and loving to His creatures, will be the same to you for ever.   Act well and righteously, and await the end with trustful, loving faith."

Wise men will learn to wait.   We have not long to wait. It needs no mighty strain on faith, to feel and know that when the soul returns to Him from whom it came, all problems will be solved, all doubts removed without the adventitious aid of those misguided and misguiding folks who seek to reconcile.

Till then let truth remain.   Seek not to hide the fact. You cannot stay the progress of discovery, nor put a skid upon the wheels of science; and even if you could, the *truth* will yet remain.   The truth is our heritage.   The "things which are revealed belong to us, and to our children for ever."

THE END.

INDEX.

U

INDEX. 291

r
l
a

st
n

l

n

l

l

l

l

l

l

l

st

n

n

l

l

l

l

l

l

l

l

l

l

l

l

l

WERTHEIMER, LEA AND CO., PRINTERS, CIRCUS PLACE, FINSBURY CIRCUS.